DINGHY DROP

DINGHY DROP

279 Squadron at War 1941–1946

Tom Docherty

Pen & Sword
AVIATION

First published in Great Britain in 2007 by
Pen & Sword Aviation
an imprint of
Pen & Sword Books Ltd

ISBN 978 1 84415 482 1

A CIP catalogue record for this book is
available from the British Library

Typeset in Palatino by
Phoenix Typesetting, Auldgirth, Dumfriesshire

Printed and bound in England by
CPI UK

Pen & Sword Books Ltd incorporates the Imprints of Pen & Sword Aviation,
Pen & Sword Maritime, Pen & Sword Military, Wharncliffe Local History,
Pen & Sword Select, Pen & Sword Military Classics and Leo Cooper.

For a complete list of Pen & Sword titles please contact
PEN & SWORD BOOKS LIMITED
47 Church Street, Barnsley, South Yorkshire, S70 2AS, England
E-mail: enquiries@pen-and-sword.co.uk
Website: www.pen-and-sword.co.uk

Contents

The Publishers have included several historically
important wartime photographs that cannot be
reproduced to our usual high standards. It was
felt that they were of sufficient interest to the
reader to be included.

Introduction

The first developments in air sea rescue (ASR) began with the use of aircraft as offensive weapons in World War I. Aircrews were provided with extremely basic life-saving equipment such as lifebelts, and rescue from the sea depended very much on passing ships. By the 1920s ship- and carrier-borne aircraft had been equipped with flotation gear, so, at the very least, there was a possibility of the aircraft remaining afloat until rescue could be effected. By 1925 the aircrews best equipped to survive a ditching were those who operated flying boats as they had been provided with a triangular inflatable dinghy by this time.

Until 1935 the RAF had a limited rescue capability provided by launches used on gunnery ranges and by flying boat and seaplane stations, but this was not a really satisfactory situation, so, in 1936, with war looming, trials began with high-speed launches and fifteen launches were initially ordered. Also in 1936 the Air Ministry began seriously to consider aircrew survival over water and by 1938 pneumatic dinghies were being fitted to land planes.

Up till this point rescue of ditched aircrew was carried out, in the main, by launches of the Marine Section of Coastal Command, the Royal National Lifeboat Institution (RNLI) and passing merchant vessels and fishing boats. In 1939 additional high-speed launches were procured to cover home waters and the organisation came under the control of Coastal Command. In the early months of the war the launches were used to locate downed aircraft but communication between launches and searching aircraft was a problem yet to be resolved. At this point there were no dedicated search and rescue aircraft, and individual squadrons would carry out the search for their missing comrades alongside any other operational aircraft that could be spared.

Following the Battle of Britain the RAF went over to the offensive with fighter patrols, attacks on barge concentrations and the enemy's capital ships in French ports, as well as low level shipping strikes by the aircraft of No. 2 Group. In addition Bomber Command kept up its raids, all of which combined to cause an increase in the number of losses to ditching and parachuting over the sea. Following substantial losses in October 1940 an Air Sea Rescue Directorate was established at a meeting in January 1941 which was placed under the control of Coastal Command with representatives at each of the command's group headquarters. The Directorate was commanded by Air Cdre L. G. Le B Croke with Capt C. L. Howe RN as his deputy. Under the umbrella of the Directorate was an organisation comprising ASR aircraft, RAF and RN high speed rescue launches, the Royal Observer Corps (ROC), RNLI, mercantile marine, coastguard service and the police. All of these organisations were to be actively involved in the sighting, reporting and rescue of downed aircrew. The search and rescue areas of responsibility fell within the boundaries of Nos 15, 16, 18 and 19 Groups, dividing the coastal waters into four areas.

The responsibility of the rescue services covered only the waters out to a distance of 20 miles and relied upon the fast launches and initially a small number of Lysanders, which carried dinghy packs on the bomb carriers attached to the undercarriage. By May 1941 the control of this small Lysander force had passed to Fighter Command and gradually the strength increased to four squadrons, Nos 275, 276, 277 and 278. By July 1941 these squadrons were also receiving numbers of Walrus amphibians, which were capable of alighting if conditions were sufficiently smooth to rescue survivors.

These units were limited to close-in operations and deeper search required the services of operational aircraft, which often could not be spared in numbers large enough to make a comprehensive search. This situation was remedied in September 1941 when approval was given for the formation of two longer-range squadrons, Nos 279 and 280. No. 279 Squadron (Sqn) was formed on 16 November 1941 at Bircham Newton in Norfolk and was initially equipped with Lockheed Hudson Mk III aircraft for (ASR) duties.

In the period leading up to the formation of these two squadrons there had been much work done in relation to air-dropped survival equipment and aids and equipment carried by the fighters and bombers to be used in the event of ditching. Air-dropped equipment such as the Lindholme dinghy dropping gear, the Bircham barrel and the Thornaby bag was developed. These contained such items as water, food, first-aid kits and distress signals. The Lindholme gear was especially useful as it comprised five parts – one dinghy and four stores packs joined together by lines. The contents of the packs would be progressively improved as experience was gained and feedback from survivors was examined.

In addition many trials were carried out to establish how best to locate and assist the survivor in his dinghy. Colour was an important factor in locating the survivor and yellow was found to be the best; consequently, dinghies, life vests, skullcaps and other rescue equipment were produced in this colour. The survivor in his dinghy was also provided with a variety of aids to assist rescue: pyrotechnic signals, signal torches and whistles, and flourescine bags containing green dye, which spread out over the sea.

Dinghy development continued alongside those other aids and they began to be equipped with telescopic masts, flags and radios. In addition bombers carried homing pigeons, which could be released with a position report.

The squadron was the first to employ airborne lifeboats, which it carried beneath the bellies of the portly Hudsons. As early as 1940 thought had been given to some type of self-propelled boat, which could be air dropped to survivors and in which they could make their way to safety. Early plans were for some type of glider-boat, but this was abandoned due to technical difficulties and it was not till January 1942 that a practical boat, fitted with oars, sails and engines, was put into production with the intention of slinging it under the bomb bay of the Hudson and dropping it by parachute. The boat was 20 feet in length and designed with integral buoyancy chambers to stop it from capsizing. The chambers were inflated by carbon-dioxide bottles, which were triggered by the action of the parachutes opening. On striking the sea rockets would fire out either side with a line attached, which would enable the survivors to grab hold of the line as they drifted onto it and thus reach the boat. The rocket would fire the line some 200 feet. In addition a rocket fired sea anchor, or drogue, was fitted to stop the boat drifting away. The first twenty-four airborne lifeboats were ordered in November 1942.

Another problem which had to be addressed was the means of communication between the searching aircraft and surface vessels, a problem which was exacerbated by the different frequencies and radio types used by operational aircraft and ships. In September 1941 the decision was taken to equip all rescue craft, air and surface, with VHF and HF radios. Following this, rescue co-ordination was much improved.

During its stay at Bircham Newton the squadron was at the forefront of many of the ASR trials and developments and it sent detachments to several locations, including Reykjavik in Iceland and St Eval in Cornwall. Its main role during the period from April 1942 until December 1943 was to provide ASR cover over the Western Approaches. The Reykjavik detachment would become No. 251 Squadron on 1 August 1944.

In October 1944 the squadron re-equipped with Warwick Mk I aircraft and moved to Thornaby in the north-east of England. By now its ASR net was cast wide and there were detachments at Tain, Fraserburgh, Wick and Banff (all in northern Scotland) and Reykjavik. Its main role now was to provide ASR cover for the Coastal Command strike wings operating from airfields in northern England and Scotland during their attacks on enemy shipping off the Scandinavian coastline. The Warwick Mk I was replaced by the Mk II in November 1945 and Hurricanes and Sea Otter amphibians joined the strength during 1945.

The squadron moved once more in September 1945, to Beccles in Suffolk later re-equipping with the Lancaster ASR Mk III. A detachment was sent to Burma from December 1945, becoming No. 1348 Flight. The squadron itself was disbanded on 10 March 1946.

By the end of the war some 5,721 RAF and US aircrew had been saved by the Air Sea Rescue Service in the waters around the UK: 1,998 of these were Americans. One of the busiest periods for US rescues was in July 1943 when 139 crew members out of a total of 196 were picked up, 78 out of 80 being picked up on 25 July. During its four and a half year existence many a bomber and fighter crew from both the RAF and USAAF had reason to thank the members of No. 279 Squadron for their safe return from the bitter seas, and though the squadron's motto was officially 'To see and to be seen', it could just as easily have been their unofficial motto – 'Anywhere for a dinghy'.

CHAPTER ONE

November 1941 – April 1942

At the beginning of November 1941 Britain no longer stood alone against the might of the German war machine. The Russians had been drawn into the war with Hitler's invasion of the Soviet Union, but after making steady advances the Germans captured Yalta, in the Crimea on 9 November. The Russians had their backs against the wall and it appeared only a matter of time before they were defeated. The situation for British and Commonwealth forces was not a lot better. Two days after No. 279 Sqn was formed Operation Crusader was launched in the Libyan desert. Within a week Rommel had halted the British offensive and broken through the 8th Army's rear and once again the British were on the retreat. British naval power had also had another serious blow struck against it when U-81 torpedoed and sank the aircraft carrier *Ark Royal*. Unable in 1941 to contemplate an invasion of the Continent for some time Britain would have to rely on the forces of the RAF to carry the offensive to the enemy. To do this it would require every aircrew member it could muster and with losses to ditching eating into this highly trained cadre the newly formed ASR squadrons would have a vital role to play.

No. 279 Sqn could probably have been said to form at Bircham Newton on 16 November 1941 when F/Lt F.E.G. Rashleigh DFC arrived from No. 1 PRU at Benson by private car. Squadron personnel and aircraft until his arrival were, in the words of the squadron diary, 'precisely nil'! The following day the first aircraft, Hudson Mk III V8999, arrived from No. 24 Maintenance Unit (MU) at Ternhill. It was loaded with a large amount of Wireless Telegraphy (WT) equipment for the squadron. In addition to the radio equipment several Browning and Vickers gas-operated (VGO) machine-guns arrived. For several days neither accommodation nor hangar space was available, and owing to the insecurity of the Hudson arrangements were made to store the weapons and equipment in the decontamination centre.

On 18 November another Hudson, T9394, arrived and F/Lt Rashleigh made the first flight by 279 Sqn on a local flying sortie of two hours, thirty-five minutes. Three days later two new arrivals turned up in the form of F/O F. Barrett and Sgt C.E. Singleton, an air gunner and Wireless Operator/Air Gunner (WOp/AG) respectively. Both were posted in from No. 407 Sqn at North Coates. The 22nd saw the arrival of a third Hudson and F/Lt Rashleigh and F/O Barrett flew up to North Coates to meet the newly designated Commanding Officer (CO) of 279 Sqn, S/Ldr V.H.P. Lynham, who was not due to take over until 27 November. Frank Rashleigh wrote to his mother on 22 November and his enthusiasm for his new posting is obvious.

Darling Mother,

Many thanks for your letter. I have been frightfully busy the last ten days, but there is no real excuse for the tardiness of this letter because I have since been promoted to Flight Lieutenant, apart from being posted here.

I am forming a new squadron! No. 279. Duties Air-Sea rescue (ASR) with twin engined bomber – & other incidental jobs! At the moment I am the only member of the Sqdn – or was. Two air gunners turned up today. My second aircraft arrived today. (Brand new from the US, name: Hudson) I tried her out this afternoon & christened her. The first two 'kites', A279 & B279 are called 'Queen of the Air' & 'Flying Pig' respectively. You wouldn't believe the difference possible in flying characteristics in two machines that are identical down to the last rivet. I'll tell you more about the job when there is more to tell. There is one rather interesting possibility. With good luck and due judgement, the latter covering a multitude of sins & vices, I should get command of a flight. In which case I should be made acting (paid) Squadron

Leader. Which <u>would</u> be rather a feather in the headgear, considering age and what not.

By the 26th accommodation had been arranged in two offices located in one of Bircham's A-type hangars, one of which was used to store equipment, the decontamination centre now being full. The squadron had also taken delivery of thirteen Hudson Mk IIIs by this date. The following day three more offices were acquired for storage in No. 2 Hangar and the squadron strength was four pilots, one observer, five WOp/AGs, one WOp/ME and seven ground staff. Over the following days all of the paraphernalia required by an operational squadron began to arrive and personnel numbers also increased to sixty.

The CO, S/Ldr Lynham, arrived on the 29th and the personnel, now numbering seventy-nine, were allocated to A and B Flights. By the following day the squadron had 131 men and the CO had managed to negotiate the complete take-over of No. 2 Hangar for the sole use of 279 Sqn. The flow of aircraft, personnel and equipment continued in the early days of December, but there was little hope of any flying due to the poor weather.

The first days of December saw the Germans only 5 miles from the Kremlin but the real hammer blow to British morale was the unexpected Japanese attacks on British and American bases in the Far East. Within a week the Japanese had attacked Pearl Harbor, leaving the American fleet in ruins. The Japanese forces stormed

One of the hangars at Bircham Newton (via Carl James/HAiB).

through Shanghai, Hong Kong, Malaya and Singapore, as well as landing in Thailand. By the end of the month the battleship *Prince of Wales* and the cruiser *Repulse* had been sunk off Malaya and Hong Kong had been captured and the Philippines had been invaded. The only good news for Britain was the lifting of the siege at Tobruk and the recapture of Derna and Benghazi. Against this background the first training flights since Rashleigh's were made on 7 December and the thoughts of the squadron personnel turned to the hope of some Christmas leave. Meanwhile the groundcrew, under F/Sgt Venemore, set to fitting dual control equipment to Hudson T9401:D.

To the great joy of the aircrew the dual control was ready the following day and training commenced. Two days later the squadron received instructions to hand over its dual control Hudson and two trained crews and some ground crew to another unit. Despite the best efforts of the CO to have the order cancelled, the postings went ahead, throwing the training programme into turmoil. The squadron did not let the loss of aircraft and personnel deter them, however, and throughout December they pressed ahead with training. The squadron celebrated its first Christmas at Bircham Newton by flying till mid-morning and then the senior NCOs (SNCOs) were entertained in the officers' mess, following which both officers and SNCOs made their way to the Airmen's Mess to serve Christmas dinner, calling in at the sergeants' mess on the way.

January 1942 saw the Japanese continue their rampage, pushing the US-Filipino force onto the Bataan peninsula, landing in Borneo and the Celebes, occupying Rabaul and forcing British troops to fall back to Singapore Island. There was better news in North Africa with the recapture of Sollum on the 12th and Halfaya in Cyrenaica on the 17th. Once again, though, the British victories were to be short-lived, Rommel counter-attacked on the 21st and by the 29th had recaptured Benghazi. The transport of supplies from the USA would also be dramatically affected, not only by the demands of the Pacific war but also by the shift of the U-boat war to the east coast of America.

Undeterred by all this the squadron continued to build its strength and carried on training. By the first day of 1942 it had eighteen aircraft on strength and had flown 148 hours in its six-week existence. Accommodation was satisfactory and equipment sufficient, American tools for the Hudsons being the only things in short supply. The 2nd saw a bonus in the form of thirty-six more groundcrew posted in from 407 Sqn at North Coates, which was in the process of manning with Canadian personnel.

The squadron carried out its first operational standby on 8 January when F/Lts Rashleigh and Barrett and Singleton and Harrington manned Hudson T9414:V, though no sortie was flown. On the 9th P/O L.J. Whittaker force-landed his Hudson at Swanton Morley on one engine after suffering an engine failure and difficulty with the flaps. The CO was noted in the squadron

A vertical aerial view of the hangars at Bircham Newton taken in 2004.

diary to be 'well pleased with this effort'. Until now the squadron had been busy receiving aircraft, equipment and personnel and, having had some time to settle in and carry out some training on the Hudson, the CO took the opportunity to brief the aircrew on their operational role.

By the 10th the squadron was being plagued by oil cooler unserviceability, so much so that the flying training programme was severely disrupted. Serviceability was further set back by damage to another Hudson when Brookman overshot the field on landing at Detling; luckily the damage was minor. On 14 January the squadron received another blow to its training when it was ordered to detach six Hudsons on loan to Horsham St Faith for six weeks. Concerns were raised as to whether any would return. On top of this a further four Hudsons were scattered across the country at Detling, Manby, Swanton Morley and Skellingthorpe. The latter returned on the 16th, flown by P/O Whittaker. He had been to Skellingthorpe for briefing on the use of Lindholme gear, which would be the primary rescue aid used by the squadron. Its purpose was to provide equipment and rations, air dropped, to sustain ditched aircrew until surface vessels could arrive on scene and effect a rescue.

The procedure followed by the squadron crews would be to fly at not more than 1,000 feet and on sighting a dinghy, drop smoke floats to mark the position. The smoke floats would also help in determining wind strength and direction. The Lindholme gear, consisting of one large and four small containers roped together, would then be dropped from the bomb racks so that it would drift onto the survivors position. The containers were buoyant and would spread out to a length of 280 yards. On impact with the water the centre, largest container automatically deployed and inflated a new dinghy. The survivors would then grab the ropes and haul themselves to it, and it would provide larger and hope-fully better accommodation than the possibly holed and damaged original. Once on board the new dinghy the survivors could then haul in the other yellow containers, which held a variety of equipment including food, drinks, clothing and pyrotechnics (See Appendix V).

Poor weather curtailed flying for the next few days until the 19th, when yet another Hudson was damaged. Sgt Jackman made a very heavy landing at Docking, badly damaging the under-carriage. The 22nd saw the squadron's first operational sortie when F/O Tyrrell was sent out on a search. Unfortunately nothing was found. On the 26th it was announced that the squadron was officially operational. The following day F/Lt E. Fitchew and P/Os Heywood and Long all flew operational patrols, although the sorties were treated as operational training until all of the crews were fully trained. On the same day the CO was promoted to wing commander and on the 28th he flew his first operational patrol with the squadron.

On 29 January Brookman, flying Hudson N and F/O Tyrrell in T9414:V flew an unsuccessful search. Three sorties were flown on the 30th during which Sgt Garrard, on a buoy patrol, twice hit the sea in very bad visibility. He got away with it but had not been helped by his instruments 'going haywire'.

February saw the Japanese bombing Port Moresby in New Guinea and landing in Singapore, followed by the surrender of British forces on the island. They also invaded Sumatra and Bali and were only 100 miles from Rangoon in Burma by the 22nd. On the home front the only items of good news were the appointment of Air Marshal Harris as Commander-in-Chief (C-in-C) Bomber Command and the successful paratroop raid on Bruneval on the 28th, during which vital radar equipment was captured. Just prior to the arrival of Harris at Bomber Command the bombers had gone on an area bombing offensive. Harris would nurture this force and area-bombing techniques alike and as the force grew more and more crews would end up in the icy seas. No. 279 Sqn was going to have a busy future.

LAC Ernest Farrow, who joined the squadron at Bircham Newton in 1942, recalled life and operations there.

During the time that I was posted to 279 Squadron we were based at Bircham Newton in Norfolk, the nearest airfield to Germany proper in the British Isles. The squadron was engaged in Air Sea Rescue work and was equipped with Lockheed Hudson aircraft, which were fitted with the latest version of ASV radar equipment. This was serviced by Canadian technicians seconded to 279.

The aircraft carried in the bomb bay two 'Large Life Rafts', which were dropped by parachute to downed aircrew, who were located floating in their much lighter dinghies. I understood that these heavy-duty rafts were equipped with a signal device, which enabled Air Sea Rescue vessels to quickly locate them. Several rescues were made using this equipment.

Bircham Newton was a peacetime airfield, with permanent built hangars, barracks etc. It was a major overhaul facility and, so as not to attract German night bombers, night flying was not permitted. All our night flying was done from our satellite airfield, Docking, about six miles from Bircham. When Bomber Command's airfields in Yorkshire were fogged in their aircraft were diverted to Docking, where we were required to carry out the 'Between Flight Inspections' so that these aircraft could return to their bases as soon as the weather cleared. The big worry was that Docking and Bircham Newton were so close to Germany that these bombers were serviced quickly and got out of harms way. We were kept very busy, especially in the summer, when it did not get dark until 2200 hrs.

Patrols continued into February, often hampered by poor weather. On 11 February the squadron's first member, F/Lt Rashleigh, was posted to Catfoss as an instructor, being long overdue for a rest from operations. (It had also been discovered that he had been posted to the squadron by mistake and should never have been at Bircham Newton!)

On 12 February the *Scharnhorst* and *Gneisenau* broke out of Brest. When the news leaked out the squadron felt sure that it would be called upon any moment. The following day, Friday the 13th, the squadron carried out five unsuccessful search sorties during which Hudson V8993:J, flown by Sgt Garrard, failed to return. Garrard, Sgts Redhead, Schulty and Logan were the squadron's first casualties. On St Valentine's Day 1942 F/Lt Tyrrell, known as 'Happy' to his colleagues, was returning to Bircham Newton from Thorney Island when his Hudson collided with a tree. Tyrrell managed to keep it flying and landed safely at Woodley, near Reading. No one was hurt. 'Happy' Tyrrell had to suffer much leg pulling.

Accurate navigation was one of the keys to a successful search and since mid-January S/Ldr Ingle had been attached from No. 16 Group to instruct the squadron in navigation techniques. During the period of his stay he gave many navigation lessons to the crews.

On 17 February two Hudsons, T9414:V and T9394:C, carried out searches, but the only excitement was the sighting of an enemy aircraft, possibly an Me 110, off Cromer. The weather restricted flying to buoy patrols over the next few days and the

only point of note recorded in the squadron diary was the introduction of soap coupons on the 19th – it would appear that
hygiene was to be rationed! Several searches were flown over the
next week with no result, although on 28 February P/O
Somerville sighted an empty dinghy during a search. He also
sighted a floating mine, which he attempted to sink. The
squadron had yet to find or rescue any ditched aircrew but March
would see a change of fortune. Indeed, on the first day of
March three Hudsons piloted by F/Lt Tyrrell, P/O Zumar and
F/Sgt Spencer were out on searches when Tyrrell saw a dinghy
with two aircraft circling it. He was lucky to spot it as he was
searching in the dark. Such was the rarity of a 'find' at night that
Group requested a full report on the incident. It read as follows:

> *Aircraft 'V' was detailed to search for a dinghy believed to be about
> nine miles off Sheringham. The aircraft was airborne at 0015
> hours on the 1st March 1942 the visibility then being fair. There
> was a certain amount of mist and at 4,000 feet there was cloud esti-
> mated at three tenths. The aircraft set course for the area to be
> searched and arrived on ETA. There was two or three miles when
> looking into the moon but visibility was otherwise bad. The dinghy
> was located by the flashing of the torches of the occupants.*
>
> *The possibilities of air sea rescue at night as suggested by this
> trip appear to be as follows: calm sea, no haze and at least half moon
> are essential before a night search is attempted. An extra member
> of the crew is definitely required for look-out purposes. Flares are
> of little help in locating a dinghy but are useful to enable it, when
> found, to be held. Flame floats, however, should be carried.
> Searches should be made into the moon at a lower altitude than in
> daytime say 400 feet. Pre-arranged R/T and Very pistol combina-
> tion should be arranged to contact surface craft in the vicinity.*

Much work would be carried out over the coming months and
years to advance the ASR techniques employed in the rescue of
downed aircrew, and the squadron would be in the forefront of
this development.

Despite the grim news filtering back from the fighting in the
Far East, with Java abandoned and Rangoon surrounded, and the
equally difficult conflict in North Africa and the Mediterranean,
where the island of Malta had suffered greatly in 1,600 air raids,
the irrepressible humour of the squadron still managed to shine

through. During the first week of March a film crew visited it to make a film on behalf of the Air Ministry. Several aircraft flew out over Hunstanton so the film crew could get shots of them departing on searches. P/O A.A. 'Gus' Henderson was filmed in the cockpit for pilot close ups and the squadron diary noted that he 'is now hoping to be re-mustered as a film star'! Whilst the filming progressed several real searches were flown with no success, though Henderson, whilst searching on the 10th, found an oil patch, two wheels and other wreckage. The following day Hudsons flown by Sgt Marchand, F/Sgt Spencer, P/O Somerville and P/O Heywood all carried out searches and all found patches of oil and floating wreckage. Heywood came across the sad and lonely sight of an empty, capsized dinghy.

Over the preceding weeks the groundcrew, that hardy, over-worked and underappreciated group had been working extremely hard keeping the Hudsons in the air. Their efforts did not go unnoticed by the CO and he had a notice read out to them at flight parade on the morning of Saturday, 14 March. It read:

During the past week 279 squadron has been called upon to make more operational sorties than during any week since the formation of the Unit.

On every occasion the aircraft involved have been off sharp on time. This has only been made possible by the punctuality and keenness of the ground crews. On numerous occasions they, and the Instrument Repairers, Electricians, Signals and Armourers, have been called upon to work continuously throughout the night in order to have aircraft ready by dawn.

I want to convey to all NCOs and aircraftmen in 'A' Flight, 'B' Flight and 'Maintenance' Flight, my appreciation of their whole-hearted co-operation.

Signed Lynham
Wing Commander
Commanding 279 Squadron

Since 10 March the squadron had moved into No. 1 Hangar, a squadron hangar, which was a great improvement on the previous accommodation, a maintenance hangar. The main improvement was in the provision of office space, the CO commented that 'The chief (and perhaps only) person to really benefit is the adjutant, P/O Nealand, who gets an excellent office.' On 15 March P/O Zumar, P/O Somerville, F/Sgt Jackman and P/O R McKimm all carried out searches and though all four found wreckage there was no sign of life. Four days later the squadron suffered another aircraft loss when F/Sgt Long crashed at Woodley. Luckily none of the crew was hurt.

The squadron commenced dinghy trials on 20 March under F/Lt Tyrrell. They were conducted to establish drift of a dinghy; it appeared that they would drift with the current rather than the wind direction. F/Lt Tyrrell carried out a search patrol on 26 March during which he sighted a Ju 88. It closed to attack his Hudson and he turned to meet and attack it scoring hits. The following day six search sorties were carried out, but all that was found was a small amount of wreckage. P/O McKimm crashed his Hudson on return to Bircham Newton, but the crew escaped unhurt. Two days later it was the turn of Sgt S.K. Scott to wreck his Hudson in a crash at Bircham Newton. Once again the crew were uninjured. If nothing else the Hudson was a sturdy design.

Searches continued to the end of the month with no success and the squadron was involved in a second series of dinghy trials, during which P/O Cowling observed results which confirmed that the dinghy would drift with local tidal streams rather than the wind direction.

By April British and Commonwealth forces in Burma were in full flight towards India and news on the American fronts was no better with the fall of the Philippines. By mid-April Malta had suffered 2,000 air raids and been awarded the George Cross for its bravery. Allied morale was given another fillip by the news of Colonel Jimmy Doolittle's courageous B-25 bombing raid on Tokyo on the 18th. Closer to home the *Luftwaffe* was not quite a spent force and German bombers commenced raids on Britain's historic cities; these raids, known as 'Baedeker Raids', resulted in Bath, Exeter, Norwich and York all being attacked towards the latter end of the month.

April Fool's Day 1942 saw four searches carried out. During one F/Sgt Long, flying T9405:U, had his port engine catch fire. The fire was quickly extinguished with the fire extinguisher, but not before pieces of the engine flew off. Long made a forced landing at Horsham St Faith. The dinghy trials continued and with a very rough sea and a wind gusting 40–50 mph the dinghy was found to be extremely steady and shipped only a few pints of water. Unfortunately, almost without exception, all of those on

S/Ldr Mandow, Medical Officer at Bircham Newton, who assisted in the dinghy trials carried out by 279 Sqn (See Appendix VI). (Eunice Ravell Collection via Lyn Gambles)

the accompanying tender were seasick and the trial was abandoned as the tender made its way through a vicious squall to sheltered waters. The trial once again confirmed the results of previous observations.

The 12 April saw the squadron lose another Hudson, V8996:X, in a bad crash at Ringstead during a night-flying sortie. The pilot was Sgt Somerville, and his observer Sgt Sprung was badly injured.

On 21 April eight of the squadron's Hudsons were out on searches. P/O R. M. Lacy in T9414:V sighted an empty rowing boat with its oars shipped and Sgt Jackman flying Hudson V9031:P came across an empty dinghy. The sight of so much wreckage and empty dinghies must have been extremely frustrating for the crews on these sorties.

The 28th was a sad day for the squadron. F/O Heaton and P/O Hides were sent to Coltishall for the funeral of Sgt Logan, a member of Sgt Garrard's crew, which had been lost on 13 February. Logan was recovered from the sea on 26 April.

At the end of April the squadron began detaching aircraft to other airfields, an occurrence which would become the norm over the remaining years of the war. Three aircraft and crews were detached to Sumburgh, via Kinloss, arriving on the 28th. The last day of the month saw further searches, this time for the remains of a burning aircraft. Nothing was found, but later in the day a further search revealed small pieces of wreckage and sadly no survivors. The squadron could only hope for more success during the coming summer.

CHAPTER TWO

May – October 1942

Anew force arrived in Britain in May 1942; the US 8th Air Force, the first contingent filtering into the country on the 12th. The build-up of the air force would be slow, mainly because of the constant demands for transfer of units and equipment to other theatres of war, but eventually it would grow to become a formidable force. Very many members of this future force would find themselves at the mercy of the unforgiving sea following a ditching and be grateful to 279 Sqn for their deliverance.

May 1942 would bring the first real successes to the squadron, but not before S/Ldr Pye managed to damage severely Hudson T9408:D. Pye had been taxiing to dispersal when one wheel fell into a hole caused by ground subsidence. The Hudson tipped over onto a wing tip and was damaged. It had to be despatched to 43 Group for repair.

There was great jubilation on 4 May when the squadron carried out its first successful rescue. P/O Lacy, captaining Hudson T9414:V, took off from Docking to carry out a night ASR patrol following a fix received from a Wellington in distress. The Hudson reached its last known position at 0516 hours and Lacy dropped flame floats to assist the search. He circled the position for six minutes and then set course for the position of the previous fix obtained from the Wellington's transmissions. His intention was to fly up and down the track of the Wellington until daylight. Two white flashing lights were sighted at 0524 hours but after circling the position for four minutes the crew concluded that they were their own flame floats flickering on the surface as they died out.

Lacy resumed the original track and at 0528 hours the turret gunner, P/O H.T. Calvert, sighted a signal distress marine (SDM) 2 miles dead astern. He quickly alerted Lacy, who altered course. One minute later he dropped another flame float. A few minutes later another SDM was sighted about three-quarters of a mile from the flame float. Lacy flew over the SDM position and sighted a dinghy in its glow. He dropped more flame floats and Sgt W. Adams, the W/Op, got off a sighting report. The Hudson crew then lost sight of the dinghy, but they then sighted the tail fin of the ditched Wellington, still floating above water. Setting course downwind from the wreck they resighted the dinghy which contained six occupants. Four of the ditched crew stood up at the approach of the Hudson and in the words of the squadron diary 'expressed great joy (and who blames them)'.

Lacy dropped a Lindholme dinghy to the survivors and eventually their dinghy drifted onto it. Two more 279 Sqn Hudsons arrived on the scene about an hour later and at 0839 hours two launches arrived and picked up the ditched crew. Captained by F/O Skarpetowski, it was from No. 305 (Polish) Sqn based at Lindholme. The Wellington had been one of two of the type lost along with three Halifaxes from a force of eighty-one aircraft despatched by Bomber Command to raid Hamburg that night. It is perhaps appropriate that the squadron's first successful rescue with the Lindholme dinghy was of a Lindholme based crew! They were fortunate in that the Hudson sighted them within an hour of the ditching, thus saving them from many desperate hours, or even days, clinging to life in their dinghy.

The squadron diarist was obviously a man of some humour as he recorded the arrival of S/Ldr H.F. Binks on posting from Silloth on 10 May as follows: 'A good looking boy with wavy hair and a devil with the women – favourite flower "hops".' Obviously no further comment was necessary!

The Squadron gunnery officer, F/Lt Barrett and seven others departed for a 'cats eye' Course at Felixstowe on 17 May. On the 22nd P/O Henderson of B Flt managed to overshoot the runway in his Hudson and ended up across the road. Luckily no one was injured. On 24 May a second 'cats eye' course at Felixstowe was attended by P/O McKimm and seven others. Although fifteen searches were carried out throughout the month, none was successful. The focus of the squadron's attention was on an initial rumour that they were to be moved to Langham followed almost as quickly by notification that they would move to Docking to make room for No. 235 Sqn. The airmen were profoundly disturbed by this news, as life at Bircham Newton was good, with no bomb-dump duties, stretcher-bearer or gas duties, or duty corporal etc to make life tedious. To their great relief the move was cancelled on the 29th. The following night Bomber Command carried out the first of the 'thousand bomber' raids against Cologne, dropping 1,455 tons of bombs onto the city and its surroundings. Luckily, the services of the squadron, to search for downed crews, were not required.

Throughout May, and indeed in previous months, 279 Sqn had gained a reputation for putting on the best dances on the station. In fact, such were the comments in the squadron diary that the reader might wonder what sort of discipline was maintained at Bircham Newton, or how higher authority hoped to contain the exuberance of young crews, whose life expectancy was short and who intended to make the most of their time. Following one dance the diary recorded the following: 'Who was put to bed by the padre? Whose girlfriend wore no knickers and why? Whose girlfriend hid herself in —?' and the following gem:

P/O X; "Meet my wife, P/O Y."
  P/O Y; "Pleased to meet you Mrs X, any wife of P/O X is a friend of mine."

Following the second 'thousand bomber' raid on Essen on the night of 1/2 June the squadron was airborne before dawn on 2 June with P/O Lacy and F/Sgt Spencer flying patrols in V8979:W and T9405:U respectively. Searches were carried out in two areas with a total of ten Hudsons. During one patrol Sgt Scott in T9414:V and Sgt Werrin, flying V9031:P, sighted a dinghy with six men on board 35 miles off the Dutch coast. They then came under attack from two Me 109s. Hudson P/279 sustained several hits during the attack, P/O Allan, the observer, and Sgt Parsons, the gunner, were injured. Both continued to man their guns and Parsons claimed one of the Messerschmitts destroyed. Werrin evaded the fighters skilfully and, with the rudder unserviceable and over 100 holes in the Hudson fuselage, managed to land safely at Eastchurch. Sgt Scott and crew were more fortunate and escaped with no damage. Sgt White, loosed some bursts off at one of the German fighters at a range of 300 yards. F/Lt Fitchew flew down to Eastchurch later in the day to pick up Sgt Werrin and his W/Op, Sgt Buller, whilst Allan and Parsons were taken to hospital. A further search by F/279 later failed to locate the drifting dinghy.

The following day the search continued and P/O Whittaker and S/Ldr Pye both carried out night sorties, during which coloured pyrotechnics were sighted in the probable position of the dinghy. The following morning Sgt Marchand and his crew were off before dawn in Hudson F/279 to continue the search. Shortly afterwards four more Hudsons were airborne to search for another ditched crew. After reaching the search area they dispersed to widen the search and at 0650 hours Sgt A.W. Campbell, the observer on board N/279 flown by Sgt Faux, spotted distress signals. Closing on them they soon discovered a dinghy with six men on board. N/279 was not carrying a Lindholme dinghy and could offer no assistance to the ditched fliers, other than to continue circling their position. W/Op Sgt Darwin got off a sighting report to base, which was intercepted by Sgt Guthrie, flying T9405:U. Arriving on scene at 0735 hours, Guthrie dropped his Lindholme dinghy to the crew of F/O Mandala, who had ditched their Ingham based 300 (Polish) Sqn Wellington 35 miles east of Cromer two hours before their sighting by Sgt Faux. The Poles had scattered flourescine marker dye and this showed up well from 3,000 feet, assisting in their location. The lucky crew was seen to transfer to the Lindholme dinghy and two hours later they were successfully picked up by rescue launches. Mandala's Wellington was one of four lost, along with seven other types, in a raid on Bremen by 170 aircraft of Bomber Command.

The dinghy sighted on the 2nd was known to be still afloat and close to the enemy coast. With a potentially difficult rescue and the risk of the Germans using the dinghy as bait for their fighters the squadron was given an escort of four Spitfires from No. 610 Sqn for their Hudsons. The search was planned for dusk and W/Cdr Lynham and his crew took off in Hudson T9400:B from Ludham. Unfortunately, they failed to find the dinghy and returned to land at Docking. P/O Senior and his 10 Sqn Halifax crew were not to be abandoned to the enemy, however. The RN sent two high-speed launches out to pick up the crew. Making a dash past several enemy E-boats they recovered five of the six crew members, one of them seriously injured, and returned them safely. Only one of the crew, the rear gunner, was lost when he failed to get out of the ditched Halifax. The Halifax was one of thirty-one bombers lost from the second 'thousand force', which had bombed Essen on the night of 1/2 June. Reports filtered back to W/Cdr Lynham later that the crew would not have survived their three days in the water had it not been for the successful drop of the Lindholme dinghy by 279 Sqn.

In the early hours of 9 June P/O Field put his Linton-on-Ouse-based 35 Sqn Halifax down on the sea 45 miles east of Orfordness. The seven-man crew scrambled out of the doomed aircraft and into their dinghy and settled down to await rescue. No. 279 Sqn launched six aircraft in two waves of three to commence the search. S/Ldr Binks in Hudson T9399:R soon sighted them and wireless operator P/O Cowling sent out a sighting report. Very soon the Halifax crew had the heartening sight of not only S/Ldr Binks, but five more of the squadron's Hudsons arriving and circling their position! At 1022 hours two rescue launches arrived and the airmen and their dinghy were taken on board for the journey back to Yarmouth. Later W/Cdr Lynham and S/Ldr Binks drove down to Yarmouth to meet the crew and obtain information about the rescue. They found them to be in good spirits and doing well.

The following day was a disappointing one for the squadron. S/Ldr R. Pye, on a pre-dawn patrol in T9414:V, sighted some Very lights. This resulted in four search sweeps totalling fourteen sorties being flown, all to no avail as nothing was found. On 12 June a four-aircraft search was commenced after a dinghy was sighted by a Beaufighter. The search was called off when it transpired that it was empty. The following week was taken up with training sorties, during which Sgt Guthrie managed to damage S/279 in a taxiing accident after a night landing at Docking.

The squadron was able to take a well-earned rest on the 19th when a party was held in the sergeants' mess. The guests included members of the four crews from 10, 35, 300 and 305 squadron's successfully rescued by No. 279. An excellent dinner was provided and earlier in the day a BBC Recording Unit interviewed several of the squadron aircrew. Following the party the squadron got back to the serious business of ASR. On 23 June Sgt Watts managed to crash Hudson T9405:U at Bircham Newton on return from a search.

Three days later, following the 'thousand bomber' raid on Bremen, the squadron expected to be busy and, sure enough, they were. During the morning two rescues were effected. The first was of the crew of a 12 Operational Training Unit (OTU) Wellington, captained by P/O Morrison, which had ditched 10 miles east of Cromer. Morrison's was one of four aircraft to ditch that night. P/O Lacy and his crew in K/279 sighted the dinghy 5 miles off Cromer and soon two trawlers arrived to assist. The tail of the submerged Wellington was still visible on the surface and one of the trawlers attempted to take the aircraft in tow! The second aircraft was Wellington Mk II Z8528:SM-R from 305 Sqn at Lindholme. Its Polish crew, captained by P/O Szybka, only had to endure three hours in their dinghy. Found by Sgt Marchand in E/279, they quickly received a Lindholme dinghy, which landed only 5 yards away. Unfortunately, the Poles were unable to reach it. They were later picked up by a high-speed launch. The tragedy that night in the heavy seas was the loss of the Wellington's second pilot G/Capt S.J. Skarzynski, Lindholme's station commander. Szybka and his crew could hear him calling for help for over thirty minutes but were unable to locate him due to lack of effective control over the dinghy in the heavy seas. Skarzynski, who had established a pre-war record for the lightest aircraft to cross the Atlantic, from St Louis du Senegal to Natal, in RWD-5, was later washed up on the German coast.

Training and inconclusive searches continued to the end of June and on the 29th A Flt was detached from Bircham Newton to Benbecula, taking with them Hudsons A, B, E, F, H and V. The following day a flight of Ansons from No. 280 Sqn arrived to replace the Benbecula detachment.

By the end of the month the Germans were continuing to advance through Russia and the Crimea and the Japanese rampage through the Far East was seemingly unstoppable. On top of this British forces in North Africa had fallen back on a line at El Alamein and following an unsuccessful counter offensive had settled into a defensive position on that line. The members of the squadron could do little but listen to the glum news and concentrate on the job at hand.

The first day of July saw three Hudsons out on a search, but Sgt Marchand in K/279 had to turn back after twenty minutes due to engine trouble. Unfortunately, the other two crews also turned round with him. Luck was with the survivors though as their dinghy was later spotted by a Beaufighter from 235 Sqn.

There was little activity, other than training, until 9 July when a fellow ASR squadron, No. 280, had their first success in finding a ditched crew with their Ansons. Three Hudsons from 279 Sqn later relieved the Ansons over the ditched crew. On 14 July F/Lt Tyrrell carried out a search for a ditched Halifax crew off Wells but nothing was found.

A visiting party came from Oakington to learn about ASR and amongst them was an officer from the USAAF. With the arrival of the Americans in Britain it would only be a matter of time before they began to supply 'trade' to the ASR squadrons. The following day four of the crews detached to Benbecula returned to Bircham Newton, whilst Sgt Scott and F/Lt Tyrrell and their crews were detached to Leuchars.

Hudson J/279 was crashed at Stornoway on the 16th, but once again the squadron was lucky as no one was injured in the incident. F/Lt Geoffrey White was the WOp/AG on this aircraft, flown by F/Lt Fitchew. White had flown sixty-six sorties with 279 Sqn and this was the last of thirty-seven flown with Fitchew. He recalls: 'We crash landed at Stornoway with the total destruction of the aircraft by fire. The crash was caused by u/s brakes.'

Six days later, on the 22nd, six aircraft were out on searches. F/Sgt Jackman and his crew, Sgts MacGregor, Bastow and Bishop, sighted a dinghy with two men on board 34 miles east of Yarmouth. The survivors were P/O Majcherczy, the captain of Wellington Mk IV Z1472:GR-H of No. 301 (Polish) Sqn, based at Hemswell, and his WOp/AG Sgt Jablonski. Following a raid on Duisburg, during which twelve of the 291 bombers dispatched were lost, the Wellington had been out on an ASR search. They were attacked by two FW190s and three of the crew were badly injured. Majcherczy was forced to ditch the Wellington at 1235 hours losing the badly injured crewmen in the process. The dinghy was sighted just over four hours later by Jackman and the rescue of the survivors was completed by high-speed launches an hour and a half later at 1830 hours. By now the Squadron's score of successful rescues stood at seven dinghies and thirty-seven aircrew saved.

Following this rescue, the fourth of a Polish crew, there was much speculation as to why the Poles seemed to ditch successfully and British crews did not. The CO declared that he was beginning to see red at the lack of successful British rescues!

The Benbecula detachment continued throughout July and the Squadron was further scattered when the CO, S/Ldr Pye and P/O Somerville and crews detached to Iceland on the 26th.

The early days of August 1942 saw immediate success when P/O Somerville and his crew in H/279, operating from Reykjavik, sighted three ships' lifeboats 60 miles south-west of the Westmaan Islands on the 2nd. They contained twenty-three survivors from the SS *Flora*, which had been torpedoed and sunk. Somerville directed a trawler to the boats and the survivors were rescued. August also saw much movement, with P/O McKimm, Sgt Faux and Sgt Woolford and crews being detached to Thorney Island. The following day they were moved to Chivenor, where Zumar, Werrin and Scott joined them. The Icelandic detachment returned to Bircham Newton the same day, having staged through Wick on the 14th.

Success was not long in coming for the Chivenor detachment, Sgt Woolford and crew in N/279 sighted two dinghies 10 miles off Land's End on the 16th. They had been found earlier in the day by other aircraft and the survivors were subsequently picked up by two high-speed launches (HSLs). The same day Faux and McKimm, in Y/279 and D/279 respectively, sighted two dinghies about 60 miles off Brest. Faux dropped a Lindholme dinghy and then both crews returned to base and reported the position. On the following day Zumar, Werrin and Scott took off from Chivenor to relocate them. Zumar and his crew in H/279 sighted them; one was empty, but the other two contained five and two survivors respectively. Six of the seven were the survivors of Wellington D/172 Sqn from Chivenor. This crew, F/Os Triggs and Badham, P/O Devonshire and F/Sgts Cartwright and McLean, had been in the dinghy for six days after ditching. The seventh survivor, F/O Watson, was the co-pilot and sole survivor of Sunderland B/461 Sqn, which had crashed and sunk in an attempt to rescue the Wellington crew. Two HSLs were directed to the scene and picked up the survivors. Later that same day three of the Chivenor detachment returned to Bircham Newton. The rest of the detachment returned on the 19th.

The US 8th Air Force carried out the first all-American

bombing raid of the war in Europe on 17th August with a raid on Rouen in France. The crews did not require the assistance of the ASR squadrons on this first operation but they would be grateful for their help in the near future. Two days after this the great amphibious raid on Dieppe was mounted, but, despite fierce air battles, the squadron's assistance was not required.

The squadron was only to have a few days together at Bircham Newton before the crews were on their travels again. On 23 August a four-aircraft detachment with the crews captained by Jackman, Forge, Marchand and Werrin flew down to St Eval in Cornwall. It was led by recently promoted S/Ldr Tyrrell. Later that day F/Sgt Jackman and Sgt Werrin, in F/279 and H/279 respectively, were sent out to search for a crew of a ditched Whitley but returned with nothing to report.

A major search commenced on 28 August after a report from the crew of Beaufighter J/236 Sqn that they had sighted a dinghy with two occupants 30 miles off Texel. Three Hudsons were dispatched to search for it but found nothing. During the night a further three crews went out but also returned with negative results. The following day Sgt Marchand, F/O Stevens and P/O Scott took off at dawn, escorted by a single Beaufighter, to continue the search. This time they were successful and Stevens in V/279 sighted the dinghy. Scott in S/279 managed to obtain a good D/F fix of the position and Marchand, flying A/279, dropped a Lindholme dinghy to the survivors. Stevens then homed rescue launches to the position. During the rescue Marchand managed to drive off a Dornier Do 24 with his front guns when it attempted to land near the dinghy. No hits were observed, but the Dornier made a hurried retreat into the haze. The survivors were S/Ldr Jay and Sgt Kent of 236 Sqn based at Oulton. They had ditched their Beaufighter, P/236 at 1510 hours the previous day.

The detachments continued to come around thick and fast. Stevens, Farrar, Zumar and crews were off to St Eval on the 30th, and Woolford set off for Benbecula the same day. A surprise addition to the squadron strength arrived during the searches of the 28th in the form of a Wellington. It was hoped to commence trial flights in this novel acquisition as soon as dual controls had been fitted.

LAC Ernest Farrow remembers the many detachments of Squadron aircraft and personnel.

279 had permanent detachments at two airfields. Two aircraft were based at Benbecula in the Outer Hebrides covering the Western Approaches, a route used by Ferry Command flying aircraft from North America. The second deployment was to St Eval in Cornwall, where the Squadron covered the Bay of Biscay. Several successful rescues were made in this area. One that was not successful involved a Canadian pilot, Flying Officer Zumar, whose brother was lost over the Bay of Biscay. F/O Zumar flew three six-hour missions and was prepared to fly a fourth until ordered to stand down due to fatigue.

The St Eval detachment was always reinforced from Bircham when dignitaries were flying back to or away from the UK. On one occasion Winston Churchill, who had been to a conference in North Africa, was well covered by at least five aircraft. I was also at St Eval when three German generals, who had been captured in the Western Desert, were flown back to Britain for internment.

Our Squadron also had temporary detachments to Leuchars in Fife covering Beaufighters equipped with torpedoes, who were attacking shipping of the coast of Norway.

By September 1942 the tide was slowly beginning to turn against the Axis. The Allies were by no means on safe ground yet but fierce fighting in North Africa saw the 8th Army holding its own against the Germans and Italians, whilst in the Far East Australian and US forces pushed the Japanese out of Milne Bay and began to capture Guadalcanal. In Burma the British forces began a counter-offensive against the Japanese in the Arakan. The Germans had more success advancing towards Stalingrad but countering this the Russians crossed the Volga north-west of Moscow, capturing territory previously lost. Towards the end of the month, in a portent of successful raids to come, RAF Mosquitoes made a successful low-level attack on the Gestapo HQ in Oslo.

While these momentous events were taking place the squadron was racking up a few little victories of its own, as well as some tragic losses.

The detachment at Benbecula, which had commenced on 29 June, at long last had a successful search on 5th September when Sgt Faux, flying Hudson V/279, spotted a dinghy with a single occupant of the north coast of the island of Coll in the Hebrides.

In fact there were two survivors from a Sunderland, O/228

Sgt Faux of the Benbecula detachment was successful in finding the crew of a ditched Sunderland, similar to this one, on 5 September 1942. He successfully homed a pinnace to the scene and two survivors were picked up. (Via A Rodgers)

Sqn, P/O Ruffell and F/Sgt Scroggs. The rest of the Sunderland's eleven-man crew was lost, though seven bodies were recovered later. Faux managed successfully to direct Pinnace 98 to the survivors through poor visibility and a heavy swell.

The squadron suffered another loss on 8 September. Sgt Farrar and crew in Y/279 took off from St Eval in company with Zumar's crew, flying T/279 to carry out a search. In the search area three Arados were sighted and a short, sharp combat ensued during which Zumar's crew managed to fire off about 1,100 rounds. No hits were observed on the enemy aircraft and none was received in return. During the fight Y/279 was last seen making for cloud cover by Zumar. On the return journey he received a call to divert to Chivenor due to the worsening weather at St Eval, and landed there safely at 2035 hours. With the weather closed in, Sgt H.T. Farrer attempted to land at St Eval but crashed and burnt out only 1 mile short of the airfield. Australians Farrer, F/O L.W. Waters and F/O J.J. Holloman and F/Sgt J.D. Granger, a Canadian, were all killed in the crash.

On 11 September the Hudsons were out on searches again, with two bodies being found floating in the water. The CO and S/Ldr Pye flew the Wellington, which had now been fitted with

WAAF of Bircham Newton MT Section 20 September 1942. Rear L to R: Pauline Lendon, Doris Beck, Flip Hart, Peggy Rushby, Joan Pratt, Mary Leonard, Gladys Veysey, Pat Cox, Dorothy 'Don' Walmesley-Cottham, Renee, Doris Crutchfield, Nora Whitley, Lil Tod, Yetta Zwart, Betti Williams. Middle L to R: Betty Wright, Ann Grover, Taffy Griffiths, Jean Fraser, Chippy Fensome, Betty Benson, McKenzie, Marjorie Whittaker. Front L to R: Vera Thorne, Joan Booth, Ruth Hearnshaw, Kathy Barlow, Sylvia Hiles, Tommie Thompson, Margaret Crawford. (Eunice Ravell Collection via Lyn Gambles)

dual controls. Several inconclusive searches were flown over the following days and S/Ldr Pye added another exotic type to his logbook when he flew a dual-controlled Albemarle on the 23rd. The following day he flew the Albemarle again, accompanied by with S/Ldr Tyrrell. On the 25th Tyrrell, F/Sgt Forge and Sgt Faux were once more detached, this time to Beaulieu in Hampshire. On the last day of the month the CO flew the Albemarle and it was reported that he 'did not enjoy it'!

The tide really began to turn against the Axis in October 1942 with the invasion of north-west Africa, Operation Torch, which began on 8 October. Montgomery squeezed the Axis forces from the east in the second battle of El Alamein, commencing on 23 October and turning into a full scale Axis retreat. In the Far East the Japanese suffered several reverses. In the Battle of Cape Esperance they lost a cruiser and three destroyers on the 11th. The fighting on Guadalcanal continued, culminating in the complete destruction of the crack Japanese 2nd Division. On the 26th a large reinforcement convoy was destroyed by US naval forces in the Battle of Santa Cruz. In addition to these victories the Japanese were also pushed back in both the Solomons and New Guinea. The Germans, meanwhile, were slowly beginning to bleed themselves to death against the defences of Stalingrad.

The first searches of October were carried out on the 2nd, and on the 3rd three Hudsons searched for a missing MGB with no results. Five Hudsons searched for another missing MGB on the 6th but nothing was sighted other than a Carley float and wreckage. The following day saw six aircraft on a North Sea search with no result and the diversion of five of them to Donna Nook and the sixth to Manby due to poor weather at Bircham Newton.

On 8 October F/Sgt Scott and crew, flying from St Eval, sighted a dinghy 1 mile off Pendeen Light in Cornwall. Four hundred yards from it they observed two men wearing Mae Wests. Shortly afterward a lifeboat arrived on the scene and picked up the dinghy and both men, who were unfortunately dead. The following day brought a new experience to some of the squadron's crews when two Stirling crews from 7 Sqn at Oakington arrived to examine the Lindholme rescue apparatus. S/Ldr Pye and two others were able to do a circuit in the Stirling.

On 10 October Henderson, D.H. Boxall and McKimm were all promoted to F/O. McKimm was on leave, but the other two treated some colleagues to a celebratory drink in the mess. One of the two provided a round of lemonade instead of gin and had to pay for his joke by having the lemonade poured down his neck!

Searches continued day and night with no success. The Wellington was still on the strength, being flown again by S/Ldr Pye on the 15th and again on the 18th with Spencer. The Wellington and Albemarle would both see frequent use over the following days as squadron pilots were taken on training flights. The month ended with the squadron saying farewell to a large contingent of Australians when P/Os T.E. Allen and

D.R. Hicks and SNCOs Werrin, Jackman, Mackenzie, Quin, Voysey, Gribble and Scott were all posted home to Australia. During the month the Hudsons had flown 385 hours with a further nine hours being flown by the Wellington and one by the Albemarle.

CHAPTER THREE

November 1942
– April 1943

November opened with a very successful day for the St
Eval detachment on the 1st. P/O Wherrett, F/Sgt
Spencer, and F/O McKimm and crew in B, V and Q/279
respectively, sighted a dinghy with four occupants about 115
miles south-west of the Scillies and S/Ldr Tyrrell flying P/279
and Sgt Mogridge in R/279 also had successful sightings of a
dinghy with four occupants 70 miles south-west of the islands.

The four survivors furthest out were the crew of Whitley 'V' of
No. 10 OTU from St Eval captained by Sgt Wright, which had
ditched on the night of 29/30 October. The other survivors were
F/Sgt Wright and Sgts Blincoe and McEwen. The co-pilot and
bomb aimer were lost when the aircraft sank after ditching. The
Whitley came down after the starboard engine failed at 500 feet
due to a glycol leak. P/O Wherrett dropped a Lindholme dinghy
to them. During the afternoon F/O Henderson and crew went out
to relocate the dinghies and sighted two Ju 88s attacking a
Wellington. Henderson wisely took evasive action and moved
well away from the enemy aircraft. His air gunner, Sgt Lumley,
saw a flash and a pall of smoke, which seemed to indicate that the
Wellington had been shot down. That night Sgt Marchand took
off from St Eval to relocate and shadow the dinghies but was
unable to locate them. The next morning three Hudsons went out
and managed to locate the dinghy containing F/Sgt Wright's

crew, a Polish destroyer later picked them up. The crew had been in their dinghy for seventy-six hours. A corvette had earlier picked up the survivors of the other ditching sighted by Tyrrell and Mogridge. This was also a No. 10 OTU Whitley, coded 'D'. When Tyrrell and Mogridge arrived on the scene the dinghy was being circled by two other OTU Whitleys and after Tyrrell dropped a Lindholme dinghy to P/O McGubbin, Sgt Sherry, Sgt Dagnall and Sgt Stewart the two Hudsons circled for three and a half hours. This crew was in the dinghy for eighty-four hours and the co-pilot died of injuries sustained in the ditching before the corvette picked them up.

There was some excitement at Bircham Newton on the 4th when Sgt Rowe swung Hudson C/279 on take off and the under-carriage collapsed. The Hudson burst into flames but the crew managed to escape to safety.

For the next week there were few operations and those that were flown were unsuccessful, but on the 13th a search commenced when three Hudsons from St Eval were ordered to look for a missing Whitley crew from No. 10 OTU. It was un-successful initially but on the following day P/O Stephenson worked out a new search area which resulted in the sighting of six survivors in a dinghy 170 miles south-west of the Scillies. P/O J.P. Heywood and crew, who were searching in company with McKimm and Marchand, spotted the dinghy. P/O Holmes and the crew of Whitley Q/10 OTU, Sgts Pond and Ramshaw, F/Sgt Dorman, Sgt Tombe and P/O Jeffrey had ditched the previous day. A Lindholme dinghy was accurately dropped to the survivors, who were subsequently picked up by the Polish destroyer L26 the next day. This was the same destroyer that had picked up the survivors on the 2nd.

On 16 November Whitley P/502 Sqn ditched but was fortunate enough to be watched all the way down by another Whitley. Four Hudsons – F/O McKimm in V/279, F/O Henderson in Z/279, F/Sgt Marchand in P/279 and F/Sgt Spencer flying X/279 – were dispatched and found the crew in two dinghies. Two Lindholme dinghies were dropped, but P/O Biggar and his crew only managed to secure one of them. The squadron seemed to be doing a good trade with the Polish and when not finding Polish aircrew survivors was directing Polish destroyers to rescue aircrew. The following day the Polish destroyer which had picked up two previous Whitley crews also picked up Biggar and his men.

The squadron held a dance to celebrate one year of existence on the 16th but was not able to rest long on its laurels as the following day a search commenced for a US B-17 which had gone missing on a flight to North Africa with General Duncan of the USAAC on board. Fitchew and Oakes took off in the afternoon on the first of a long series of searches. S/Ldr Tyrrell followed that night with another search, but with no success. The following day Hudsons from Bircham Newton and St Eval were out in force and the search continued for several days. On the 23rd they were assisted by Liberators of the US 404th Sqn before the search was finally called off.

The squadron lost the use of another Hudson on the 27th when Sgt Price swung Z/279 on take-off. Fortunately it did not catch fire after the crash and the crew escaped unhurt. The Hudson suffered damage to the airframe and one of the engines.

On the last day of the month the Squadron almost lost another Hudson, and this time the crew too. P/O Heywood, flying L/279, sighted two FW 190s, which quickly attacked the lone Hudson. The fighters sped in from below and astern and opened fire, scoring hits on the Hudson. The rudder and port aileron were damaged and WOp/AG F/Sgt Orr had one of his turret guns put out of action and was wounded in the head. The other gunner, Sgt Groome, was also injured. Heywood made for cloud cover and managed to shake off the fighters and making a safe landing, despite the damage, at Bircham Newton.

Due to the rear gunner having to spend some time in hospital a preliminary combat report was produced using information provided by the gunner in his hospital bed and the pilot, P/O Heywood.

Pilot Officer Heywood in aircraft 'L' was flying on an easterly course one mile to port and slightly behind aircraft 'N'. Both enemy aircraft were sighted and identified at approximately 700 yards range. Aircraft 'L' opened up fully and headed for 'N' intending to formate, but both aircraft turned to starboard. Enemy aircraft on the port side started attack from port quarter and port side, gunner of Hudson fired a burst at approximately 400 yards. Rear gunner instructed pilot to do a steep climb turning to port and own aircraft successfully evaded fire from this attack. Second enemy aircraft immediately came in from starboard quarter and carried out an attack from astern and below. At this stage through haze 'N' and 'L' lost contact. It also wounded rear gunner and through hits in the turrets put one gun u/s. Starboard side gun was also hit and jammed magazine. Hudson then climbed ahead without rudder control and entered cloud at about 2,500 feet. During this climb more attacks were carried out either three or four in number, and it was then found that the intercom had also been rendered u/s in this first attack. Pilot was only able to hear rear gunner very faintly and was in any case unable to take evasive action. Those subsequent attacks were all carried out from below and astern and consequently rear gunner was unable to open fire excepting on the last attack when enemy aircraft appeared to think that rear gunner must be out of action. On this attack he came in to 30 yards and enabled rear gunner to get in a burst at that range as he came up dead astern instead of underneath. Although the rear gunner cannot definitely claim hits, the enemy aircraft then broke off his attack and allowed Hudson to gain cloud cover. The estimated time of combat was three to four minutes.

No. 279's sister squadron No. 280 lost an Anson on 8 December and two crews commenced the search that night. The search continued the following day and the dinghy containing the survivors was sighted by Beaufighters. Three Hudsons were taking part in the search and they dropped two Lindholme dinghies to the Anson crew but they failed to secure them.

On 9 December the squadron became involved in trials of an airborne lifeboat with the Cunliffe Owen Company at Eastleigh near Southampton. The CO flew the boat under T/279, whilst S/Ldr Pye, F/O Boxall, P/O Keay and F/Sgt Vennimore observed from Cunliffe Owen's test aircraft. When the boat was dropped over the Solent near Cowes the parachutes failed to open and it was smashed to pieces.

Over the remainder of its existence the airborne lifeboat would play a vital part in the squadron's daily activities and it is worth relating here its development and design. The original lifeboat was designed by yachtsman and yacht designer Uffa Fox. Following the capture of his son by the Germans he set his mind to the development of an airborne lifeboat. Using a combination of paper and jam from his daily tea he constructed a model which was dropped from an upstairs window to test the concept. Fox immediately took his idea to Lord Brabazon, who approved the plan. Fox moved his bed into his office to work twenty-four hours

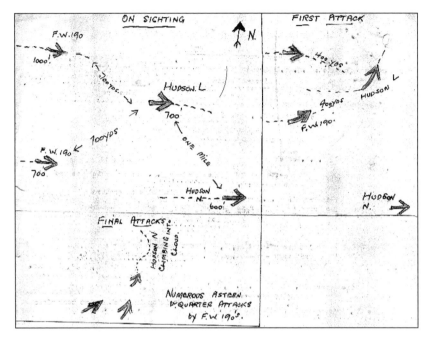

A graphic depiction of P/O Heywood's combat with two FW 190s on 31 November 1942. The diagram was attached to the combat report.

A fine view of a Lockheed Hudson carrying an airborne lifeboat. This particular aircraft is shown in RCAF service. (Public Archives of Canada via C Charland)

a day, seven days a week on his projected 23 foot boat. Three weeks later the first boat was complete. Painted grey it was equipped with watertight compartments and bulkheads, a dagger board for sailing and self-bailing slots. Also included were a navigation locker with charts and tide tables and a medical locker (which also contained rum!). The wood used in the construction was elm or mahogany; later plywood would also be used. The boat was equipped with a sailing rig and an auxiliary engine and after successful trials it was produced in versions of varying lengths from 24 to 50 feet. A wireless transmitter receiver was also fitted for two-way telegraphy, with the aerial run out by a kite or in some version fixed to the mast. For the initial trials Fox himself was placed in a rubber dinghy in the Solent and after the lifeboat had been dropped successfully he climbed aboard, started the engine, stepped the mast and sailed to shore. The airborne lifeboat would be used many times during the war and afterwards and save many lives.

The following day the weather closed in whilst four aircraft were out on a search and two, flown by Henderson and Wilson, diverted to Leuchars, where F/O Henderson had the misfortune to run N/279 over a defective drain cover, causing the under-carriage to collapse.

For the next week the squadron carried out inconclusive

Lockheed Hudson V9158:OS-T was used in trials of the Cunliffe Owen produced airborne lifeboat. (Air Historical Branch (RAF))

searches from both Bircham Newton and St Eval and then on the 17th F/O McKimm found a dinghy with five occupants some 200 miles south-west of the Cornish base on a night search. In the early hours of the following day P/O Spencer and crew continued the rescue of the survivors, but were unable to relocate the dinghy. Three more Hudsons set out during daylight on the same task but had no luck in locating the survivors. However, on the night of the 19th McKimm and Marchand set out to continue the search and this time the dinghy was located and Lindholmes were dropped. The search continued until the 24th when F/O Henderson sighted a corvette off Cape Cornwall, which signalled that the five survivors in the dinghy had been picked up.

Sgt Kingsford, the captain of 502 Sqn Whitley 'G' and his crew had much to be thankful for on Christmas Day 1942. In the early hours of the morning he was forced to ditch, but had the good fortune to have his pyrotechnics spotted by P/O Wilson and crew patrolling in Hudson K/279. They were seen about 12 miles away

Ground crew of 279 and 320 (Dutch) squadrons and Bircham Newton support staff celebrate Christmas in the blackout in December 1942. Second row from front, seated third and fourth from right, Stanley Melbourne Gambles and Eunice Ravell. (Eunice Ravell Collection via Lyn Gambles)

at 0830 hours and just under an hour later the dinghy was found. Two Lindholme dinghies, one of which inflated upside down, were dropped to the Whitley crew by K/279 and A/279 and Kingsford's crew managed to secure both and all of the attached containers. At 1430 hours, after 11 hours in the dinghy, the survivors were picked up by a launch.

Christmas Day at Bircham Newton was celebrated in traditional fashion with all the officers serving Christmas dinner in the WAAF and airmen's messes. On 30 December the Wellington and Albemarle, which had been used for training, were collected by the Air Transport Auxiliary (ATA) and returned to an MU. By the last day of the year the squadron had found a total of fifteen dinghies containing seventy-four aircrew and three lifeboats with twenty-three seamen making a total of ninety-seven lives saved. There was great enthusiasm amongst the crews to reach three figures before the Squadron had been operational for twelve months and with two months to go they were hopeful that this would come to pass.

By now there had been a considerable turnover in the personnel of the squadron and few of the originals remained. The latest postings came on Boxing Day when S/Ldr R.Y. Tyrrell and his crew were posted to 407 Sqn and it was announced on the last day of 1942 that W/Cdr Lynham would be leaving at the end of January.

It had been a highly successful year for the Allies in that they had been able to stem the Axis advances and in many cases

During 1942 the squadron operated an Albemarle and a Wellington in the training role. This Wellington is a Coastal Command aircraft with the ASV radar mounted in a chin radome under the nose. (Via A Rodgers)

reverse them. Equally the squadron had had a successful first year of existence learning to use the skills and equipment required for ASR. The following year would inextricably link the squadron with the Hudson, the Lindholme dinghy and the airborne lifeboat and bring many successful rescues.

S/Ldr Tyrrell's replacement was S/Ldr Mossford, who arrived with his crew from Silloth on New Year's Day. On 7 January W/Cdr Lynham was awarded a DSO but the celebrations were somewhat marred by the loss of Sgt W.M. Arnold and his crew. He had taken off that evening at 1820 hours from St Eval in Hudson Mk III V9031:A to carry out a search off the Lizard and failed to return. The Hudson's image faded from radar at 1913 hours and three minutes later a fire was seen on the sea at that position. Sgt Arnold and his crew, fellow Australian Sgt R.W. Paradise, Sgt J.D. Sclater, a New Zealander and Sgt R.F. Bannister were considered to be an experienced crew, having joined the squadron in November 1942.

The citation for Lynham's DSO read:

Since its formation in 1941 Wing Cdr Lynham has commanded No. 279 Squadron. This officer has trained many crews for day and night search operations and they have been directly responsible for the successful rescue of 55 members of aircrews and 23 seamen, often despite enemy opposition. This officer has displayed great enthusiasm and magnificent powers of leadership and organization.

On the 16th another of the 'old hands', F/O Heywood, was posted to Silloth and in his place the squadron received F/Lt Home RCAF and F/O Sherwood. On the following day W/Cdr B.G. Corry DFC arrived from No. 16 Group HQ to replace W/Cdr Lynham.

The weather closed in at St Eval on 21 January whilst S/Ldr Mossford and Sgt Oakes were out on patrol and it was with some difficulty that Oakes managed to land back at base. S/Ldr Mossford, however, had the misfortune to suffer W/T and R/T failure and his crew was forced to bale out. They came down near Swansea, with one crew member landing in the sea and having to swim ashore. The Hudson V9046:F, flying on automatic pilot flew on for a further 60 miles, crashing into a hill in Radnorshire.

W/Cdr Lynham left the Squadron on the 22nd and W/Cdr

Corry officially took command. The weather, which had caused so much trouble the previous day, failed to improve on the 22nd and although F/O Henderson and Sgt Oakes managed to take off on patrol from St Eval, the weather had closed in by their return. Henderson diverted to Chivenor and landed safely, but Oakes, like S/Ldr Mossford the previous day, had W/T and R/T failure. The crew baled out 8 miles north of Bodmin with Oakes leaving the aircraft at well below parachute safety height. He landed heavily but luckily was not seriously injured. The Hudson, V9042:P, crashed out of fuel.

The strength of the Allied bombing raids began to increase in 1943 and on 27 January the US 8th Air Force made its first daylight raid on Germany. For Bomber Command the war was becoming increasingly a technological one and on the 30th the bombers made first use of H2S ground mapping radar equipment.

The aircrew of No. 279 Sqn knew little of these developments, and although many of them had flown tours in Bomber Command, they were now flying the relatively obsolete Hudson in a role which, until the introduction of ASV radar to assist with searches, required little in the way of bombing technology.

The squadron's run of ill luck continued into February with yet another loss. Two Hudsons departed from Bircham Newton on the 4th to search in the North Sea for the crew of a Liberator reported to be in distress. F/O C.G. Crawford, who was leading the pair, decided to return a short distance off Happisburgh when he suffered W/T and intercom failure. F/Sgt Marchand, one of the squadron's most experienced pilots, was flying E/279 and was observed to follow Crawford as he circled Happisburgh before being lost to sight. Crawford's crew assumed that he had turned for base and headed for home. They failed to return at ETA, however, and at 1720 hours an SOS was picked up. Along with Marchand's usual crew was W/O Slugoski, acting as navigator. He was not the usual navigator, but he had no crew of his own and was filling in on this fateful trip. He went missing along with Marchand, F/Sgt Preece, F/Sgt Evans and Sgt Gendron. Although searches were carried out by crews from the squadron and from Nos 280 and 320 Squadron's nothing was found.

The weather played its part in yet another Hudson loss on the 5th. F/O Henderson and crew took off from Leuchars in V/279 to search for some MGBs about 150 miles out in the North Sea.

The squadron badge, approved by HM King George VI in January 1943. (E. Farrow)

Their troubles started when the automatic pilot became unserviceable. Contact was not made with the MGBs and a signal recalling them to base was received. On the return trip Henderson encountered severe weather conditions and the weather over Leuchars was extremely bad. Unable to get in to the airfield the crew baled out, unfortunately with the loss of air gunner Sgt Pertus, who came down in the sea and was drowned. The others sustained only minor injuries. On the same day the detachment at St Eval moved north to Davidstow Moor in Wales.

February 1943 was fast becoming the Squadron's unluckiest month. The 11th saw yet another loss when Sgt Neil crashed D/279 attempting to land at Leuchars. The Hudson had two crews on board and three of the occupants sustained injuries. F/O Tidswell broke his nose, Sgt Whitney suffered concussion and Sgt

Paterson was badly bruised. The Hudson was severely damaged in the crash.

As always the squadron was at the forefront of ASR development and on 17 February F/O Crawford flew S/279 from Davidstow Moor with an airborne lifeboat slung under the bomb bay on the first operational search with a boat fitted.

On 19 February a protracted search for the crew of a ditched Hampden commenced. S/Ldr Pye took off to search for the crew of O/415 Sqn 45 miles east of Orfordness but was unable to locate them. The survivors had the frustration of hearing W/279 pass overhead three or four times but were unable to signal due to the loss of their Very pistol. The Squadron continued to search for the survivors throughout the day in cooperation with Ansons of 280 Sqn and Hudsons of 320 Sqn but still nothing was sighted. In the early hours of the 20th two crews took off to search for another crew, this one from a ditched Wellington, but nothing was seen. During the afternoon it was reported that Beaufighters from North Coates had found the Hampden dinghy and S/Ldr Pye took off in K/279 to relieve them. Owing to the inaccurate position report the dinghy was not located but the Hampden crew were fortunately found by a Walrus from Martlesham Heath which rescued them that evening.

The 'gremlins' were not content with their bag of crashed Hudsons, and took one more on the 27th. P/O Wilson crashed taking off from Bircham Newton in J/279. Luckily the crew escaped with only slight burns.

The last day of the month saw another success for the squadron when F/Sgt Watts and crew in K/279 found a dinghy with six occupants at position 5402N 0335E. Sgt M.F. Gray and his 419 Sqn Halifax crew had ditched in the early morning of the 28th, returning from a minelaying sortie off the Friesian Islands. Theirs was the only aircraft lost from ninety-one taking part in the operation. Unfortunately they had to leave when they reached the limit of their endurance, though a Hudson of 320 Sqn and a Wellington relieved them. Later Sgt Passlow took off to take over from the 320 Sqn aircraft, but the survivors were picked up by launches before he arrived on the scene. The pick-up had its own problems when the first two launches sent out ran short of fuel before reaching the dinghy; however a second pair of launches from a base on the River Humber successfully picked up the crew.

March 1943 was a very disappointing month for the squadron,

which carried out numerous searches, all of them inconclusive. On the 29th another crew was lost when Hudson S/279 crashed into the sea off St Ives. The pilot, F/O Gibbs was rescued, but died of his injuries later. The remainder of the crew, F/Sgt Long, F/Sgt Povey, F/Sgt Bacon and F/Sgt Fletcher, were lost.

By the end of March the squadron's aircraft establishment had changed considerably. Initially equipped with the Hudson Mk III there had been a gradual trickle of replacements as the aircraft was developed and improved and the squadron now held three marks of Hudson: nine Mark IIIs, one Mark V and nine Mark VIs.

April began at Bircham Newton with the squadron involved in two parades. The first was on the 1st to celebrate the twenty-fifth Anniversary of the formation of the RAF. The following day the squadron formed up again on parade to have its crest, approved by HM the King, presented to them by the Air Officer Commanding (AOC) No. 16 Group. The first two weeks of the month brought nothing but inconclusive searches, but the crew's frustrations were relieved by the news on the 16th that long serving F/O McKimm had been awarded the DFC; this was the first to be awarded to a squadron member.

Amongst those joining the Squadron during this period was Sgt Dougie Whittaker, observer on Geoff Curtis' crew. He recalls the early days of his tour: 'By early April there were many Australians on the Squadron and we did a lot of formation flying with Lynn Bedford from Wagga Wagga. On 22 April we were joined by No. 1401 Flt at Bircham Newton and we carried out our first operation on 27 April.'

By the end of the month the ever-changing aircraft establishment now stood at eight Hudson Mk IIIs, three Mark Vs and five Mark VIs as the newer Mks V and VI replaced the Mk III.

CHAPTER FOUR

May – October 1943

By May 1943 the war situation was markedly different from a year previously. The Germans had been pushed out of North Africa, and the 6th Army had surrendered outside Stalingrad. The RAF began to bomb the island of Pantelleria as part of the preparations for the invasion of Sicily, and in the middle of the month the famous 'Dambusters Raid' led by W/Cdr Guy Gibson was carried out. Bomber Command also made its heaviest raid of the war so far on Dortmund, dropping 2,000 tons of bombs. Half of Wuppertal was destroyed in another raid and the bombers were now engaged in the Battle of the Ruhr. The USAAF meanwhile was keeping busy with raids on Antwerp, Kiel and St Nazaire.

Following its involvement in the trials of the airborne lifeboat with Cunliffe Owen and flying the first operational sorties with the boat the Squadron had its first success with the new equipment on 5 May 1943. F/Sgt Bowman of No. 102 Sqn, based at Pocklington, ditched his Halifax returning from Dortmund on the night of 4/5 May. This had been the largest non-thousand bomber raid of the war to date and the first major attack on Dortmund. Thirty-one bombers were lost, including Bowman's, and a further seven crashed in bad weather at the bomber bases.

Luckily for Bowman and his men an aircraft of No. 1401 Met Flight sighted the dinghy and sent a signal, 'Am over dinghy, north-west of Bircham, position 5340N 0129W'. F/Sgt Mogridge and crew were quickly airborne from Bircham in W/279 with an

No. 279 Sqn aircrew in 1943. F/Sgt Ted Rusby 1st right. F/Sgt
Mogridge 4th from right. (Helen Barnard)

airborne lifeboat slung underneath. On reaching the dinghy
Mogridge successfully dropped the lifeboat 30 feet from it and
Bowman's crew climbed aboard. Thirty minutes later they had
the engine started and were given a course to steer for Wells.
Mogridge stayed overhead shadowing the boat which was
making a steady 6½ knots. F/O Wilson, who had also reached the
scene, left Mogridge after taking photographs of the lifeboat drop
and returned to base. At 1130 hours F/Lt Fitchew was airborne
in D/279 to relieve Mogridge, but W/279 had to leave the lifeboat
due to fuel shortage before he arrived. D/279 found the lifeboat,
still making a steady 6½ knots, now only 16 miles from Wells, but
just then the engine failed and though Bowman's crew hoisted
the sail, there was so little wind that they were barely making
headway. Eventually an RAF launch picked up the crew, two of
whom were injured, and landed them at Grimsby. The launch
crew moored the lifeboat to a buoy when it began to break up
against the launch. The following day Mogridge and his crew
visited the survivors in the Royal Naval Hospital in Grimsby and
found them all to be in good spirits, even the WOp, who had been
hit in the eye by the Halifax's TR9 radio set!

LAC Ernest Farrow recalls the first successful use of the
airborne lifeboat.

In 1943 the first Hudson was fitted with a life boat, which was slung under the bomb bay and dropped, suspended by three parachutes. It was a source of amusement on the squadron that it was always the officers who flew the 'Boat', no doubt wanting to have the honour of being the first one to drop same. Unfortunately for them they had no luck, but the first time a Flight Sergeant pilot flew the boat he made a successful drop and went in the record book accordingly.

The first operational drop of the airborne lifeboat was reported in a Times newspaper article on 31 May 1943:

LIFEBOAT DROPPED BY PARACHUTE

NEW AIR-SEA RESCUE DEVICE

FROM OUR AERONAUTICAL CORRESPONDENT

An airborne lifeboat, dropped by parachute from an air-sea rescue Hudson air raft of RAF Coastal Command, recently saved the lives of the crew of a Bomber Command Halifax who were drifting in their dinghy in the North Sea.

The lifeboat was dropped from about 1,000 feet, and it came to rest on the water only about 20 yards from the bomber crew's dinghy. The lifeboat was fitted with engines and soon the airmen were travelling towards England at a speed of six knots. The course to steer was signalled by the Hudson, and for most of the journey the crew had an air escort. About ten miles from the English coast the lifeboat was met by a naval vessel. The Halifax crew had been forced to 'ditch' their aircraft after it had been damaged in the recent raid on Dortmund.

The new type of airborne lifeboat was specially designed for dropping by parachute, and it is carried under the fuselage of the aircraft. Its development is largely due to the research work of Group Captain E.F. Waring DFC, AFC, Deputy Director of Air-Sea Rescue. When dropped by the aircraft it falls as gently as a man descending by parachute, and no matter how it strikes the water, the boat will right itself. Special buoyancy tanks keep it afloat and prevent it from capsizing even in the roughest weather. In compartments in the hull are stowed the two motors, and full changes of clothes, medical supplies, food, and pyrotechnics. There is also a good supply of petrol. The lifeboat, which can carry several persons, also has a portable wireless set, as well as sail and oars in case the engines break down.

The next few days passed fairly routinely until the 13th when the squadron became involved in a search and rescue which saw not only crews flying searches but also squadron members becoming involved in the sea rescue too. A Flying Fortress had been outward bound for an operational sortie when one of the 0.5 inch guns ran away whilst being warmed up by one of the gunners, resulting in the starboard tailplane being almost completely shot away and the rear gunner being hit by a bullet in the groin. The Fortress captain ordered the bombs to be jettisoned into the sea and flew back over his base at Grafton Underwood where six of the crew baled out, including the wounded gunner, who was dropped from a static line. All six made a safe descent and the pilot, finding the Fortress increasingly difficult to fly, turned out to sea again with the intention of baling out over the coast and allowing the Fortress to crash into the sea. *En route* to the coast two more of the crew baled out over King's Lynn, landing safely. The damage to the aircraft put the autopilot out of action and attempts to lash the controls in place were unsuccessful so the captain and the co-pilot, Lt Gorse, stayed at the controls until the aircraft started to break up.

While this drama was being played out a rescue launch had left the coast earlier in the day carrying, in addition to the regular crew, W/Cdr Corry, OC 279 Sqn, W/Cdr Burwood, OC 280 Sqn, S/Ldr Pye and F/O Keay of 279, and S/Ldr Basson the controller at Bircham Newton. In addition the launch also carried a bomber crew from the OTU at Cottesmore. The launch was also towing an airborne lifeboat to give the bomber crew practice in its use.

On the way out W/Cdr Burwood, S/Ldr Pye and F/O Keay sat in the towed lifeboat, which, being rudderless and with its buoyancy tubes deflated, capsized, throwing the occupants into the sea. Fortunately all were able to swim to the overturned lifeboat which the launch crew had cut away as soon as the accident occurred. They climbed onto the boat using the hand-rails and were soon transferred to the launch. W/Cdr Burwood apparently found his pipe and sunglasses no hindrance during his immersion, for both were still firmly in position as he climbed aboard the launch! F/O Keay had the most difficulty as he was hampered by the heavy gumboots he was wearing and the fact that he ended up underneath the lifeboat when it capsized. Lying on his back he kicked off the boots and swam downward and sideways to get clear, surfacing 30 feet away from the boat. The boat was later recovered.

During the afternoon Y/279, which had been out earlier in the day in a search off Great Yarmouth, during which a petrol tank and parachute were sighted, was airborne again after reports of a Flying Fortress breaking up in mid-air and falling into the sea off Cromer. During this search they sighted wreckage and were informed by a rescue launch, one of two in the area, that one body had been found.

At about 1615 hours the Fortress was seen to break up and W/Cdr Corry immediately ordered the airborne lifeboat cut away. The launch made top speed to the area where the wreckage was seen to fall, several miles away. Two parachutes were seen to descend from the doomed Fortress and a bearing was taken on them whilst course was altered toward them. As they entered the area where the wreckage had fallen an empty dinghy and other equipment was sighted, the launch picking up the dinghy.

After half an hour of fruitless searching a Stirling appeared and began to circle the launch before setting off towards a position in the wreckage area, all the while signalling with an Aldis lamp. The launch followed it, which was being handled most skilfully at low level by its pilot. After a short while another RAF pinnace appeared on the scene, homed to the Stirling and joined the search. The pinnace, from Wells, found the co-pilot, Lt Gorse, and after treatment on the boat he recovered fairly rapidly from the effects of shock and immersion. Following this rescue a message was received that the Sheringham lifeboat had picked up the pilot, Capt. D. Rodgers, but that he had died shortly afterwards from shock and exposure.

With the survivor recovered the launch with the 279 Sqn group on board recovered the airborne lifeboat and, despite it being waterlogged, carried out some sailing tests, from which some useful lessons were learned. The boat trip ended with the party from Bircham Newton and the rescued co-pilot being rowed some 2 ½ miles to the shore at Wells in the lifeboat, as the launch could not get back into Wells owing to low water. Lt Gorse was entertained in the mess at Bircham Newton and flown back to Grafton Underwood the following morning.

The ASR squadrons of the RAF were not the only units engaged in rescuing downed aircrew and the Germans had similar units to rescue their own men and any unlucky Allied aircrew that they happened across. Often survivors would be scooped up from under the guns of the enemy and on occasion the ASR squadrons would arrive on the scene to begin a search or rescue only to find the enemy already circling the dinghy. This was the case on 15 May when F/Sgt Mogridge took off to search for dinghies which had been sighted by Beaufighters about 40 miles off Borkum and a good 200 miles from Bircham Newton. Piloting Hudson W/279 he reached the search datum, only to find a Dornier Do 24 circling there. At a range of 800 yards the Dornier opened fire on the Hudson. Mogridge closed to 300 yards and fired a short then a long burst, which he observed making strikes on the starboard hull engine and wings of the Dornier. During the exchange of fire the navigator, F/Sgt McGregor, was wounded in the left thigh and a single bullet entered the turret, killing F/Sgt Rusby. Breaking off the engagement Mogridge made for Bircham Newton. After landing it was discovered that the Hudson had suffered bullet holes in the tailplane, the port side, the astrodome, the perspex nose and the tail. F/Sgt Mcgregor was taken to hospital in Ely and a funeral service was held at Bircham Newton on the 18th for F/Sgt Rusby, who was buried at Brookwood Cemetery on the 20th. The following combat report was submitted:

> F/Sgt Mogridge in aircraft 'W' was flying on a westerly course and went to investigate circling aircraft. F/Sgt Mogridge notified his crew of its position and told the rear gunner to keep watch on the enemy aircraft. To this he replied 'OK, I can see it'. On approaching enemy aircraft it immediately went down to deck level, the enemy aircraft then being on port bow ahead. Still closing identified it as a Do 24. At about 800 yards the enemy aircraft rear gunner opened fire, white trace and white smoke was seen. F/Sgt Mogridge's position at that moment was 10 degrees from astern and his rear gunner appeared to have been hit because no word was passed from the gunner to pilot after the Do 24 enemy aircraft first burst. The enemy's rear gunner appeared to be allowing a considerable amount of deflection so F/Sgt Mogridge closed to the

attack, range being 600 yards. A short burst was given at 600 yards range closing rapidly. At about 400 yards F/Sgt Mogridge throttled back and gave the Do 24 a long burst. A cry was heard by F/Sgt Mogridge and he therefore broke off the attack to starboard. Evasive action was taken at the same time the enemy aircraft mid-turret opened fire with a long burst. The deflection used by the enemy aircraft mid-upper turret seemed very wide. F/Sgt Mogridge then ascertained the damage and was informed that the navigator was wounded in the thigh. On this information being received F/Sgt Mogridge called the rear gunner on the intercom and received no reply. The aircraft was then on a course of 310 degrees. F/Sgt Kidd applied first-aid to the navigator and immediately afterwards tried to extricate the rear gunner, F/Sgt Rusby, from the Boulton Paul turret but was unsuccessful because the rear gunner was resting on the fire and engaged lever and the turret was on the port beam.

LAC Ernest Farrow, one of 279 Squadron's ground crew, recalls the return of this aircraft to Bircham Newton.

A 279 Sqn crew. 1st left F/Sgt Rusby, others unknown. (Helen Barnard)

I was on duty one Saturday night awaiting the return of one of our aircraft when it appeared suddenly overhead, firing red flares. He landed, and instead of coming to the dispersal site, taxied directly to the Control Tower, where the emergency vehicles were standing. The aircraft had been shot up, the radio system damaged, the navigator wounded in the leg and, sadly, the rear gunner was dead. We learned later that one bullet had hit him in the heart area, causing him to bleed to death.

Without the assistance and hard work of the squadron ground crews and support staff at Bircham Newton it would have been impossible for 279 Sqn and the other squadrons based there to carry out their operations. Amongst the support staff were many WAAF, a large number working in the motor transport (MT) section and the station sick quarters (SSQ). Cpl Eunice Ravell worked in both sections and provides a useful insight into the daily working of these sections in support of the operational squadrons.

In 1941 I was posted to RAF Bircham Newton, so it was 'goodbye' to the MT Section at RAF Hook, the barrage balloons and the south, and with my kit bag on my left-hand shoulder, gas mask and tin hat on my chest, gas cape and ground sheet on my back, and great-coat over my right arm, I was taken by lorry to the local railway station and dispatched to Heacham, between Sandringham and Hunstanton.

I arrived at Waterloo Station and then went by underground, which was packed with rows of sleeping people and small family groups – night workers and the homeless, and people using it as a permanent air-raid shelter. It was a sad sight.

F/Sgt T Rusby, killed in the fight with a Dornier Do 24 on 15th May. (Helen Barnard)

At Kings Cross, I caught the train for Norfolk. 'Caught' was the operative word, because it was just leaving and I hurled myself into the nearest carriage. Unfortunately it was 'First Class' and was bristling with braid and 'scrambled egg' – i.e. Brigadiers, Admirals and Air Vice Marshals. They all looked appalled. It was sacrilege for such a thing to happen. A humble 'erk' being catapulted amongst them – travelling FIRST CLASS! The air was charged as in an H.M. Bateman cartoon from 'PUNCH', when someone drops a terrible brick. Not a word was said, a very small space was made for me on the edge of the seat and we travelled all the way in silence.

It was dark by the time I reached Heacham, and because of the 'black-out' and a stormy night, it was PITCH dark. I got out of the train, unable to see a thing and not knowing which way to turn. After groping around for some time and not hearing a soul anywhere, a voice shouted in the distance: 'Anyone here for Bircham Newton?' 'Yes – oh yes- there's me. Wait for me, wait for me.' I yelled in relief.

I had to cross the line following the direction of the voice, and in my haste and anxiety to get there, I misjudged the edge of the platform and fell onto the line. I tore my stockings and scraped my shins painfully and my 'luggage' was everywhere. Some of the equipment I was carrying, however, helped to pad the fall, and I wasn't hurt much but very shaken and muddy.

Eventually I got to the truck that had been sent for me and was bundled into the back by two eerie forms, who shut me in with a clang of the tailboard and went round to the front to get in the cab and drive me eight miles to my new destination.

I enjoyed Bircham Newton, although it was sprawling and windswept, and miles from anywhere. We had to have bikes to get around on. The Transport Section was a friendly collection of as many women as men – about a hundred of us altogether. The women were billeted in what had been the airmen's' married quarters in peacetime – small, semi-detached houses in rows, set apart from the main camp; with 6 to a house.

My roommate was Dorothy Walmesley-Cottham ('Don' for short), with Joan Pratt and Dot Stribling next door; and we were all ambulance drivers. The job suited me fine. We had 24 hours on duty and 24 hours off duty and we joined in with life at the sick quarters. There was a dental surgery, an operating theatre, a dispensary, two doctor's surgeries and a mortuary.

Cpl Eunice Ravell in Bircham
Newton MT yard in 1943. (Eunice
Ravell Collection via Lyn
Gambles)

> *Every morning there were rows of
> miserable patients on sick parade,
> and the smell of ether, and the
> medical talk at meal times – all
> bringing waves of nostalgia for my
> childhood. I felt very much at home.*
>   *As an ambulance driver every
> day was different. Some days we were very busy, some days we
> had nothing, but we always had to be ready to take off at a
> second's notice. Calls sometimes came from the airfield that a
> plane was in trouble and injured crew had to be collected. Planes
> often landed that had been shot up. A 'crash' fire-tender and a
> 'crash' ambulance stood by for every aircraft, and if there was an
> alert of some difficulty on board, we both had to crawl our
> vehicles across the grass to try to meet it at the exact spot at
> which it seemed it would land; as sometimes seconds counted in*

Bircham Newton
SSQ staff 1942. L
to R: Fred, Dot
Stribling, Ethel
Gisby, Bee,
Grace, 'Don'
Walmesley-
Cottham, Denny.
(Eunice Ravell
Collection via
Lyn Gambles)

getting the crew out. Ely, about 50 miles away in Cambridge-shire, was the nearest civilian hospital and serious cases for surgery had to be taken there.

After a time I was promoted to corporal, and taken back into the Motor Transport Section. This meant I had to take parades, do night duty in the Transport Office and dispatch drivers and to jobs as needed. I also had to move my sleeping quarters to an NCO's bunk in the barrack block in charge of twenty-four noisy WAAFs, and keep tabs on the drivers who were supposed to be servicing or washing their vehicles. The Wash and Repair Bays were right at the end of the yard and somewhere you skived to for a natter. If anyone came, you just had to disappear under your machine with a grease gun in your hand or stick your head under the bonnet and be checking your oil, water or battery.

Later when I was in charge of the MT Stores and the repair mechanics from these bays came in and out all day long, getting supplies or ordering new parts for vehicles, one Corporal seemed to need more than anyone else, and we discovered eventually that he was building a car for himself on the side, out of RAF spares.

Medical and MT Staff at Bircham Newton SSQ. L to R: Denny, Lil Tod, Esther, Hans, Eunice 'Neen' Ravell, Joe, Trot and Johnny. (Eunice Ravell Collection via Lyn Gambles)

The Bircham
Newton
ambulance crew
1942. L to R: Joe,
Trot, Esther, Ann
Grover. (Eunice
Ravell Collection
via Lyn
Gambles)

The local pub was called the 'Norfolk Hero', about a mile and a half from the camp, and it was downhill to cycle there, and uphill to cycle back, which was the wrong way round for drunks! It was a spartan place, with a stone floor and benches all round, and a blazing fire in winter, where they got the poker red hot and plunged it into a bucket of slap ale, to mull it, and then ladled it all round into everyone's mug. It was matey and warming, the air thick with Norfolk accents, and after a time one of the locals would get up and do a clog dance on the stone floor, while others clapped to the rhythm.

On 26 May F/O Crawford and his crew took Hudson A/279, equipped with an airborne lifeboat to North Coates, where the King and Queen visited the following day. F/O Crawford and his crew were presented to them and the King took a great interest in the survival equipment available in the airborne lifeboat.

On Friday, 28 May 1943 a Whitley of No. 10 OTU crashed into the sea at 4945N 0815W. The crew managed to scramble out and into their dinghy, which was then found by Sunderland O/461 Sqn. The Sunderland attempted to land but crashed, killing one of the crew. The next day another Sunderland, E/461, found the dinghies, landed and took on the survivors. It was unable to get off, however, as it developed engine trouble. A third Sunderland arrived and some time afterward F/O Sherwood turned up in Hudson K/279 to find one Sunderland on the water and the other circling at 200 feet. Sherwood managed to contact a destroyer and home it to the scene, signalling to the circling Sunderland that it was on the way. The destroyer took aboard the twenty-eight survivors and took the Sunderland under tow. The survivors included those of the Whitley, the crashed Sunderland and the other Sunderland with engine trouble. After some time the crippled Sunderland was repaired and managed to take off with a skeleton crew.

Sherwood was involved in another successful rescue the next day. Beaufighters returning from patrol reported sighting a dinghy and Sherwood and his crew set off in F/279 carrying an airborne lifeboat at 1759 hours to commence the search. An hour and a half later in position 5005N 0803W they sighted a dinghy. As they closed on it they discovered that there were in fact two dinghies containing five and one survivors respectively. The survivors were from a Whitley of No. 612 Sqn, based at Chivenor, and F/Sgt Earnshaw and his crew, who had taken to the dinghies thirty-six hours earlier, appeared to be in good spirits, waving at the approaching Hudson. Sherwood climbed to 2,000 feet and sent a sighting signal to base. Shortly afterward a Walrus and a Sunderland appeared and began to circle the dinghies. Leaving them to shepherd the survivors F/279 went to find some rescue motor launches (RMLs) and homed them to the survivors who were picked up a short while later. Sherwood then set course for base, but on the way back he came across a Walrus on the water with its engine stopped and its crew up on the nose. He sent a sighting report of this aircraft, which was being circled by two Spitfires and an Anson, before returning to Bircham Newton.

The air war began to hot up in June with the issue of the 'Pointblank Directive' to RAF and USAAF chiefs of staff. Bomber Command carried out 'shuttle raids' to Friedrichshafen, with the bombers landing at bases in North Africa and then returning via a raid on Spezia in Italy. The USAAF for its part carried out its first daylight raid on the Ruhr, bombing Huls.

The first search in June, by F/O Reade and crew in H/279 from Davidstow Moor was for a BOAC aircraft which had gone missing *en route* from Lisbon. It had been carrying the famous actor Leslie Howard, who had been on a lecture tour on behalf of the British Council, and Kenneth Stonehouse, Reuters' Washington correspondent. The airliner had been attacked and shot down by Ju 88s. No trace of the aircraft or survivors was found. Reade landed at Predannack.

On 9 June four crews set out to search for a dinghy but had to return due to very poor visibility. The dinghy contained the survivors from a Beaufighter of 143 Sqn. F/O Pardun and Sgt Hoskins had been flying at very low level that evening, when they hit the sea and crashed. They were dazed after the crash but managed to get out onto the wing of the Beaufighter, which stayed afloat for just one minute. Pardun then swam to the dinghy supporting his still dazed navigator. Several aircraft were heard in the vicinity that evening and then at 2100 hours a Lancaster appeared, which the Beaufighter crew believe spotted them, as it turned onto a reciprocal course. No rescue came that night, however, and on the following day several aircraft were heard in the fog. No. 279 Sqn got four crews airborne but the weather still severely hampered the search. At 2100 hours Pardun and Hoskins thought they were saved when an ML was sighted only ½ mile away, but it turned away without seeing the dinghy. After dawn on the 11th the survivors sighted some Beaufighters and heard more launches and then A/279 and D/279, which were airborne on the search, intercepted a message from the dinghy's emergency radio. F/O Jones of No. 280 Sqn, who had also been searching in company of two more 280 Sqn Ansons found the dinghy at 0941 hours that morning and Pardun and Hoskins were later picked up by RML and brought safely to shore.

The detachment at Davidstow Moor moved to Harrowbeer on 9 June and carried out its first search from there on the 14th, unfortunately without result. On 12 June Hudson F/279 left Harrowbeer for the long journey to Vaagar in the Faeroe Islands, routeing via Stornoway and arriving there on the 14th. F/O Sherwood in F/279 had been detached to this northerly location to search for the crew of a US Catalina which had been wrecked in a crash whilst attempting to pick up the crew of a ditched 206 Sqn Fortress 150 miles north west of Vaagar. On the 16th at 2013 hours F/279, carrying an airborne lifeboat, was over the two dinghies, which were 2 miles apart. Sherwood circled the positions, dropping smoke floats, and made a run up to one of

them dropping the lifeboat from 750 feet. Unfortunately the parachutes failed to open and the boat crashed into the sea. Its forward
rocket operated and after the crash one of the buoyancy tubes
remained floating. While this drama was being played out two
Fortresses, a Catalina and a Hudson (from Iceland) arrived and
began circling. The Hudson dropped a Lindholme dinghy
and then departed. F/279 returned to Vaagar and after landing
F/O Sherwood examined the Hudson and found that the static
line for the lifeboat parachutes had not been attached, causing
their failure.He returned to Bircham Newton on 20 June.

Amongst those on the Harrowbeer detachment was Sgt
Dougie Whittaker who recalls some of their sorties.

> We moved to a satellite station at Harrowbeer in Devon on 15 June
> which we used for regular sweeps over the Bay of Biscay. Our first
> sortie in the Bay of Biscay was on 16 June – no joy. On the 23rd
> we found wreckage in the bay but no bodies.
>
> The airfield was actually the village green and a Typhoon detach-
> ment was there as well. Harrowbeer is three miles from Yelverton
> and bays were built in, into which the aircraft were stationed at the
> side of the cricket pitch.

One of the highlights of the month at Bircham Newton was the
appearance of a squadron newspaper named the *Windsock*.
The first issue included articles on 'gremlins', Malta, the story of
a Fortress which force landed at Bircham after a raid on Kiel and
the outgoing CO's farewell message. The squadron diary records
that 'no writs for libel had been received an hour after publica-
tion'! The remainder of the month passed quietly with no
successful searches.

July 1943 found the Germans launching Operation Citadel and
the great tank battle at Kursk. Fortunately they made few gains
and suffered heavy losses to the Russians, who stood their
ground. The Soviets immediately counter-attacked. US and
British forces invaded Sicily on the 10th and by the 20th the Italian
forces on the island had surrendered *en masse*.

The squadron had a fruitless fortnight in the first half of July
with Dougie Whittaker's crew locating a dinghy with three
bodies on board off Wells next the Sea and then on the night of
14/15 July W/Cdr Bray DFC of No. 12 OTU at Chipping Warden
set off for Rennes in Wellington Mk III BJ702 on a Nickel sortie

(leaflet dropping). The Wellington crossed the coast a mile or so off track but course was altered for the target. Whilst crossing the Mortain-Dom front region at 16,500 feet the port engine was hit by predicted flak and badly damaged. Bray tried to continue but, unable to maintain height, he was forced to turn back. Recrossing the coast at 0135 hours they encountered more light flak but were not hit. They had, however, lost 2,000 feet in evasive action, height they could ill afford to lose. Over the sea the leaflets were jettisoned, unfortunately carrying away the W/T trailing aerial in the process. The W/Op transmitted an SOS and the identification friend or foe (IFF) was switched on to assist in fixing the location of the bomber for rescue assets. With the crippled Wellington impossible to control Bray ditched her at 0210 hours off Cap d'Antifer, sustaining a broken nose. Another crew member, P/O Parkinson, was also injured. The crew clambered into the aircraft dinghy and spent the next day and a half paddling towards England, but due to the strong current, they made little headway. They had seen several aircraft pass overhead as they waited for rescue and had fired Very lights at some. As their emergency rations dwindled their hope of rescue did likewise. Then a formation of Typhoons led by W/Cdr Scott spotted the dinghy and signalled its position. ASR swung into operation and a 279 Sqn Hudson was ordered off.

F/O Wilson was airborne in W/279 from Bircham Newton at 1025 hours and proceeded to Tangmere where he picked up an escort of Typhoons from No. 486 Sqn at 1143 hours. Wilson then made his way to the reported position off Cap D'Antifer where the dinghy was sighted after only fifteen minutes. W/Cdr Bray and his crew waved as the Hudson arrived and, flying at 140 knots and a height of 700 feet dropped the airborne lifeboat.

Wilson reported a slight shudder as the lifeboat left the Hudson, dropped by the navigator, F/O Hender, and the three parachutes were seen to develop well. On landing it came to rest slightly nose down, as the inflation gear did not fully function, but the rocket did work, deploying the drogue. As the lifeboat hit the water the Wellington crew were seen energetically paddling towards it. Whilst the rescue was taking place 486 Sqn was fending off a formation of fifteen FW 190s which had come up to fight. At 1244 hours Wilson set course for Thorney Island, still escorted by the Tangmere Typhoons, who were keeping a close eye on the enemy coast for activity. In the

F/O Sherwood and crew, operating from the Faroes, attempted to rescue a Catalina crew by airborne lifeboat on 16 June 1943. The Catalina had crashed attempting to rescue the crew of a ditched Fortress similar to the one shown. Another Catalina was also involved in the rescue attempt, as were two more Fortresses. (Via A Rodgers)

event the Germans declined to take part and W/279 landed at 1317 hours. Wilson reported that 'it looked like a lovely day in France'. The Wellington crew transferred to the lifeboat and made their way under their own steam to a point midway across the Channel where they were intercepted by HSLs and brought safely into Newhaven. No. 486 Sqn, who had spotted the dinghy, were later presented with the centre keel-board of the airborne lifeboat and it was polished, varnished and used as a squadron scoreboard.

Dougie Whittaker, flying in Sgt Curtis' crew, recalls this successful rescue on the 15th involving F/O Wilson:

We were on patrol with F/O Wilson when we found ten bods in two dinghies just off Le Havre. They had ditched a Fortress after a

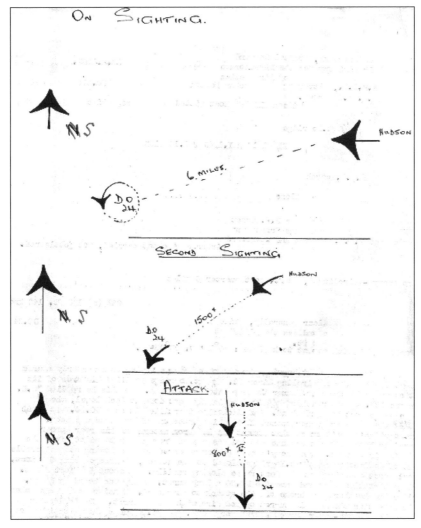

A diagram of the air combat between F/Sgt Mogridge in Hudson W/279 and a Dornier Do 24 on 16 May 1943 which was appended to the combat report.

daylight raid on Germany. Wilson dropped an airborne lifeboat –
all saved. I do not recall seeing the FW 190s but the Spitfires were
in attendance. [There is some confusion over the number of aircrew or the date of the incident that Whittaker recalls. Either it was the Wellington crew that was rescued or a Fortress crew on another date.]

As the scale of operations increased throughout 1943 with Fighter Command carrying out sweeps over occupied territory, Bomber Command's strength and hitting power increasing and the USAAC beginning to raise the tempo of its operations, despite constant diversions of its squadrons to North Africa, the ASR organization found itself becoming busier and busier. No. 279 Sqn was no exception to this increase in tempo and over the months to come they would have success upon success in finding and rescuing ditched aircrews.

Their next success came on 18 July when F/Sgt Mogridge, airborne from Harrowbeer in Hudson U/279, sighted the survivors of ditched Hampden P/1401 Flt less than an hour after they had gone down. P/O Parkinson and his crew had been on a meteorological reconnaissance sortie when their port engine failed and they ditched in the North Sea. The Hampden crew quickly abandoned the aircraft through the escape hatches; the nose was going under in ninety seconds, followed by the tail after two minutes. U/279 was airborne at 1037 hours and sighted an oil patch at 1052 hours followed swiftly by the sighting of a two-star red Very cartridge. The dinghy containing the Hampden crew was 15 miles off the Lincolnshire coast. Two good fixes were obtained and an HSL was spotted heading towards it. At 1215 hours it picked up the crew, later landing them at Immingham. The squadron diary notes that 'the navigator of the Hampden, P/O Fettes, retained his log and gave his Met report, though it was a few hours later than usual'!

On the night of 24/25 July Bomber Command carried out Operation Gomorrah, when 728 bombers dropped 2,300 tons of bombs on Hamburg in only forty-eight minutes, losing only twelve aircraft. Hamburg would suffer seven air raids over a period of six days from both Bomber Command and the 8th Air Force. The days that followed would see the squadron involved in many searches for ditched bomber crews. Following the night raid the Americans carried out another daylight raid on the city and over the next two days 101 British and American airmen would be rescued. Nineteen of the US bombers taking part in the raid were reported missing. A huge search and rescue operation involving HSLs, Walrus amphibians, lifeboats, trawlers, fishing smacks, aircraft of Bomber, Fighter and Coastal Commands and the dedicated ASR aircraft commenced and at one point more than seventy search aircraft were in the air.

No. 279 Squadron's biggest day to date came on 26 July. After an early search by Mogridge and his crew south of Lowestoft for the missing crew members of a Lancaster (which subsequently landed safely at base, although some of its crew had baled out) a half submerged, empty dinghy was sighted and an HSL homed to it. With further reports of dinghy sightings four Hudsons were dispatched, led by F/Lt Stevens, to investigate. On reaching the search area they found over twenty Danish fishing vessels, well outside their permitted fishing area. There was a suspicion that they might be carrying aircrew survivors.

In the afternoon W/Cdr Corry took W/279 out to search for a dinghy sighted 65 miles north of Ameland. He was accompanied by F/Lt Pederson in O/279. On the way to the search area Corry sighted a ditched Flying Fortress about 35 miles north-east of Cromer. The bomber, from the 327th BS had only just ditched and all ten of the crew was in the process of transferring from the wings to the dinghies. One of the survivors appeared to be unable to board the dinghy and was clinging to the side. W/Cdr Corry dropped his airborne lifeboat, which came down 100 yards from this crew. At 1505 hours the first dinghy load had successfully transferred to the lifeboat, which they paddled over to the second dinghy. Ten minutes later the ditched Fortress sank and simultaneously W/279 was able to signal to an MTB that he had dropped a lifeboat to the survivors and set course for base, leaving Pederson circling the survivors. Whilst circling, Pederson's gunner tried to sink one of the empty dinghies but only succeeded in deflating it.

At 1806 hours the lifeboat signalled, 'Send boat, motors . . .'. O/279 replied, 'Motors under hatch.' The lifeboat responded, 'Motors u/s.' O/279 then signalled, 'Launch on way' and continued to circle the survivors. At 1915 hours they sighted an HSL six miles to the south-west and guided it to the lifeboat. The Fortress crew were picked up and taken to shore with the lifeboat in tow. Pederson then returned to base.

W/Cdr Corry, who had returned earlier, sent out another lifeboat-equipped Hudson to the original search area. F/Lt Fitchew in U/279 and Sgt Curtis in V/279 were actually airborne before Corry landed and flew to the position off Ameland where Bomber Command reported Halifaxes circling dinghies. On the way two dinghies were sighted, tied together and containing eight US airmen, 16 miles north-north-east of Cromer. Fitchew decided that Curtis should stay with these survivors, who were from a ditched Fortress of the 322nd BS 91st BG, and went on to Ameland. The Fortress was 42-3119 'Destiny's Tot' flown by Jack W Hargis. They had taken off as a spare aircraft from Bassingbourn to fill any gaps in the group formation due to unserviceability. No gaps appeared so Hargis decided to fill a slot in another group heading for Hanover. After bombing they turned for home but Hargis soon broke formation and began to descend over the North Sea. He warned his crew to prepare for ditching and they assembled in the radio compartment, where the radio operator was sending SOS signals. The ball turret hit the water first and then the Fortress ploughed to a halt. The crew quickly escaped through the radio room hatch and the pilots climbed out of the cabin windows. Working their way along the wing they launched two dinghies, five men in each as the Fortress sank from sight. Then two Spitfires arrived and circled the dinghies for a while.

Curtis climbed to get a fix after dropping his Lindholme containers, which the survivors reported to have landed 'almost a bulls-eye between our two dinghies'. They managed to reach them and climb in. At 1845 hours a Walrus appeared and picked up some of the survivors. This was followed a short time later by another Walrus, which collected the remainder.

Sgt Dougie Whittaker was Sgt Curtis' observer and recalls this sortie.

> *Three of us in formation, led by F/Lt Fitchew were sent to try and pick up some bods in two dinghies off the Norwegian coast. We found two dinghies tied together and we dropped some smoke floats and a Lindholme dinghy into which all eight piled and then we called for help and circled for two hours until an amphibious Walrus picked them up. Felt elated.*

Meanwhile Fitchew continued toward Ameland in U/279 and at 1839 hours he sighted a Halifax and followed it for several minutes until he found five dinghies tied together containing eight airmen. A second Halifax was circling the dinghies. Fitchew dropped his airborne lifeboat within 30 yards of the survivors and two of them paddled their dinghy over to it and climbed aboard. They then returned to pick up the other survivors and

An airborne lifeboat drops on its parachutes towards a ditched B-17
and its crew on 26 July 1943. Note the crew on the wing and in two
dinghies floating nearby. (USAAF via A McLeod)

were successfully underway by 1916 hours. The Fortress, from
the 410th BS 94th BG had been attacked and shot down by three
FW 190s crossing the Danish coast and all except one of the crew
managed to escape the ditched Fortress which broke in half on
hitting the sea and sank in fifteen seconds. At 2006 hours the
gaggle of Halifaxes and the Hudson were joined by a third
Halifax and shortly after that by three Fortresses. It would appear
the survivors were well protected! A short while later the lifeboat
came to a halt when the engine failed, but the aircrew managed
to hoist the sail and began to prepare to row. At this point Fitchew
had to return to base but left the three Fortresses circling them.
The survivors managed to restart the engine and it ran all night
at one third throttle. At 0730 hours a Danish fishing vessel took
the crew on board and set course for England. The lifeboat was
also hauled aboard. While the survivors were being looked after

by the Danes the search for the lifeboat was continued first by F/O Pederson in O/279, followed by W/Cdr Corry, who found the fishing vessel and homed HSLs to it. Some time later two HSLs intercepted it and after a bottle of rum had been consumed the Danes continued to England, landing the survivors at Yarmouth at 2245 hours.

On 28 July the ten crew of a Fortress of the 544th BS 384th BG ditched 15 miles north of Ameland. F/Sgt Palmer was airborne at 1605 hours in Hudson W/279 carrying an airborne lifeboat and accompanied by F/Sgt Mogridge and crew in O/279. At 1728 hours they sighted the dinghy with the survivors on board and two searching Mitchells. The Americans waved enthusiastically as Palmer dropped the airborne lifeboat 50 yards from them, and they began paddling towards it. Once aboard they got the engines started and W/279 gave them a course to steer by Aldis lamp. One Mitchell remained circling as the Hudson departed.

Another of the Squadron's stalwarts left that day. Posted overseas with his crew. S/Ldr Pye had been with 279 Sqn since 1942 and he took with him F/O Cave, F/Sgt Adams and F/O W.G. Knight. The following day his replacement, S/Ldr H.G. Mossford arrived to take over B Flt.

The lifeboat which had been dropped to the Fortress crew on the 28th, was found in a stationary condition on the 29th and an aircraft from the squadron successfully dropped supplies and petrol to the survivors, who managed to get underway again. Visibility was very poor during the day and the shepherding Hudsons lost sight of the lifeboat at least three times during their patrols. Luckily, after the last loss of contact the survivors were picked up by an HSL bringing the rescue to a successful conclusion.

On 30 July a Mitchell of 226 Sqn at Swanton Morley, coded 'Q', was attacked by eight enemy fighters while it was circling a dinghy 50 miles north of Terschelling. Both engines caught fire and the pilot immediately ditched. He and one crew member failed to get out but three others, P/O Eyton-Jones, Sgt Bishop and Sgt Lecomber managed to escape from the sinking aircraft and swam 10 yards to the drifting dinghy. Another aircraft reported the ditching and F/O Crawford set out in Hudson W/279 in company with O/279 to find the survivors. On reaching the scene Crawford was attacked by two Messerschmitt Me 210s but they did not succeed in damaging or shooting down the Hudson, which escaped. On return to base Crawford submitted his combat report.

F/O Crawford in Hudson W/279 in company with F/O Wilson who was leading in Hudson O/279 was flying at 150 feet, course 058 (T) when his operator reported several blips on the radar ahead at five miles. At five miles range four aircraft were sighted visually and were seen to be circling an aircraft which was ditching. The crew of 'W' immediately assumed the circling aircraft to be hostile and took up action stations, the pilot maintaining the same course and heading towards the ditched aircraft. The turret gunner of 'W', who, as had been agreed before take off, was to control both aircraft in case of attack, immediately asked to be switched over to 'Transmit' on the TR9 and began his commentary. As the range closed he identified the enemy aircraft as Me 210s, reported this and gave their position – Green Bow up 1,000 yards. The enemy aircraft formed up in line astern and appeared to be about to make a diving attack. 'W' was stepped up to 400 feet still formating on 'O's Red Quarter and both pilots warned to prepare to corkscrew. This was washed out when the enemy aircraft began to climb and take up a new position in the sun and on the Red Quarter. Maintaining their line astern formation they commenced a diving attack from 3,000 feet and 1,000 yards range. 'O' was told to step up and at 800 yards the controller ordered a climbing turn to port. The pilot of 'O' was concentrating on searching for survivors from ditched aircraft and had not switched over to TR9. He therefore remained on Green Bow flying slightly down. Enemy aircraft opened fire at 600 yards, closing to 550 yards, then breaking away down and across the Green Quarter. Their shots all went behind and below. No hits. 'W's navigator who was manning the port side gun fired five short bursts from 600–350 yards. The turret gunner fired one burst only at 400 yards, the enemy aircraft being hidden for the most part by the port fin and rudder. The turret gunner of 'O' also managed to fire two fairly long bursts, although in his case too, the enemy aircraft were mostly lost to sight behind the port fin and rudder. No strikes were observed. Enemy aircraft disappeared on southerly course after attack.

W/279 set off again later for a night search for Eyton-Jones and his surviving crew members but had no luck. In daylight P/O Watts took off from Bircham Newton on R/279 to rendezvous

Beaufighters of the North Coates Strike Wing escorted P/O Watts'
Hudson during the search for P/O Eyton-Jones' ditched Mitchell. (Via
A Rodgers)

with a Beaufighter escort at North Coates and proceeded to the
search area. Three Beaufighters were soon sighted circling three
dinghies at the last known position of the survivors and Watts
successfully dropped an airborne lifeboat to the survivors. Eyton-
Jones and his men climbed aboard, but unable to start the engines,
they hoisted the mast and sail, which took them southwards.
Watts signalled them a course to steer before departing. Later
more aircraft went out to find and shepherd the survivors but
failed to find them. During a rough night in the dinghy during
which they had to ride out a storm, Eyton-Jones and his crew
were picked up by an RML and finally brought safely to shore on
3 August. A successful conclusion, but as we shall see shortly this
crew were lucky to survive.

Dougie Whittaker was on ASR patrol again on 31 July. 'We
covered eight Spitfires on patrol but could not assist one which
was shot down.'

Sorties such as this one were very disappointing and frustrating for the crews involved whose whole *raison d'être* was the
saving of life.

P/O Eyton-Jones' Mitchell was not the only one shot down. On
1 August three Hudsons led by F/Lt Fitchew set out to find the
crew of one which had been shot down by enemy fighters during
an ASR search. The survivors were believed to be 65 miles north-
west of Borkum. At 1647 hours in position 5431N 0347E Fitchew's
crew in G/279 sighted two dinghies tied together, one of them
containing three survivors. The aircrew in the dinghy fired

pyrotechnics as the Hudson approached and at 1653 hours F/O Pederson, in Hudson N/279, dropped an airborne lifeboat, which landed successfully 80 yards downwind of the dinghies. The crew was seen to board the boat, but did not even examine the engine hatches, let alone start the engine or hoist the sail. Fitchew remained with the lifeboat after the other two Hudson's departed and when he left at 1956 hours the lifeboat was still stationary.

Early the following morning three Hudsons set out to relocate the Eyton-Jones crew but had no luck. A further search was mounted and F/O Tait in N/279 had better luck, finding the lifeboat at 0924 hours. He reported that all the occupants seemed lively. The mast had been rigged and snapped during a tremendous storm the previous night and had been replaced by an oar. The drogue had been insufficiently effective in keeping the boat bow-on to the enormous waves and the crew had thrown the sail into the water to act as an additional drogue to prevent it foundering. When Tait found them, the lifeboat was hove to and, unfortunately, he lost sight of it as he climbed for a fix. He failed to relocate it and had to return to Bircham Newton, short of fuel.

Another effort was made in the evening, led by F/Sgt Neil. They found a Halifax circling in the area, which led the two Hudsons to the lifeboat, which was still hove to. One of the Hudsons managed to call up an RML, which was given a position for the lifeboat and a distance and course to steer.

Just before midday on the 3rd F/O Wilson and crew were able to relocate the lifeboat and Wilson was able to contact two HSLs to whom he gave directions. He then proceeded to drop sea markers between the lifeboat and the HSLs. By a coincidence he was replaced on scene by P/O Watts, who had dropped the airborne lifeboat to Eyton-Jones and his crew and at 1524 hours he had the satisfaction of seeing an RML towing it towards England, where they landed the crew at Gorleston that night. The squadron later received a message from the CO of No. 226 Sqn. 'The crew say they felt confident in their dinghy and the boat dropped as aircraft were visible most of the time. They wish to express their particular gratitude to the aircraft which dropped their boat and to the launch that rescued them.' The unfortunate crew of the other Mitchell, who had made little attempt to help themselves once aboard the lifeboat, was never found.

By August 1943 Bomber Command's Battle of the Ruhr was drawing to a close, but a new battle was about to begin for Berlin.

In addition the US 8th Air Force was building in strength all the time and sending out larger formations to more distant targets. Coastal Command maritime patrol and strike aircraft were out in force and Fighter Command were harrying German air and ground forces regularly. All of this meant more aircraft and crews returning in trouble, with wounded crew members, shot up aircraft and often precious little fuel. The icy waters of the English Channel, the North Sea and the Atlantic Ocean would claim a good many of them. No. 279 Sqn and the rest of the ASR organization would do their best over the coming months to pluck the fortunate ones from these dangerous seas.

One lucky crew was that of a No. 2 OTU Beaufighter from Catfoss, which ditched violently after engine failure and sank in twenty seconds 40 miles north-east of Flamborough Head. F/O Myatt was soon airborne with the Bircham Newton station commander as second pilot and reached the scene to find two Beaufighters circling the survivors. Myatt spotted the two dinghies at 2038 hours with one man in one and the other clinging to the side of the second. F/O Myatt climbed for a fix and then swept down to drop his Lindholme dinghy. The occupant of the first dinghy paddled towards it and Myatt remained circling. At 2146 the Hudson crew sighted an Aldis flashing and turned towards it to find an HSL, which was homed onto the dinghies and successfully picked up the two survivors, F/O Mottram and P/O Phillips. Unfortunately, Mottram, the pilot, died soon after being brought ashore.

On 9 August the squadron received a copy of a message, which had been sent from the Secretary of State for Air to the AOC Coastal Command. It read.

> *The War Cabinet have charged me to express to you their admiration of the magnificent work performed by the Air Sea Rescue organization during the recent heavy air battles. Many gallant American and British aircrews owe their lives to their constant diligence and unflinching devotion to duty. They are making an indispensable contribution to the growing Allied air offensive.*

Tragedy struck once more in an unfortunate accident on 17 August. First Lt Moore USAAF and F/Sgt Flanagan, who had both joined the squadron with their crews a few days earlier, were practising circuits in Hudson U/279 when Moore swung badly on take-off and the Hudson crashed and burst into flames. Flanagan sustained severe burns in the crash and died in Ely hospital the following morning.

On 19 August F/O Pederson was scrambled in Hudson L/279, in company with F/Sgt Neil in A/279, to search for the crew of a

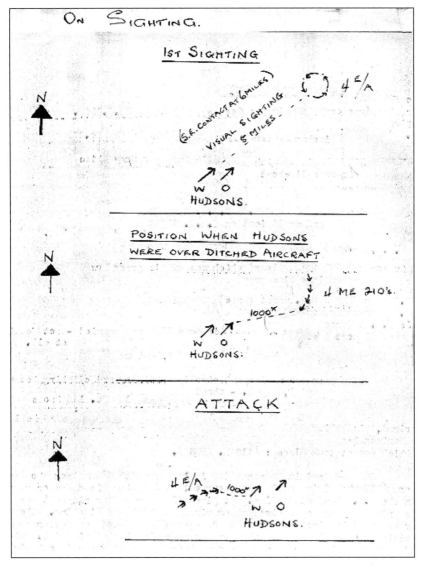

The combat report diagram from the 30 July 1943 battle between W/279, O/279 and four Me 210s.

Flying Fortress of the 96th BG, which had caught fire during the assembly procedure for a raid on Woensdrecht airfield. The crew baled out and the B-17 came down at Wolferton Sands in the Wash. Pederson sighted the burning bomber on the foreshore and after circling for a while it was seen to blow up. Shortly afterward L and A/279 were recalled to base.

Six Hudsons, led by F/O Myatt in L/279, took off at 1830 hours from Bircham Newton to search for a dinghy 20–50 miles east of Southwold. Three-quarters of an hour later Myatt sighted an empty dinghy and a minute later received a message indicating that the survivors were aboard a Walrus, which was unable to take off. Myatt was ordered to guide a boat to the location but five minutes later received a further message that rescue had been effected. The empty dinghy was fired on and left to sink.

On 22 August F/Lt Fitchew led a search of five Hudsons, including R/279 carrying an airborne lifeboat, in the morning to locate a dinghy with two occupants reported to be approximately 50 miles north of Terschelling. A parallel-track search was commenced and less than two hours later one of the Hudson crews spotted a red pyrotechnic on the port beam. Two minutes later they were over the dinghy and at 1118 hours F/Sgt Bedford in R/279 dropped his airborne lifeboat to the survivors. Unfortunately the drop was a disaster, one parachute opened fully, another only partially and the third not at all. The occupants of the dinghy paddled towards the lifeboat and one man climbed aboard and began to examine it. He signalled that it was unserviceable, while the second man, apparently injured, lay in the bottom of the dinghy. The survivors abandoned any hope of using the lifeboat and drifted away in the dinghy.

At 1515 hours another search set out from Bircham Newton led by F/O Tait and including another lifeboat-equipped Hudson, F/279, flown by F/O W. Clark. The abandoned lifeboat was sighted first at 1721 hours in a waterlogged condition and just over twenty-five minutes later the dinghy was relocated. Clark dropped his lifeboat and this time all went well, with the boat landing 40 yards from the dinghy. Both occupants boarded it and managed to start the engines, though they stopped shortly afterward. Hudson D/279 set off to look for any HSLs in the area but found none and F/279 departed for base a short while later. F/O Myatt in K/279 stayed with the lifeboat and saw that the occupants had managed to restart the engines and set off steering an erratic course to the west. They appeared to be having difficulty with the rudder and were trying to steer using an oar. K/279 left them at 1938 hours while three Beaufighters continued to circle them.

The following day an effort was made to relocate the lifeboat but the six Hudsons searching had no luck. During the search it became evident that the Germans had noticed all of the activity. Two Ju 88s put in a brief appearance and it was later discovered that the survivors had been picked up by a Dornier Do 24 sent out by the Germans. The rescue ended tragically, however, when some Flying Fortresses came on the scene and shot the Dornier, carrying the survivors, down in flames.

Sorties flown by the Hudsons of 279 Sqn often took the crews close to enemy occupied coastlines in the search for survivors of ditched aircraft and consequently brought them within range of German fighters and military vessels, which were equally keen to get their hands on the ditched crews. These searches often resulted in dogfights between escort fighters and the enemy. Often the Hudsons would search without the benefit of a fighter escort and on those occasions were at great risk of being shot down in any encounter with a German fighter. Following the night raid by Bomber Command on Berlin on 23/24 August 1943 one such encounter occurred.

Two Hudsons took off from Bircham Newton to search for a crew of five in a dinghy in the approximate area of 5500N 0500E. Hudson H/279 was flown by F/L Fitchew with F/O Scott, P/O O.V. Burns and P/O Field as his crew and Hudson R/279 was flown by F/Sgt Neil accompanied by F/O Whapham, F/Sgt Pennington and F/Sgt Gourlay. Approaching the search area they encountered two Stirlings circling the dinghy in position 5449N 0440E and a few minutes later F/Sgt Neil successfully dropped his airborne lifeboat, which came to rest within a few yards of the dinghy. The survivors transferred from the dinghy to the lifeboat and shortly afterwards the Stirlings departed.

This had been F/Sgt Neil's first operational lifeboat drop but he and his crew had little time to enjoy the success. Thirty minutes later, as the Hudsons continued to circle the lifeboat, two Messerschmitt Bf 110s appeared and began to fire upon the survivors in the lifeboat. Fitchew and Neil closed up together and began to take evasive action, taking up a westerly heading in the hope of outrunning the German fighters. Shortly after the commencement of the attack Fitchew lost contact with Neil and flames and a large column of smoke were observed on the surface. R/279 had been shot down.

Running for base Fitchew had the added worry of a further seven Bf 110s arriving on the scene and a running battle developed, with the Messerschmitts making attacks from the rear, port and starboard. During the fight P/O Burns managed to get off about 700 rounds at the Germans and though no hits were claimed it was observed that one of the fighters had a stopped engine. By skilful evasive manoeuvring Fitchew managed to escape the fighters and returned with his crew intact and only two hits to the underside of the starboard aileron.

Whilst Fitchew and Neil had been fighting the Messerschmitts two other Hudsons, had been ordered off to relieve them but were quickly recalled due to the enemy fighter activity in the area. The fate of the survivors in the lifeboat is unknown. At base F/Lt Fitchew submitted his combat report.

F/Lt Fitchew in Hudson H/279 in company with F/Sgt Neil in Hudson R/279 was circling an airborne lifeboat dropped by F/Sgt Neil when F/Lt Fitchew at 1625 hours sighted two aircraft in the circuit. They were immediately identified as Me 110s. F/Lt Fitchew immediately gave 'Action Stations', the range of the enemy aircraft being 700 yards, and they were crossing aircraft 'H' nose to the Red Bow. The enemy aircraft appeared to dive onto the airborne lifeboat at extreme range.

Hudson 'H' continued to turn to port endeavouring to formate with Hudson 'R' and at the same time the rear gunner in Hudson 'H' reported to his pilot that there was another aircraft on the Red Beam down 2½ miles. This was later identified as another Me 110. Hudson 'R' who was due west of Hudson 'H' was also turning steeply to port on to a westerly course, the range between aircraft 'H' and aircraft 'R' being 1,000 yards. Closing to 500 yards aircraft 'R' was now on aircraft 'H's Red Quarter. The range was decreased rapidly to 300 yards by the pilot of aircraft 'H' throttling back.

At this moment the enemy aircraft singled out a target each and closed to the first attack from the Red Quarter up 700 feet, opening fire at 1,000 yards. Both Hudsons turned in to the attack and did a diving turn to port. Hudson 'H' opening fire at 800 yards with a short burst. As the range closed the rear gunner in aircraft 'H' gave the enemy aircraft a long burst at 400 yards closing as the enemy aircraft broke off the Attack at about point blank range on the Green Beam. The range between the Hudsons was still about 300 to 400 yards.

The enemy aircraft attacking aircraft 'H' immediately committed himself to a second attack from the Green Quarter 700 yards up 700 feet. Aircraft 'H' did a diving turn to starboard, corkscrewing, undulating, throttling back and weaving and the attack was broken off on the Red Quarter. The rear gunner fired whenever possible. The third attack was made from 1,000 yards dead astern. The rear gunner ordered the pilot to undulate at 600 yards during which period the gunner was able to fire a number of short bursts. At about 250 yards the pilot throttled back and did a diving turn to starboard down to sea level, whereupon the enemy aircraft overshot to port but quickly recovered and made his fourth attack from the Red Bow to Red beam at 900 yards.

Aircraft 'H' turned in to the attack and the enemy aircraft broke away on the starboard beam above aircraft 'H' at about 150 yards.

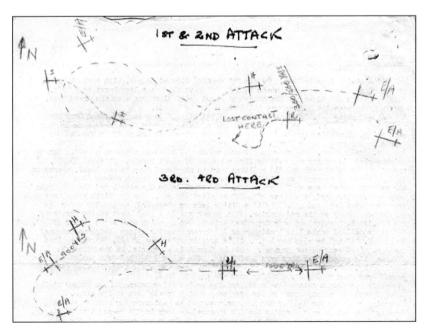

The first four attacks by the Me 110s during F/Lt Fitchew's running battle on 24 August 1943.

The enemy aircraft fifth attack was made from the Green Beam and aircraft 'H' did a diving turn to starboard, so passing underneath the enemy aircraft to break away on the Red Quarter. The gunner got in a good burst on the breakaway. The Messerschmitt's sixth attack was made from dead astern, during which period the gunner of aircraft 'H' saw a pall of smoke 3 to 4 miles away 10 degrees Green Quarter astern, which was assumed to be aircraft 'R' and he also saw four Me 110s crossing the bows of aircraft 'H' making into the sun. (A/G wearing sun goggles). This he immediately reported to the pilot who informed his gunner that they were four of seven enemy aircraft. The other three enemy aircraft had just peeled off towards aircraft 'H' but passed Red beam up 1,000 feet and the other 4 enemy aircraft peeled off and passed Green beam up 1,000 feet. Nothing more was seen of them.

Meanwhile the astern attack developed, evasive action being taken and the gunner firing short bursts and a long burst on the breakaway, which was to port at 150 yards. Formating again on the Red Bow the enemy aircraft endeavoured to manoeuvre for another attack from Red Bow but on each occasion the enemy aircraft appeared to turn in 'H' turned towards the attack, eventually the enemy aircraft made a poor effort and crossed to the Green Bow carrying out the same tactics, eventually turning to attack. 'H' made a diving turn into the attack, passing underneath the enemy aircraft. The rear gunner and Green side gunner got in bursts as the enemy aircraft crossed on Green Beam and Quarter exposing the underside of the fuselage. Pilot on this attack thought that port engine was windmilling as though out of action. The engagement finished. 'H' set course for home at 0 feet. Throughout the action the height was between 0–700 feet.

LAC Ernest Farrow recalls Fitchew's return to base.

On another occasion one of our aircraft based a Bircham Newton was searching off the Dutch coast when it was attacked by German fighters. The pilot, F/O Fitchew, a regular peacetime officer, took such evasive action, that although the aircraft was damaged by enemy fire and covered with engine oil, he returned to base. We all thought he must have flown the Hudson upside down to escape.

While Fitchew and Neil were struggling with the Messerschmitts F/O Tait, in Hudson D/279, was carrying out a patrol when he sighted a 280 Sqn Anson circling an area of wreckage and three survivors. An empty Lindholme dinghy was nearby but the survivors were making no attempt to reach it. Tait dropped another Lindholme dinghy, but once again the men in the water made no attempt to get to it. At 1510 hours the Hudson managed to contact two RMLs and homed them to the survivors. Just over two hours later the launches came into view and the survivors were taken on board at 1750 hours. Tait then turned for home with fuel becoming short. Unfortunately two of the three survivors died after being rescued.

Hopeful of finding survivors from F/Sgt Neil's crew of Hudson R/279, which had been shot down the previous day, the squadron attempted a search of the area on the 25th. Three Hudsons were sent out to the area and a fighter escort of eight Mustangs from 309 Sqn were led out by S/Ldr D.T. Downer in a fourth Hudson, acting as navigation aircraft. The search was a failure, however, as the Mustang leader signalled to Downer as they reached the area that they had insufficient fuel to remain in the search area and would have to return to base. Downer led the Mustangs back to the coast and they then set course for their base. The three Hudsons, who had planned to carry out a parallel track search of the area, spent some time searching for their escort before setting course for base.

The last day of the month was marked by a five-aircraft search in the morning, led by newly promoted S/Ldr Fitchew, for Danish fishing vessels escaping from Denmark. F/Sgt Oakes in Hudson D/279 found five boats and WO Mogridge in K/279 found four more. Bircham barrels and Thornaby bags were dropped by the Hudsons to assist the Danes in their escape and several were seen to be picked up.

The month had been relatively unsuccessful for the squadron due to the losses in dogfights and accidents, and the failure of the airborne lifeboat drops to recover survivors, many of whom were never seen again.

September saw the spirit of the Squadron in need of a boost and it came in the shape of a successful rescue on the 2nd and the 4th September. On the 2nd Dougie Whittaker was involved: 'A Typhoon pilot had been forced to ditch soon after take-off and we found him and contacted base who sent a Walrus of 276 Sqn to pick him up OK.'

Also on 2 September, F/Lt Stevens on detachment at

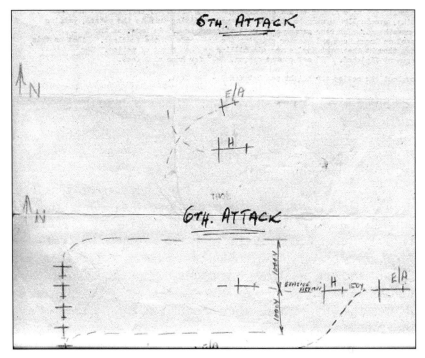

The final attacks on 24 August 1943.

Harrowbeer, was airborne at 0745 hours to carry out a search off the Ile de Bas. Just before reaching the area an unidentified aircraft was sighted and, discretion being the better part of valour, Stevens turned away and set course for home. A few minutes later, though, his escort of eight Typhoons was sighted and he resumed course for the search area and at 0806 hours sighted a Walrus on the water alongside a dinghy. The Typhoons circled until the Walrus took off and Stevens set course for Harrowbeer.

On the night of 3/4 September Bomber Command dispatched 316 Lancasters and four Mosquitoes to attack Berlin. Losses were high, with twenty-two of the Lancasters failing to return. Amongst them was a Lancaster of No. 106 Sqn, based at Syerston and captained by S/Ldr Howroyd, which ditched in the North Sea.

It was attacked over Berlin by a Messerschmitt Bf 110 night-fighter at 2329 hours just as 'bombs gone' was called over the intercom. Sgt Mackenzie, the rear gunner, was fatally wounded in this first attack. Howroyd immediately took violent evasive action. The next burst of fire from the nightfighter fatally wounded the bomb aimer, P/O, Saxby and damaged most of the electrical instruments. Intercom, emergency intercom, IFF, compass and radio were put out of action, though the radio was quickly repaired. The Messerschmitt carried out four more attacks and as it broke away on the last of these it presented a perfect target for mid-upper gunner Sgt Kelly, who fired a long and accurate burst into its belly. Kelly was firing without sights as these had been shot away by a cannon shell, which had also temporarily blinded him. The nightfighter went into a steep dive, held in a cone of searchlights as it dived to its doom.

Howroyd set course for England, but unaware of the compass failure strayed well off course, something that was only discovered as they passed over the east coast of Sweden. By the time the Lancaster reached the Dutch coast it had only 40 minutes of fuel remaining. Howroyd continued, with little chance of reaching England, transmitting distress messages in the hope of being picked up. His harness had been shot away during the attack and when the decision to ditch was made his flight engineer, Sgt Sergeant, lashed him into his seat with a length of oxygen tubing. As the Lancaster descended through 1,000 feet all the engines cut out and an engineless ditching seemed inevitable, but at only 10 feet off the sea the engineer managed to switch over to tanks containing a few more gallons of fuel. The engines picked up at the last moment giving Howroyd some control and enabling him to make a perfect ditching. The crew felt hardly any shock on impacting the water and were able to escape the doomed Lancaster with almost all of their gear. The mortally wounded rear gunner was lifted out after a hard struggle but the crew were unable to extricate the dead bomb-aimer, who went down with the aircraft when it sank many hours later.

Good fixes were obtained from these signals and F/O Tait and P/O Watts got airborne at first light to search for the Lancaster, which had ditched 130 miles north-east of Bircham Newton. The Hudsons arrived in the search area and on the sixth leg of their search both crews simultaneously sighted the still floating aircraft. Fixes were obtained and a sighting message passed back to base as F/O Tait dropped his Lindholme gear. On receipt of the sighting message two more Hudsons were airborne to relieve the first pair. P/O Watts met these aircraft at the halfway point and led them to the dinghy. WO Passlow, in W/279, dropped an airborne lifeboat to the survivors at 1114 hours and the first two Hudson then set course for base.

The wounded rear gunner had survived the ditching and was lifted into the dinghy by the others, but sadly he died about an hour later. The remaining five survivors transferred from the dinghy to the lifeboat, which had landed about 60 yards from them, but no effort was made to start the engines. One of the circling Hudsons flashed a course to steer by Aldis lamp but received no acknowledgement. F/Sgt Palmer in the second Hudson remained circling the lifeboat and contacted some RMLs, which gave him an ETA of 1630 hours. Unfortunately Palmer had to leave the scene at 1425 hours unaware that two more Hudsons were on the way.

Howroyd's crew found little difficulty in transferring from the dinghy to the lifeboat but they found that the parachute lines had not fallen clear and despite efforts to cut them away the lines fouled the propellers, preventing them from starting the engines. They hoisted the sail but the wind was not helping them make much headway.

The two relieving aircraft, flown by F/Sgt Bedford and WO Gale, were airborne at 1345 hours and proceeded straight to the lifeboat position. They soon found it and, remarkably, the Lancaster still floating nearby. They managed to establish contact with the RMLs and homed them to the lifeboat, which they reached at 1630 hours, taking the survivors on board. The survivors, one of whom was injured, were landed at Immingham the next day and a message of thanks and appreciation was received from 106 Sqn for the quick work in rescuing the crew.

On 6 September 1943 the US 8th Air Force carried out a raid on Stuttgart using the B-17s of the 1st and 3rd Bomb Divisions. The raid was a costly fiasco during which cloud frustrated the attacks on various objectives and many of the formations became separated. The 1st Wing suffered especially due to many of its short-range B-17s running short of fuel and crash landing in England or ditching in the sea. Twelve B-17s, carrying 118 crew, ditched and, remarkably, all of them were rescued by ASR.

Among them was the crew of the 92nd BG crew captained by 1st Lt Prusser. On ditching they found one of the two aircraft dinghies torn to shreds and all crowded into or clung onto the remaining dinghy. The overloaded dinghy lay heavy in

The USAAF A-3A liferaft as used by crews of the B-17, B-24, B-25 and B-26. (USAAF via A McLeod)

the water, with three men clinging to the side and proved impossible to steer. The ten man crew waited for rescue.

Around midday F/O Clarke was airborne from Bircham Newton headed for Tangmere in Hudson W/279. After briefing there he was airborne again at 1619 hours with an escort of four Mustangs heading for a position 8 miles west of Cap d'Antifer. Just over half an hour later W/279 was overhead the dinghy after sighting a pyrotechnic and turned into wind to drop the airborne lifeboat.

Unfortunately Clarke was forced to make the run directly into sun and the boat landed 100 yards away from the survivors in the dinghy. Prusser and his men made determined attempts to paddle the waterlogged and overloaded dinghy toward it but by the time Clarke turned W/279 for home they had made no progress. They never reached the lifeboat, which continued to drift away from them, but were fortunate to be picked up during the night by HMS *Breasdale*.

Further success came the following day when F/Sgt Bedford and WO Gale took off from Bircham Newton to search for a Lancaster crew who had ditched after turning back out to sea to jettison their bombs. The crew had previously been sighted by an aircraft of No. 280 Sqn in position 5330N 0142E. WO Gale successfully homed HSLs to the area and the crew was picked up.

There was much celebration on the squadron on 8 September following the news of the Italian surrender and celebrations continued the following day with the award of a DFC to Australian F/Lt L.G. Wilson and the promotion of McKimm to Flight Lieutenant.

By mid-September the squadron was due to begin re-equipment with Vickers Warwick twin-engined ASR aircraft and four were due to arrive for conversion. On 19 September F/O Myatt and his crew arrived to act as instructors during the conversion.

A major effort was made to locate a ditched Halifax crew on 20 September. Initially seven Hudsons took off from Bircham Newton after distress signals and a fix 45 miles west of Texel were obtained. The Hudsons searched areas to the north and south of the fix but nothing was sighted. Later a Stirling sighted the dinghy and reported it to be 30 miles west of Texel. On receipt of this information W/279 was dispatched, with an escort of ten Spitfires from Coltishall. Rough seas and fading light hampered the search and nothing was sighted. Despite the lack of success the day ended on a happier note when the navigator of W/279 was informed on his return that his wife had presented him with a son!

The Harrowbeer detachment were also busy as Dougie Whittaker recalls.

> We were now at Harrowbeer and on 20th September operated a lengthy search for two Beaufighter crews without any success. Due to fuel shortage we had to land at Predannack to complete the mission. On the 21st we directed a Walrus which picked up a ditched Typhoon pilot and by the 28th we had returned to Bircham Newton

The remainder of the month was filled with unsuccessful searches and the only points of note were the departure of V and E/279, captained by F/O Myatt and F/O Pederson, for Wick on a detachment of unspecified length and purpose. On 29 September S/Ldr Fitchew was awarded the DFC and a celebration party was held that night in the mess.

Following a search attempt on 30 September, which was

thwarted by the weather, S/Ldr Downer led a four-aircraft search to a position west of Esbjerg on 1 October. A bomber was believed to have ditched in the area on the night of 29/30 September and the Hudsons were to search for the survivors. On reaching the search area, they had just commenced the first leg when Q/279 developed engine trouble. It turned for base, escorted by S/Ldr Downer in L/279. The other two aircraft, misunderstanding the leader's Aldis instructions to continue the search, also turned for home and the second attempt to reach the survivors was a failure.

There was an unusual occurrence on 4 October when F/O Reade was airborne in N/279 from Harrowbeer. About forty minutes after take-off the airborne lifeboat suddenly fell away, landing in the sea. Fortunately a surface vessel was able to recover it and the undamaged Hudson landed safely.

On the same day a search was carried out around a position 26 miles east-north-east of Cromer, close to rescue float No. 3. The search was the result of reports of an explosion in this position, where two USAAF Fortresses had been seen circling. F/O Crawford made a thorough search of the area around the rescue float but found no sign of life either on or near it.

By now the re-equipment of the squadron with Warwicks was imminent; No. 280 Sqn were already converting from Ansons to Warwicks at Thorney Island and were to move to Thornaby to operate the type from there. The strong rumours circulating on 279 Sqn included one that they would likewise convert and move to Thornaby as Bircham Newton was unsuitable for Warwick operations. The rumoured move was not popular. The squadron members would have preferred to remain in East Anglia. Not all was doom and gloom, however, as spirits were raised by a spate of promotions over the next few days; F/Sgts Shaw Kidd and Johnson and WO Baker all being promoted to P/O.

On the 6th five Hudsons set out from Bircham Newton to search an area 70 miles north-east of Cromer for survivors from a Lancaster which had failed to return from a search the previous day. Although F/Lt McKimm found an empty dinghy and a search was made around its position there was no sign of survivors. Further inconclusive searches were carried out over the next few days.

Promotions continued to be promulgated throughout the month and included F/Sgts Jackson, Neil, Bedford and MacFarlane, who were all commissioned. As we have seen, however, F/Sgt Neil had been shot down in a fight with Messerschmitts and would never know of his promotion. P/O F.T. Lerway was also promoted to F/O.

Poor weather grounded any search attempts over the next few days and on the 12th the squadron was informed that it was to move to Thornaby on 24 October. The following day three Hudsons took off from Bircham Newton to carry out a search but entered fog and lost contact with each other. F/Sgt Oakes in Q/279 was carrying an airborne lifeboat and as he made landfall the Hudson crew felt a heavy bump, but could not ascertain the cause. When Oakes landed it was discovered that the airborne lifeboat was missing!

Fog and poor weather prevented much flying until the 15th when four aircraft went out to search for a dinghy east of Cromer. At the end of the second search leg F/O J.S. Tait, flying Z/279 and equipped with an airborne lifeboat, noticed that the Hudson was yawing and vibrating badly. The problem was caused by the sea drogue of the lifeboat, which had come out of its housing and wrapped itself around the port tailplane, fin and rudder. The Hudson very quickly became uncontrollable and Tait ordered F/O Bishop, his observer, to jettison the lifeboat. It had a normal descent and Tait's Hudson returned safely to base. The search continued but to no avail. The following day another fruitless search was carried out.

No. 279 Sqn on parade at Bircham Newton in 1943. (E Farrow)

On the 16th W/Cdr Corry led a party from the squadron to Thornaby to inspect the facilities prior to their move there on the 24th. On the 18th serviceability problems again hampered a search. Four aircraft set out to search an area 140 miles north-east of Cromer, led by F/O Crawford. After six search legs Crawford's gauges indicated he was short of fuel so he returned to base, handing over leadership of the search to P/O Bedford in M/279. On landing it was discovered that the fuel gauge had been giving a false reading. The remaining aircraft continued the search but sighted only Danish fishing vessels. Later F/O Tait in V/279 and F/Sgt Curtis in Z/279 carrying an airborne lifeboat returned to the search area but only managed to complete two legs before darkness fell making it impossible to continue the search.

By 19 October the Squadron had been informed that it was to remain at Bircham Newton operating Hudsons for the time being and that the move to Thornaby and re-equipment with Warwicks had been postponed. Over the following weeks many sorties were flown searching for survivors from various aircraft but apart from sightings of wreckage no successful rescues were made.

CHAPTER FIVE

November 1943
– April 1944

The early days of November were marred by poor weather and it was not until the 4th that operations recommenced with a four-Hudson search led by P/O Bedford. No results were obtained and the following day four more aircraft set out at first light, this time led by F/Sgt Palmer, to search the same area north-east of Cromer, where pyrotechnics had been sighted. During a thorough search of the area nothing was found other than some debris and an aircraft wheel. A second search was carried out by three Hudsons led by F/Lt Crawford for the crew of a ditched Beaufighter, finding only wreckage and an aircraft wheel once again. In the afternoon W/Cdr Corry led a further search for the Beaufighter crew but the search was finally abandoned due to failing light and the Hudsons landed at Docking.

A typical sequence of events causing a squadron Hudson to be scrambled during this period is recalled by Dougie Whittaker.

We would be on stand-by in the crew room playing cards, shove halfpenny etc. and the phone would ring. We would be scrambled to get to a known ditching. Sometimes nowhere near it. Otherwise after night bombing raids over Germany by Bomber Command we did regulation searches over specific areas of the North Sea, often nothing found. If we saw anyone in the water we told base who told us to stick around. They contacted ASR boats, which came to my given position.

The squadron suffered another loss on 13 November when M/Sgt Courson, an American, and his three English crewmembers failed to return from a navigation exercise in Hudson B/279. A second American crewmember, 1st Lt Dooley, was also lost with this crew. When they failed to return to base Warwicks of No. 280 Sqn were sent to search in the late afternoon but found no trace of them. Searches continued until the 15th with no success.

Whilst the search for B/279 was ongoing F/Lt Crawford led three more Hudsons on a search 60 miles north-east of Cromer for the crew of a ditched Fortress. Serial number 239860, it was one of a formation from the 548th BS 385th BG, based at Great Ashfield in Suffolk, taking part in a raid on Bremen. It was piloted by 2nd Lt Ben McCall and his co-pilot 2nd Lt C.L. 'Pete' Ginn. *En route* to the target it collided with another aircraft in the formation, which resulted in the loss of nine-tenths of the stabilizer and one complete side of the tailplane. The tail gunner, S/Sgt WH Butler was also lost at this point, his fate unknown.

Despite severe injuries McCall, with help from Ginn, managed to keep the bomber under control and in formation until the target was hit, then with the oxygen system knocked out descended to a lower altitude, leaving the formation. Escorting fighters attempted to shelter the stricken bomber and fought off repeated attacks, during which navigator, 2nd Lt John Replogle, shot down one of the attacking fighters.

Hoping they could make base McCall and Ginn struggled with the controls as they approached the coast of Europe where they were joined by two more damaged aircraft, a P-38 and a B-24. Ginn later said, 'The three of us must have been some spectacle. Like lame ducks, we tried to stay in formation with each other.'

The engines then began to fail and the battered bomber lost altitude, now committed to a ditching. McCall had the crew huddle together in the radio compartment prior to ditching and the radio operator, T/Sgt Stanley Easterbrook, remained at his radio sending SOS signals.

As the Fortress hit the water the nose ploughed in and submerged about 25 feet before rising to the surface. Ginn left the

Though of poor quality this photo depicts the crew of
Fortress 239860 ditched on 13 November 1943 returning
from Bremen and rescued by Hudsons of No. 279 Sqn.
Standing L to R: T/Sgt L.F. Charland, S/Sgt W.H.
Bowles, S/Sgt S.W. Easterbrook, Sgt Ward, Sgt E.J.
Berthiaume, Sgt W.H. Butler. Kneeling L to R: 2nd Lt B.J.
McCall, 2nd Lt G.A. Reed, 2nd Lt J.L. Replogle, 2nd Lt
R.E. Lambiaso. (via Gerard Berthiaume)

cockpit and released the dinghies; unfortunately, one of them
was torn to shreds by the jagged remains of the aircraft tail,
leaving only one small dinghy for all nine men. Liberators
returning from the raid spotted the ditching and sent out distress
signals to ASR, who quickly alerted 279 Sqn.

F/O Clark, piloting the No. 2 Hudson in the formation, hit a
seagull on take off, which knocked a large hole on the nose
Perspex and scattered entrails, feathers and worms all over the
cabin. Clark elected to continue and his observer, F/O O'Gorman
decided to navigate the Hudson from the aft cabin area. The crew
blocked up the hole in the nose as best they could with a cushion,
but 'Nobby' Clark reported afterwards that it was '— Cold!'
Reaching the search area the Hudsons commenced the search and

after about two minutes on the first leg Crawford's rear gunner F/O Godfrey reported sighting pyrotechnics on the port quarter. Minutes later the formation was over an American dinghy with apparently six or seven occupants (As we have seen, there were, in fact, nine).

Crawford dropped his Lindholme dinghy and containers, which the survivors were able to reach, and then climbed for a fix. During the climb his aircraft developed engine trouble and, signalling his intentions to the other aircraft, he set course for base. Shortly afterward his engines picked up and he turned Y/279 back to the dinghies. F/O Wilson then dropped another dinghy from K/279 but the result went unobserved due to the visibility deteriorating. The survivors reported that of the two dinghies dropped one was punctured and useless. The weather worsened as the survivors huddled in the dinghy in the snow, sleet and rain. McCall who had been seriously injured during the collision and the subsequent ditching had passed out in the first hours of their ordeal and later died in the arms of top turret gunner T/Sgt Lawrence Charland. The ball turret gunner also passed out, suffering from the effects of cold and lack of oxygen earlier in the flight.

By mid-afternoon F/Lt McKimm had got airborne in E/279 to assist with the search and, sighting the other three Hudsons he joined them in circling the survivors. Shortly afterward the first three aircraft departed for base and McKimm remained circling and dropping marine markers close to the dinghy. The weather worsened and McKimm was forced to leave several times to avoid violent squalls passing through the area. McKimm's radio operator had been trying to raise rescue launches in the area without success and at 1815 hours the W/Op obtained a good fix and instructions to drop flares in the area. Meanwhile, help in the form of Hudsons P and H/279, flown by P/O Pederson and F/Sgt Curtis, was on the way. The reinforcing Hudsons found the dinghy after sighting McKimm's marine markers. The new arrivals had been searching an area adjacent to Crawford's and whilst P/279 continued to search in this area until dark, H/279 circled the dinghy. With darkness both Hudson departed leaving McKimm circling in E/279 and dropping flares until, at 1930 hours, the wake of an RML was sighted heading for the dinghies. Unable to contact it, McKimm tried to assist it in locating the dinghies in every way possible; switching on navigation lights, flashing the Aldis lamp and even switching on the aircraft landing lamps. The survivors in the dinghies fired off flares in a bid to attract attention. The aircraft flare gun had been lost in the ditching, but Ginn, remembering that the dinghy was supposed to have one, searched till he found it and quickly fired off three flares. E/279 finally had to leave the scene at 2016 hours and landed at Docking. The RML, which had been on a course away from the dinghy, saw the flares and returned and picked up the survivors and landed them at Great Yarmouth at 0230 hours on the 14th. There were nine survivors in all, two of whom were kept in hospital, while the rest returned to their base.

On 17 November F/Lt McKimm in P/279 and S/Ldr Fitchew in Q/279 carried out a frustrating sortie. They were scrambled to locate and drop a lifeboat to a dinghy containing survivors, which was being circled by a Halifax. On arrival in the area they found the circling Halifax but no sign of a dinghy. Dropping marine markers they made a search of the area. Later it was established that the Halifax had lost sight of the dinghy in the rain and in any case it was empty!

Bomber Command began the long series of raids; which came to be known as the Battle of Berlin on 18 November and the squadron was kept very busy during the rest of the month. They

Parachute flares were used by downed crews to attract the attention of searching aircraft. (USAAF via A McLeod)

had little success, however, until 23 November, when four aircraft, led by F/Sgt Curtis, took off from Bircham Newton shortly after first light to search for Stirling 'J' from No. 214 Sqn based at Chedburgh piloted by Sgt Friend. The crew managed to get off a good series of signals for a fix before ditching. WO Mogridge was the first to sight the dinghy in position 5253N 0315E. Another dinghy was sighted a short distance away. Lindholme dinghies were dropped to the survivors and attempts made to contact HSLs whilst Mogridge and Curtis remained circling the dinghies until the rescue launches arrived and picked up the five crewmembers.

F/O Reade of the Harrowbeer detachment had the frustration of being unable to assist a ditched crew who at first appeared to be close to rescue, on 24 November. Airborne from Harrowbeer at 1013 hours in Hudson O/279 he set course for a search area to the north-west of Land's End. Almost three hours later a Warwick was sighted circling and Reade turned to investigate. Five men in a dinghy were seen paddling towards an airborne lifeboat dropped by the Warwick. The lifeboat was listing to one side and the aft buoyancy chamber had not inflated, but, the survivors were seen to board it. Shortly afterward the dinghy broke adrift and the helpless crew were now in a lifeboat that was sinking. Reade decided to drop a Lindholme dinghy, but could not re-locate the lifeboat. A Wellington and a Warwick also assisted in the search, but the lifeboat was not found before Reade had to set course for Harrowbeer. The search continued for a further two days without success.

Towards the end of November the weather began to deteriorate and aircraft returning from searches were often diverted to other bases or had extreme difficulty in landing at Bircham Newton. On the 27th S/Ldr Downer, who had been the last to leave a search for a missing Fortress only managed to land at base after flares had been lit to guide him in. The following day F/Sgt Curtis had a close call in poor weather when he made a heavy landing and bent the aircraft propellers. On the 29th the squadron held an anniversary dance to celebrate two years of operations and to say farewell to many members who had been posted.

December was a relatively quiet month, although the early days were plagued with engine problems. On the 4th F/Sgt Oakes took off for Docking and shortly afterwards one engine caught fire. Luckily the wind was northerly and he was able to line up with the Docking runway without having to make a risky circuit of the airfield. The engine fire went out on landing, but not before causing severe damage. The next day WO Passlow took V/279 out with three other aircraft to search for a missing Halifax south-east of Cromer. They did not find the Halifax but did come across three American-type dinghies, which they attempted to sink with gunfire, though no hits were seen. Passlow returned in poor visibility and landed on one engine.

The detachment of squadron aircraft and crews at Harrowbeer, which had been there since June finally came to an end when the crews returned to Bircham Newton on 14 December.

Docking was the scene of another incident when Hudson H/279 crashed there in a forced landing on Christmas Eve.

The Battle of Berlin raged on, with occasional forays to other cities such as Frankfurt, which received 2,000 tons of bombs on the night of 20/21 December. Berlin suffered a similar raid on the 29/30 December, the eighth attack of the battle. There were numerous searches throughout the month but no success until the penultimate day of the year when F/O Wilson in V/279 succeeded in locating the crew of a 514 Sqn Lancaster 50 miles off Great Yarmouth. Two HSLs were led to the six survivors who were picked up just after midday.

A night raid on Stettin by 358 bombers on 5/6 January brought 279 Sqn its first success of 1944 the following day. Among the losses that night was a 626 Sqn Lancaster, ME577:UM-T2 (crewed by F/Lt Belford, F/Sgts Lee and Gould, and Sgts Hill, Trinder and Newbourne). They were on their eighth operation with 626 Sqn, when they were damaged by a night fighter over the target. Losing fuel the pilot was forced to ditch in atrocious conditions at 1000 hours. They were 100 miles east of Withernsea. The crew suffered only slight bruising in the ditching and managed to escape from the sinking aircraft and thence into the dinghy. The dinghy radio was lost in the process and they had been unable to bring any survival gear from the Lancaster. Very soon they were cold wet and seasick.

Reports of the ditching resulted in F/O Gaze getting airborne in Hudson N/279 and at 1220 hours he was circling the Lancaster crew in position 5444N 0245E. The sea conditions were very rough and visibility was exceedingly poor, requiring Gaze's crew to maintain constant vigilance so as not to lose sight of the dinghy. At 1245 hours Gaze made his run in and dropped the airborne lifeboat, which landed 200 feet downwind of the survivors. Things were looking good as the lifeboat drifted towards the dinghy, but it then drifted past and was swept away. The Lancaster crew had been unable to reach it as the rocket designed to fire out the line on that side had failed.

Gaze continued to circle the dinghy until he was joined by F/Sgt Johnson in E/279 some 3½ hours later. Johnson dropped a Lindholme dinghy 50 yards away but had the disappointment of seeing it go unused. The Lancaster crew had managed to paddle within 10 yards of the it only to see it swept away from their grasp in the high seas. As dusk fell it became increasingly difficult to maintain contact and eventually the Hudsons lost sight of the dinghy. The survivors in the dinghy were in good spirits however, firm in the belief that since they had been located they would soon be rescued. They waited in the growing darkness with a good supply of Very cartridges and the pistol.

Help was indeed on the way. F/O Reade in W/279 had arrived as relief aircraft and the launches, after some discussion about the suitability of the weather for a rescue, had set out from base and were heading to the scene. Just after midnight Warwick Y/280 took over the search area and dropped sea markers and a flare, which illuminated the dinghy. Having relocated them, the aircraft continued to circle and forty-five minutes later one of the rescue launches spotted them in its searchlight and took them aboard, landing them at Great Yarmouth at 1130 hours on the 7th suffering only from the cold and wet. Belford and his crew were flown back to Wickenby by the OC 626 Sqn, Gp Capt Crummy. Sadly, they were lost on their next operation to Berlin on 27 January 1944.

Fog and snow curtailed operations for the next four days and then, on 11 January 1944, the US 8th Air Force sent out two major raids to Germany. The first consisted of 291 B-17s of the 1st BD to Oschersleben and Halberstadt escorted by 221 P-47s. The second raid, which was spoiled by the weather, was to Brunswick by 327 B-17s and B-24s escorted by 371 P-38s and P-47s. The bombers were recalled from the target and many of them bombed targets of opportunity within Germany.

To cover ASR for these raids three aircraft took off from Bircham Newton to patrol the return route. At 1350 hours a pall of smoke in position 5251N 0259E was investigated, but on arrival overhead they found an HSL was already on the scene, close to some wreckage. By now weather at base was deteriorating and a recall was sent out to the three Hudsons.

O/279 managed to land at base and E/279 diverted to Coltishall. A/279, flown by F/O Gaze, however, sighted pyrotechnics to port and turned to investigate. A B-17, A/C No. 842 *Miss Boo* of the 447th BG, flown by 2nd Lt Fouts had ditched in flames and at 1449 hours Gaze was orbiting the 10 survivors huddled in two dinghies in position 5231N 0311E. The W/Op obtained a good fix and rescue launches were soon on the way. Whilst Gaze continued to circle, concern over the deteriorating weather caused base to send another recall out. Gaze dropped a Lindholme dinghy to the survivors but it failed to inflate and on receipt of the recall signal he prepared to drop markers and delayed markers to assist rescuers to relocate the dinghies. Before he had completed his marker drops a launch was sighted and he remained overhead until the survivors were taken on board at 1709 hours. He then turned for base but diverted to Coltishall where he landed safely at 1754 hours.

The 447th BG mission summaries contained details of the mission and the ditching of *Miss Boo.*

Miss Boo *was one of the many Fortresses that took part in the large 8th AF bombing assault on the German target of Brunswick on January 11th.* Miss Boo *turned on the IP with the formation and made one run over the target. The formation started a 360-degree turn and it was in this turn that a large number of enemy fighters concentrated their attacks on* Miss Boo. *Fourteen ME 110s came in from the right and ten JU 88s from the left and turned in towards the tail. They shot their rockets first and the air around the Fortress was filling with bursting rockets. Five rockets in succession burst just underneath number three engine and it caught fire. The first wave of ME 110s turned away and the JU 88s continued on in followed by four ME 110s that came in high on the tail.*

The tail gunners says, 'The air behind us was like a forest fire caused by the cannon of the oncoming fighters.' The tail gunner picked out one JU 88 in an attack of six and started firing at it. The German fighter came in so close the tail gunner could see the spent cases and ammunition links falling into the engines. The German fighter burst into flames and spun earthward.

The above action all took place during the turn over the target. In spite of such opposition the pilot, 2nd Lt Fouts brought his ship over the target and scored a perfect hit. As they pulled away from the target large sheets of flame were observed rising from it. More fighters pressed home their attacks on the crippled Fortress. The pilot had succeeded in extinguishing the fire in number three engine by cutting off the gas but could not get it going again. Number one engine was hit by flak and the prop could not be feathered. This left Miss Boo *with only two good engines and consequently she had to drop out of formation.*

The Fortress remained under constant attack for one and one half hours from large numbers of German fighters. The right waist gunner, Staff Sergeant Louis P Szurleys, had the sight blown off his gun but continued to fire and brought down one of the fighters. The radio operator, Staff Sergeant William Trobaugh Jr, also brought down one and so did the top turret gunner, Technical Sergeant William J Wilmurth. The attacks were not all toward the tail position. Several JU 88s came in towards the nose and one was knocked out by the bombardier, 2nd Lt James C Kidd. Both the chin turret and the ball turret were hit by cannon fire and put out of action. The ball gunner, Staff Sergeant Eric Hill, tried to keep the tail gunner supplied with ammunition by carrying belts back to the tail gunner at various intervals. The

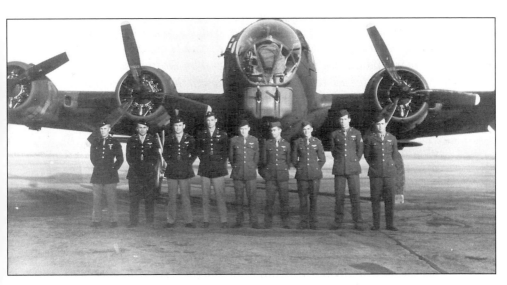

B-17 Flying Fortress *Miss Boo* and crew 58 of the 447th BG on 30 October 1943. 2nd Lt James C. Kidd is fourth from left. (James C. Kidd)

Germans had a four-engined bomber that looked like a Fortress, in the air against the crippled Fort. The plane did not come close but fired broadsides of rocket and cannon fire. The pilot of Miss Boo *had been taking evasive action all this time against both flak and fighters. This caused many of the Axis bullets to miss their mark. When the North Sea was sighted all the German fighters left, except one ME 110, that made several passes at the Fortress but took off when four P-47s showed up.*

The two remaining engines now started to falter and the co-pilot, 2nd Lt Don Lionudikas, gave orders to throw everything overboard that they could and prepare to ditch. This they did and assumed crash positions in the radio room.

James C Kidd, the bombardier, then takes up the story from the point of ditching.

The plane was broken into three parts by the crash impact. I remember dimly realizing I needed to time my exit from the radio room to the wing carefully to avoid the scissors action of the broken fuselage parts. Crew members either jumped from the wing to the dinghies or were pulled aboard from the frigid and very rough 8–10 foot waves.

Each dinghy was equipped with a box kite and a long antenna attached to a hand-cranked generator, which sent out an automatic signal. We had a hard time getting the box kite airborne – the kite was wet and the dinghy was tossed about by the high seas.

All the crew suffered from shock, although there were only minor injuries. One of the gunners was obsessed by the idea of sinking. I remember his trying to bail water out of the North Sea. When the water became so rough, we were repeatedly thrown out of the dinghy. The crew abandoned it, tied themselves together with a dinghy rope and relied on their Mae Wests. We slowly lost consciousness one by one.

My next memory is being pulled aboard a rescue boat. The crew covered us with hot towels, dipped in the sea and heated by wrapping them around the exhaust system. We were fed hot soup from a can heated by ignition of a tube in its centre. The boat set a course for the base at Great Yarmouth – the roughest ride I've ever had! When we reached the base we were treated royally, fed the best food we had ever eaten in England and given beds in the officers quarters. We were so impressed with the courage and kindness of our rescuers, who went out to sea dressed only in their jeans and turtlenecks, that when we left for our base the next morning we gave the crew all our leather, fur-lined equipment – our only means of showing our gratitude. They in turn gave each of us a picture postcard of the rescue boat signed by the crew.

To add insult to injury James Kidd was wounded on the return journey to base when the Germans bombed the train they were travelling in!

An article in the *USAAF Intelligence Summary* for 16 January 1944 entitled 'Air/Sea Rescue Total to Date: 659' told the story from the point of view of the Americans.

Superb coordination was once more demonstrated in a rescue on 11 January, when weather presented a tough obstacle. Because of lowering ceilings and visibility, A/SR organized a patrol of Hudsons to be ready for possible ditchers as heavies began to come in from the long, tough operations over Germany. One of the Hudsons had a first class MF/DF fix about 100 miles off Great Yarmouth, in the North Sea. Two dinghies were sighted, and sea markers and smoke floats were dropped. Weather was becoming so bad at base by this time that the Hudson was being called home. High speed launches were sent out at once and were homed to the dinghies by the aircraft, which then went in, though the crew didn't make their home base. The launch sighted kite and Very flares at exact position of the fix and took an entire crew of ten to terra firma. The automatic SOS on 500kcs agreed perfectly with the original fix, and the whole incident was a complete success. Cooperation and full use of technical aids paid off.

Almost as important as pulling ditched crews from the sea was training them to use their equipment properly in the event of a ditching. To that end the squadron regularly sent crews around the US bases to lecture and demonstrate to the American aircrew. F/Lt Stevens returned from one of these lecture tours on the 14 January, having instructed some 2,200 American aircrew at Wendling, Shipdham, Hethel, Tibenham, Seething, Bungay and Hardwick. The demonstrators felt that, despite occasional hardships, the sessions were well received, once in particular, when the motor starting rope of the lifeboat broke as F/Lt Stevens heaved on it. The records report that this 'went over particularly big. So did F/Lt Stevens.'

The rest of the month was plagued by poor weather and though numerous searches were carried out none was successful.

January also saw another award to a squadron member. This time it was a DFM awarded to F/Sgt G. John, a member of McKimm's crew, on the 18th. Three days later Dougie Whittaker's crew found two bodies off the French coast.

The weather in February was little better, and it was not until the 7th that the squadron got involved in a search. No. 415 Sqn had dispatched one of their aircraft, Wellington LZ655/A captained by F/Lt J.F. Acer, from North Coates on an anti-shipping Rover sortie off the Dutch coast and it had failed to return to base. With no fix to give the ASR system an exact position, the 279 Sqn standby crew, captained by F/O Nicholson, was dispatched in a night search in conjunction with a boat along the missing aircraft's probable track. Nothing was found and the next morning two pairs of Hudsons, followed by a third pair in the afternoon, continued the search but once again had no success.

A search for a missing Typhoon also commenced on the 7th and continued to the 9th with no success. On the 9th 415 Sqn provided the object of another search when Wellington HZ642/N was lost in a similar manner to A/415 lost on the 7th. In extremely poor conditions a Hudson was sent out along the missing aircraft's route just after midnight with no success.

A change of management occurred on 10 February with the departure of W/Cdr Corry to HQ No. 16 Group and the arrival of his replacement, W/Cdr N.W.C. Bindloss, from No. 280 Sqn. A squadron dance was held to say farewell to W/Cdr Corry and welcome the new CO, who had another celebration a week later when he was married. The squadron also said farewell to long-time member F/Lt Stevens who was posted to North Coates. Lt Young also left, returning to duty with the USAAF on the 8th.

Between the 10th and the 21st many searches were carried out with no success. On the 22nd F/O Goff's crew were witnesses to a tragic incident. Goff was flying J/279, one of two aircraft on patrol off Orfordness during the return of USAAF bombers in the late afternoon. He came upon the scene of a ditching in position 5200N 0240E, only to observe one of the airmen disappear beneath the waves with his parachute. The other aircraft operating was E/279 flown by F/Lt Clark, who sighted two

American dinghies containing the crew of a 323rd BS, 91st BG B-17, 42-37939 named *Sugar Blues*, ditched by 1st Lt Mariarz at 1729 hours in position 5202N 0237E. B-17 379 had been repeatedly damaged by fighter attacks and was unable to stay in formation. Descending to low altitude and barely able to stay in the air 1st Lt Roman V. Mariarz decided to ditch. The 91st BG daily summary noted that Mariarz completed the manoeuvre with rare coolness and remarkable skill. Clark's Lindholme dinghy failed in the drop, but Goff arrived shortly afterwards and managed to drop a second dinghy. The survivors were able to reach this and make use of it. During the ditching 2nd Lt Peter Delo was struck on the head by a belt of .50 calibre ammunition as they went underwater. He never flew on operations again.

J/279 departed for base and E/279 remained with the survivors until F/O Bedford in D/279 arrived as relief. A combination of flame floats and pyrotechnics enabled Bedford to locate the dinghies and both aircraft kept orbit over them until the rescue launches were sighted at 1900 hours. About an hour later, rescue complete, both aircraft returned to base. The B-17 survivors were landed at Harwich by the launches little harmed by their ordeal.

In 1997 Peter Delo related the events of the ditching and subsequent rescue to Lee Bishop.

The target run itself was routine but they were set upon by several FW 190s, too many to recall. The damage wasn't clearly known, but the cowling on No. 3 engine (just inboard on the co-pilot's side) was blown clear. Descending to low level they buzzed an electric train on the Dutch coast with Number three still spinning and the cowling missing. After falling behind, the pilot, known as 'Mazzy', and Delo decided to stay low to the ground until they could reach England. They realised, just after crossing the coast over the North Sea, that they would never make England.

They had at least one engine out and realised they would have to ditch. The radio operator had contacted ASR and a boat was expected. They ditched the plane, which went off without any problems but one. A belt of .50 calibre ammunition in the top turret had bounced out of its contained and flew forward when the B-17 hit the water, striking Peter Delo in the back of the head.

The liferafts were inflated and there was some discussion on whether the cockpit crew would go out the side windows or out

2nd Lt Peter
Delo. (L Bishop)

*through the radio compartment. The crew all got into the boats and
watched the* Sugar Blues *drift off. (Nobody actually saw the plane
sink. Years after the war a member of his crew swore that the wing-
less* Sugar Blues *had been spotted in a British scrapyard right
after 1945 and he wondered if it had drifted along, its fuel tanks
empty, to a landfall on the coast).*

*After some time in the water a plane flew over. It was getting
dark by the time they saw the lights of boats coming from opposite
coasts. They knew one was the ASR boat from England and the
other they thought was likely an E-Boat from occupied France. The
crew was worried that the Germans would get there first. The ASR
boat got there first and they jumped in as fast as they could. Delo
had fired a flare gun as the ASR boat got close and the flare actually landed on the deck of the boat. The ASR boat riddled the rafts
with a deck gun before leaving.*

*They were all soaked to the skin so the crew found them dry RAF
uniforms to wear. These were a huge joke when the crew got back
to base. Peter Delo was sent to hospital for his head injury and lost
his sight for some time afterward. He eventually got it back but
was taken off combat duty permanently. He kept the flare gun that
'saved their necks'. Some time after the ditching a large envelope
arrived for the crew from somewhere in London. It had cards and
patches made up for the crew members from the 'Goldfish Club'.
They all carried their cards and had the patches sewn under the
right sides of the collars.*

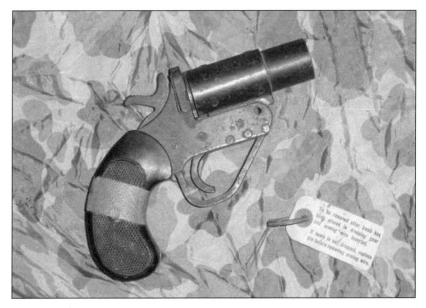

The flare gun used by Peter Delo after ditching *Sugar Blues*. Delo kept
it as a souvenir. (L Bishop)

Peter Delo returned to flying with the reserves in the 1950s and
ditched again in a P-47 in Baltimore Harbour. He died in 1999.

Though many more searches were carried out this was the last
success of the month.

On 6 March 1944 the 8th Air Force sent 730 B-17s and B-24s
escorted by 801 fighters to Berlin and other targets of opportunity
in Germany. Of these two B-17s and two B-24s ditched on the
return leg. No. 279 Sqn was providing ASR cover for their return
and at 1603 hours F/Lt Butt's crew spotted one of the reported
Fortresses (actually a B-24 42-52191 coded N+ and named *Little*

The crew of *Sugar Blues*
photographed in RAF uniform
after their rescue. One of the
crew is holding a leather jacket
with the bomber's name and
artwork on the back. (L Bishop)

Joe (or *Lille Belle*) of the 453rd BG based at Old Buckenham piloted by 2nd Lt Herman J. Meek) come down in the sea at 5207N 0230E. Both patrolling Hudsons were soon over the scene, where they observed a number of survivors clinging to the wreckage. A Lindholme dinghy was dropped but the survivors seemed unwilling or unable to leave the wreckage to swim to it. Shortly afterward two Walrus amphibians arrived and moved around the wreckage searching for survivors. Unfortunately of a crew of ten only two were picked up. Second Lieutenant Joseph G. Cyr was the only survivor. Butt returned to base and S/Ldr Downer in J/279 remained until the crew in the Walrus had completed their work. He then vectored a launch to the Lindholme, which was recovered.

On 9 March two Hudsons from the squadron were on patrol between Haisborough and Lowestoft in poor weather conditions, awaiting the return of the US heavy bombers from Berlin, Hannover and Brunswick. Nearing the end of the patrol a signal was received diverting the second aircraft, B/279 flown by F/Lt Wilson, to search for a dinghy reported to be in position 5250N 0355 E, just off the Dutch coast. Wilson set course for the area at 1650 hours and just under an hour later the rear gunner sighted a red pyrotechnic at a range of 8 miles.

T/Sgt Jerome Wodin, one of the survivors of the ditching, recalls the story of the doomed Fortress mission and rescue.

> *We were on a bombing mission to Berlin and about half way there I checked the gas, which is the usual procedure for the engineer. I noticed that the gas consumption was higher than it usually is and immediately informed the pilot. It was a ticklish spot for a decision but we had never aborted or turned back yet and we sure hated to pull one on this big assault.*
>
> *We didn't want to miss it and unconsciously we said, 'To hell with it' and kept going. We kept with the formation and I got a big kick when we dropped our bombs on 'Big B', our name for Berlin. With all that flak about us I was wondering if we shouldn't have gone back when we saw our gas dwindling.*
>
> *After unleashing our eggs we started our journey home and we kept a pretty close watch on those gas tanks. We had no idea that the reading on the gas tanks were incorrect and definitely not in our favour. We had a tailwind returning, without which, we would never have gotten as far as we did.*

Crew 35 of the 709th BS 447th BG. The B-17 they flew was
The Sack Hounds. Front row L to R: S/Sgt N. Thompson,
T/Sgt Charles V. Holden, S/Sgt Robert R. Shoita, T/Sgt
Jerome Wodin, S/Sgt Bill Tatum, Johnny Siedlicki. Back row
L to R: Co-pilot, Lt McHenry, Bombardier, Lt White, Pilot, Lt
Jurnecka, Navigator, Lt Heizelman. (C Siedlicki)

*I tried transferring fuel from one tank to another but we soon
discovered that although it read approximately fifty gallons, it was
practically empty. Then the fuel pressure dropped down to five
gallons – we quickly feathered the prop.*

*At this time we knew we were in for it and the pilot gave us
orders to throw out everything that was moveable. Though we were
approaching the sea and even though we knew the seriousness of
the situation we got quite a kick out of just dumping ammunition,
guns and everything else overboard. We ran into some flak at this
time but we paid very little attention to that.*

*Just as we left the coast another engine quit and we were
very busy all over the ship. I moved my top turret toward the
front so the pilot and co-pilot could grasp it and help themselves
out of the cockpit when we ditched. I took the flare gun, flares
and first aid kit to the radio room where we all assembled for the
ditching.*

*With all the classes that we had on ditching, I knew that we
were well prepared for it from the 'know how' standpoint. But it
is something else again when you actually have to go through
with it. At this time another engine quit and we lost sight of our*

formation. The radio man got the SOS out and we went into our crash positions. I was bent over and when I heard the alarm bell go I was expecting anything. The first shock was slight as the tail hit and then came a loud crash. I was then thrown backwards and I guess everyone else was in a mess also. But I didn't get a scratch even though the ball turret was pushed forward about five feet and through the door of the radio room against which I was sitting.

Water came rushing in from all directions but we kept calm and went out in good fashion. I couldn't release the dinghy from the radio room but we used the emergency release on the outside of the ship and that did the trick. The emergency radio was thrown out, and not knowing just how long the ship would stay afloat we got into our dinghies as soon as they were inflated and clear of the plane.

We never thought the ship would stay afloat as long as it did, about half an hour. Sometimes it is only thirty seconds before a ship will go down and we weren't taking any chances. We shoved

2nd Lt John T. White, the bombardier of 2nd Lt Joseph E. Jurnecka's 447th BG Fortress crew, which ditched and was rescued with the aid of an airborne lifeboat dropped by F/Lt Wilson and crew of 279 Sqn. (Via 447th BG Association)

off and as I saw all ten of us OK, I knew we were darn lucky. The bombardier, 2nd Lt John T. White and I got to work on the emergency radio set, filling up the balloon and cranking the radio. It was a sight seeing such a large plane just lying on that sea and suddenly the tail went up and down she went. I chuckled to myself as I remembered that we were flying the ship that my friend's crew usually flew and we had lost her.

A couple of the boys were getting seasick and I admit I had a touch of it myself. We all got busy bailing the water out of the dinghies, but we were all soaked through when we hit the water.

The Hudson was soon over two American dinghies with ten occupants only a few miles from the original position given.

Johnny Siedlicki wrote the captions on the back of these two photos: 'Boys in Our Crew – Nare, Thompson, R.R. Shoita, Jerry Wodin. (C. Siedlicki)

These were the survivors of 2nd Lt Jurnecka's 709th BS 447th BG B-17 from Rattlesden. Jerome Wodin recalls the arrival of the Hudson.

> *Soon after. A plane, a RAF Hudson bomber, came overhead and dropped us an airborne boat, which turned over as it hit the water. That plane was a wonderful sight. We thought then that it would be only a matter of an hour or so before a boat picked us up. That's what we thought. We rowed our dinghies to the boat and we all got into it, and then tied our own two dinghies to it.*

An hour after setting off on the search Wilson successfully dropped the airborne lifeboat 50 yards downwind and within five minutes the occupants of both dinghies had reached it. The survivors lashed their dinghies to the lifeboat and appeared to be well, though they made no effort to start the engines or raise the sail. Having reached the limit of endurance Wilson dropped delayed marine markers to assist relief aircraft to locate the lifeboat and turned for home, landing at Docking in the dark. With the departure of the Hudson Jerome Wodin and the rest of the Jurnecka crew were left in the airborne lifeboat.

This photo was taken from Hudson B/279 shortly after dropping the airborne lifeboat to Lt Jurnecka's ditched crew. (C. Siedlicki)

I got to work on the engines which were in the boat but they had all gotten wet and it was impossible to start them. The plane dropped some flares to identify our position and then left. We had ditched at about 4 pm and this was about two hours later. We all tried to get as comfortable as possible but it was difficult as wet as we were. We all huddled together and tried slapping each other's bare feet to keep warm and prevent frostbite that none of us relished. We were disappointed because it was getting dark and still we were out in the North Sea.

It was a rough night and we saw to it that none of us went to sleep. We tried everything to keep warm and even though we figured that we'd have to spend the night out on the sea we were pretty confident of getting picked up.

Meanwhile two more Hudsons, M/279 flown by F/Lt Ashby and U/279 captained by F/O Brown, were patrolling a line between Lowestoft and Southwold when they found 1st Lt McGuire's ditched 448th BG B-24 42-31210 *Piccadilly Ann/ Buccaneer*. It was ditched due to flak damage in position 5242N 0257E, with two dinghies containing eight survivors alongside. A Lindholme dinghy was dropped, which they succeeded in boarding. The Liberator continued to float for another forty-five

Lt Jurnecka's ditched crew make their way in the aircraft dinghies toward the airborne lifeboat dropped by F/Lt Wilson in Hudson B/279. (C. Siedlicki)

minutes before slipping beneath the waves. Forty-five minutes after the bomber disappeared a launch, which had been contacted by the Hudsons, appeared on the scene and took the survivors on board.

The airborne lifeboat dropped on the 9th and last seen with the survivors of Jurnecka's crew on board but doing little to get the engines going or the sail up, had not been forgotten and on the 10th three Hudsons made a search along its drift line. F/Lt Wilson in L/279, who had dropped the lifeboat the previous day, had the satisfaction of relocating it just as it was about to be taken in tow by an HSL. Jerome Wodin recalls the events of that day.

The morning came after endless hours and the visibility was very poor which certainly didn't help us. I tried the engine again but 'no dice'. I hated to think of spending another night out there. About ten o'clock we got our emergency radio working again and we were happy to have it putting out our SOS.

At approximately three o'clock, we saw two launches in the distance and I thought I was beginning to see things. However, we shot up two flares and the launches came toward us. It was the Air-Sea Rescue boats. We were pretty well exhausted and had to be helped on board where we immediately changed into dry clothing, and it sure felt swell. We had some hot soup on that boat that tasted better than a steak. We were taken to a hospital where one night's long rest fixed us up. After we returned to our own base we went to a rest camp for seven days.

I will never forget the date of our ditching experience, because it was my girlfriends birthday, the second anniversary of our engagement.

Crew member Johnny Siedlicki wrote of the ditching a few days later:

After coming out of Big B (Berlin) we ran out of gas and had to ditch in the North Sea 20 miles from the Dutch coast. Spent 23¾ hours in that cold sea and sure was glad to get picked up by the rescue boat. By the way, it was my 13th mission, so that's why we didn't get picked up till the next day!

The survivors were landed at Great Yarmouth that night and Wilson, together with the station intelligence officer, had the opportunity to meet them. When questioned they said that they were enthusiastic about the lifeboat drop but had made little use of its resources, even the warm dry clothing, even though they were only 35 miles from the enemy coast. They had relied on being pinpointed and collected. The squadron operations record book (ORB) notes *So they were – But!'*

There was little success over the next two weeks. On 23 March the crews of the squadron were witness to a series of tragic events. Two Hudsons, piloted by S/Ldr Downer and F/Sgt Palmer, were patrolling off Orfordness when their attention was drawn to a column of smoke in position 5157N 0246E. On reaching the scene they discovered an HSL blazing furiously with a dinghy containing three survivors alongside. They had been the victims of a 'friendly fire' incident when a Thunderbolt mistook the HSL for an E-boat and opened fire on it. The Hudsons managed to lead a second HSL to the scene, and it took the survivors on board. Then, while the Hudsons were still orbiting the scene a Mustang appeared and signalled that it wished them to follow it. S/Ldr Downer turned his Hudson to follow and was led to an area of debris and oil within which floated two survivors in Mae Wests. There was no sign of a dinghy so Downer dropped a Lindholme dinghy to the floating men. Unfortunately it failed to open. A Liberator arrived and dropped another, but this time it was dropped too far away to be of any use.

Determined to have the survivors picked up Downer climbed for a fix. Meanwhile a Walrus amphibian appeared and made low passes over the area, though it could not find any survivors. Downer covered the area again, but there was no sign of the two airmen. After another period of searching with no luck Downer was forced to return to base. Another tragedy had been played out in the bitterly cold waters of the North Sea.

Tragedy almost came closer to home on the night of 26/27 March. Hudson Mk V AM544:E took of from Bircham Newton for a search just before midnight, but crashed just outside the airfield boundary in flames. Dougie Whittaker, now a F/Sgt, and his crew mostly managed to escape with minor abrasions and cuts, though the Hudson was a total loss.

A never to be forgotten day. We took off from Bircham Newton at 1150 hours and at about 100 feet the port engine stopped and we hit the ground. The other three members of the crew scrambled clear but my head hit the dashboard and I was unconscious. Medics arrived quickly (I am told) and pulled me free. The plane then blew up. I was badly injured, so I was taken to RAF Hospital Ely and had eighty stitches in my head and face. The famous surgeon Archibald McIndoe saw me and said I would be OK. As a patient I was taken to the Royal Command Performance and shook hands with the King.

Aircrew losses due to ditching were a sad fact of the bomber war and the cruel sea took another crew on the night of 26/27 March. A Halifax had sent out an SOS in position 5255N 0255E in poor weather. Dubious about the success of a search in such conditions the squadron sent out a single Hudson, M/279 piloted by F/O Gaze, to assess conditions in the search area. At 1518 hours Gaze found an area of wreckage and aircrew in the water 2 miles from the SOS position. He dropped a Lindholme dinghy but to no avail as the Halifax crew had already died of exposure in the icy sea. Two further pairs of Hudsons were homed to the search area and an HSL brought to the scene. The HSL collected the bodies of the unfortunate Halifax crew and recovered the dinghy.

F/Lt Hollebone's logbook entry for 20 April 1944 showing the encounter with flak near Borkum. (B Palmer)

For the next three weeks the squadron carried out fruitless searches. On 19 April it was lucky not to lose another aircraft and crew. F/Lt Wilson had been patrolling a line between Cromer and Haisborough to cover formations of US bombers returning to base in darkness after a raid. The patrol was uneventful until L/279 landed at base, whereupon it was attacked by a *Luftwaffe* night fighter intruder. Fortunately its fire missed the Hudson and no damage or casualties were sustained. F/Lt Hollebone also encountered some flak whilst carrying out an ASR search off Borkum on the 20th but returned undamaged.

A quiet week of patrolling followed, but on 29 April F/O Brown and his crew set out in Hudson F/279 equipped with an airborne lifeboat and escorted by two Spitfires to search for a dinghy around 5136N 0335E. Pyrotechnics and a small light, possible from the dinghy radio, were seen and Brown made a run-in to drop the lifeboat.

Unfortunately a faulty button shield caused the observer to release the lifeboat prematurely and it landed ¼ mile away from the survivors in the dinghy. Shortly after this the Germans began to take an interest in the proceedings and searchlight batteries on Schouwen Island swept the area, illuminating the dinghy at one point. Brown dropped a message container to the survivors giving them the lifeboat bearing and distance before departing.

The attempts to rescue the survivors continued the next day when F/O Bedford in Q/279 flew out to the area with an escort of Spitfires from Manston. They quickly found the lifeboat but, unfortunately, saw no sign of the dinghy or survivors. Whilst searching, the Hudson and the escorting Spitfires came under attack from some ineffective light flak from Schouwen and the neighbouring island.

CHAPTER SIX

May – October 1944

The first week of May saw WO Oakes and his crew have a lucky escape whilst returning from a search for a missing Beaufighter. On the way back to base on the 6th the port engine of the Hudson, AE585, caught fire and Oakes had to force-land 6 miles from the airfield. The crew managed to escape from the Hudson safely although they were all shaken up by their ordeal.

Ken Border was posted to 279 Sqn in the summer of 1944 as a flight mechanic and recalls life at Bircham Newton during the run up to D-Day.

A posting to 279 Squadron as an LAC FMA in the summer of 1944 produced a travel warrant to Docking which turned out to be a tiny station on a single track branch railway from King's Lynn to Wells next the Sea in Norfolk. On arriving at Docking I caught the RAF-operated shuttle bus service that ran between a satellite airfield a short distance from the village and Bircham Newton, a few miles away where 279 was based, via the railway station, and was dropped off at the camp guardroom where I was refused entry because by that time it was evening and too late to start the routine booking-in process so I was directed to a transit hut outside the main camp for the night. Next morning I was allowed into the camp and began registering at the various points, i.e. pay accounts, medical section etc. and was eventually allocated a bed space in one of the barrack blocks before reporting to the squadron office.

As the bus had approached Bircham Newton the first aircraft I spotted on the dispersals were some old Gloster Gladiator biplanes so it was with great relief that I discovered at the office that 279 Squadron was equipped with Lockheed Hudsons and that the Glads belonged to a Met Flight! The flight sergeant to whom I reported was F/Sgt Hubbard, always called 'Chiefy', from Grimsby and whenever he had a 48 hour pass he often organised a lift to North Coates airfield, a few miles from Grimsby, in a Beaufighter being delivered there from the Coastal Command Preparation Pool which was also at Bircham.

Though the vast majority of the squadron's 'trade' came from ditching bombers, occasionally a lone fighter pilot would require their services. Fighter pilots were less well equipped to survive following a ditching as the aircraft could not carry a large dinghy or much in the way of survival equipment due to the weight penalty imposed. Lt J. Werb of the P-38 Lightning equipped 55th FG was one of 754 fighter pilots escorting 922 US bombers to Berlin, Munster and Osnabruck on 7 May. He was forced to ditch off Felixstowe when his starboard engine caught fire. He had great difficulty in escaping from his sinking fighter and lost his dinghy in the process.

F/O Bedford in Hudson G/279 was patrolling the bombers return route when he sighted a pall of smoke and turned to investigate. Arriving at the scene the crew quickly spotted Werb floating in his Mae West and dropped a Lindholme dinghy. Unfortunately it failed to inflate, but rescue was at hand as an HSL arrived on the scene, picked up the unconscious pilot and brought him safely home.

On 12 May the squadron just missed the opportunity to rescue the famous night-fighter pilot W/Cdr Bob Braham and his navigator F/Lt Gregory. Flak and a fighter attack had damaged Braham's Mosquito and he had ditched at high speed north of Cromer. The Mosquito broke in two but Braham and Gregory managed to get out of the cockpit unhurt. While the ditching was in progress P/O Curtis in A/279 was being scrambled for his second sortie of the day. Arriving over the wreckage, which remained afloat for another hour, he found Braham and Gregory paddling their dinghy towards some trawlers that had arrived on scene. The trawlers picked up both survivors and 279 Sqn's services were not required.

American fighter pilot Lt D. Noble was one of four fighter pilots to end up in the sea after escorting 888 bombers to Berlin and other targets in Germany on 19 May. He was extremely lucky that S/Ldr Downer was patrolling in E/279 close enough to see the splash of the fighter entering the sea and then to spot him descending in his parachute. Downer quickly homed an HSL to the spot and Noble was rescued.

The following day four Hudsons were sent out to search for a ditched Fortress crew, captained by Lt Julian P. Rogers of the 100th BG based at Thorpe Abbotts, in position 5440N 0640E. Rogers' B-17, named *Rogers' Raiders*, of the 350th BS had ditched returning from Berlin on the 19th. Three of the engines were knocked out by enemy fighters. As Rogers put the crippled aircraft down on the North Sea the initial impact broke the tail section away and as the Fortress hit the water, again water flooded in through the waist door and camera well, slightly injuring two crew members. All of the emergency equipment was lost in the ditching.

Two of the Hudsons were forced to make early returns but F/O Reade in K/279 and F/Lt Clark in N/279 pressed on and located the survivors in their dinghies. Clark made a successful lifeboat drop at 1312 hours and all the survivors transferred to it. Some three hours later the boat was underway on the course given by the Hudson crew, which remained orbiting until, at 2117 hours, Warwicks relieved them. WO Oakes was airborne before dawn in A/279 to relieve the Warwicks. Flying in poor visibility he managed to make contact and took over the escort of the lifeboat. Three Danish fishing boats were seen approaching the lifeboat and at 0600 hours. They took the survivors on board and took the lifeboat in tow. The fishing boats took up a course for the enemy coast so Oakes signalled base for instructions and, whilst waiting for a reply, fired across their bows to discourage them from their present course. Oakes was then relieved once more by Warwicks who shadowed them, keeping them together. The Warwicks were joined by S/Ldr Simpson in Hudson O/279. The fishing boat with the survivors on board had elected not to move again after being fired at. One of the Warwicks managed to home an HSL to the scene and the survivors were transferred at 1000 hours.

The sea was too rough to salvage the lifeboat so one of the Warwicks used it for target practice. Lt Rogers reported later that

The C-2 liferaft used by single-seat fighter pilots of the USAAF. (USAAF via A McLeod)

they had been well treated on the fishing boat with hot drinks and food being provided. Only one of the Danes spoke English and he said that the vessel's captain was prepared to remain in the area for a few days until a rescue launch turned up, if necessary. The Fortress survivors were eventually landed at Great Yarmouth in good spirits and none the worse for the ditching.

The final rescue of the month came on the 25th. For the 457th BG this was Mission 50 to Berlin. Sixteen B-17s took part. Lt Harry Stafford's B-17, 42-102965, was hit by flak over Berlin after they had dropped their bombs. Nos 3 and 4 engines were put out of action, with their propellers windmilling.

The attack left the pilot injured and unconscious and the co-pilot, Lt Bernard Yavorsky took over. The crew considered making for Sweden, but changed their minds and headed for home. Near Heligoland they were hit again by flak and lost a third engine. Dumping as much weight as possible overboard they hoped to remain airborne, whilst the radio man sent out an SOS. Stafford made a perfect ditching and all the crew were able to climb into the aircraft dinghies. F/O Goff left base at 0135 hours

2nd Lt Julian P. Rogers' 100th BG 350th BS B-17 crew. Kneeling L to R:
S/Sgt Thomas S. Guralski, radio operator; Sgt Russel E. Gately Jr, ball
turret gunner; Sgt Richard L. Kendall, flight engineer; Sgt Carroll W.
Brooks, waist gunner; Sgt Clarence F. Cherry, waist gunner; Sgt
Alfonso L. Fiore, tail gunner. Standing L to R: 2nd Lt Frederick A.
Mead Jr, navigator; 2nd Lt Julian P. Rogers, pilot; 2nd Lt Robert B.
Lawler, co-pilot; 2nd Lt Bertram C. Liberman, bombardier. (100th
Bomb Group Photo Archives via Michael Faley)

in Hudson O/279 to relieve a Warwick over the dinghy 40 miles
north-east of Cromer. By 0300 hours he had succeeded in homing
an HSL to the spot and ten survivors were taken on board and
brought to safety.

On 21 June two Hudsons, J and G/279, flown by F/Lt Pederson
and Lt Coale respectively, searched the area close to the Wash for
the downed B-24 flown by Lt Joe Salisbury. At 1746hrs they
sighted two dinghies tied together containing four survivors.
Both aircraft dropped Lindholme dinghies and the survivors
managed to board one of them. Meanwhile WO Palmer had
scrambled to relieve Pederson and Coale arriving at 2002hrs

Ten minutes later Pederson and Coale departed for base and

Palmer made his run in and dropped the lifeboat to the survivors below. The boat landed 50 yards downwind, perfectly positioned, but one of the parachutes had failed to release and the inflated canopy dragged the lifeboat downwind so quickly that the furiously paddling survivors were unable to reach it. Palmer remained in the area for a further hour trying to contact rescue launches with no success until he too left for home.

The efforts to bring the survivors to safety continued before dawn the following morning, but the first aircraft sent out failed to relocate the dinghies in the rough seas. A larger search was then organized, with the search area split into northern and southern sectors. Three aircraft covered the north but saw nothing. The crews searching to the south had better luck when WO Mouland and crew in U/279 sighted the dinghies. Overnight the survivors had managed to attach their half-submerged dinghy to one of the Lindholmes and a Q-type dinghy. Attempts were made to find rescue launches, but when these failed Mouland dropped another Lindholme to supplement those already dropped. U/279 continued to circle the survivors until

Three members of Lt Stafford's 457th BG crew are seen in this photo taken on 16 July 1944: Rear 2nd left Lt Stafford, 3rd left navigator Lt Flach, 5th left bombardier Lt Wodek. (Bernie Baines Collection via 457th BG Assoc)

F/Lt Ashby in Hudson D/279 arrived as relief. A short time later P/O Curtis in B/279 also arrived overhead. The two Hudsons remained over the dinghies until an RML was sighted and twenty minutes later the survivors were taken on board. Curtis watched the launch get underway, abandoning the dinghies, then dropped down and attempted to sink them with gunfire, but they were still afloat, though holed, when he departed the area.

Lt Salisbury related the events of that day to his son Joe.

The B-24 was hit by German fire and he had to ditch the plane in the North Sea. The crash occurred during a terrible storm in extremely high seas. He has told me several times of trying to save the crew as best he could by landing his big B-24 longitudinally on top of a swell. Unfortunately, the plane broke in half and

Lt Stafford and lead crew taken on 7 August 1944. Members of the ditched crew of 25 May are as follows: Rear 2nd left Lt Stafford, front – 1st left Sgt V.D. Naylor, 2nd left Sgt V.R. Hook, 3rd left Sgt F.M. Graven, 5th left Sgt R.H. Ridge. (Bernie Baines Collection via 457th BG Assoc)

the rear half went down almost immediately with all hands. He still mourned every one of his lost crew after fifty years. All crew members in the forward part of the plane survived, as it floated for a while before sinking. My dad was injured and so were some others. It was a terrible storm and the surviving crew were injured, cold and wet, huddling in small 2-man rubber rafts. Several hours later an RAF rescue plane flew over and dropped a rigid lifeboat. While floating down attached to the parachute, the boat's parachute lines got tangled and the boat entered the water bow first, flooding the interior. The crewmembers were unable to bail out the boat, so they remained in the rafts, but tried to use what they could of the supplies in the lifeboat. Some time later they were picked up by the RAF.

Two hours after this rescue ended two more of the squadron's Hudsons were scrambled to relieve a pair of OTU Wellingtons circling a dinghy in position 5218N 0236E. The Wellingtons had

A third photo showing members of Lt Stafford's 457th BG crew, which ditched on 25 May 1944. Rear 2nd left Harry Stafford (now a captain), front 1st left Sgt Naylor, 2nd left Sgt Hook, 3rd left Sgt Ridge, 5th left Sgt W.H. Osika. (Bernie Baines Collection via 457th BG Assoc)

set their IFF sets to the distress frequency and this assisted S/Ldr Simpson in J/279 and F/Lt Butt in H/279 to home to the dinghy. Arriving at 1447 hours they joined the Wellington circuit and twenty minutes later Butt dropped his Lindholme dinghy. It failed to inflate but the survivors, from New Zealander, P/O Nicklin's 57 Sqn Lancaster, ND741:DX-A, managed to reach and open the containers. At 1600 hours an RML was sighted and led to the dinghy. Twenty-five minutes later seven aircrew, one of whom was injured, were picked up and brought safely home.

Ken Border, an LAC with 279 Sqn recalls the events of D-Day and the summer months that followed.

I was allocated a Hudson III which was interesting as I'd never encountered American types before and some of their systems were quite different from British practice. Most of the Hudsons were Mk IIIs with Wright Cyclone engines and they were white except for the top surfaces of the wings, tail-planes and fuselage, which were medium grey. In addition there were one or two Mk IV versions with Pratt & Whitney engines which were grey/green camouflage on the top and sides with pale green undersurfaces but they were not liked by the aircrews. When the 'D-Day' stripes were painted on they obliterated the aircraft's individual identity letters on the fuselage sides so these were then painted in yellow on the outer face of each fin above the flash. In the late summer the CO ordered that smaller letters were to be painted, also in yellow, on the inner face of each fin, either P or S as appropriate as apparently some mid-upper gunners were getting confused between port and starboard when reporting to the pilot over the R/T, and about the same time an order came out that the stripes on all upper surfaces had to be over-painted grey.

The Hudson had a fixed forward-firing 303 machine gun in front of the pilot, two more in the large mid-upper turret and there were fittings at two removable side windows where a gun could be mounted. In addition most of them had a ventral gun position which was a section of the cabin floor that could be wound down to allow a gun to be fired aft by a gunner laying flat on the floor but I don't recall this ever being used. Some of the Mk III Hudsons carried an airborne lifeboat fitted under the fuselage.

Life at Bircham Newton in the summer of 1944 was somewhat hectic with 24 hour activity to keep as many of the ageing Hudsons

Lt J.D. Salisbury's 445th BG 700th BS Liberator crew, which ditched on 21st June 1944. (J Salisbury)

serviceable as possible, not always easy with no local source of spares, and if a Hudson was damaged too badly to be repaired on the squadron it was almost certain to have some undamaged components removed and replaced by defective parts before the repair party arrived. In addition to work, guard duties and various courses left little free time but a bus ran between the camp and King's Lynn every evening so a free evening could be spent 'in town' although we didn't think it was a very interesting place and didn't often go there.

Bircham Newton had been an airfield in the First World War and was retained by the RAF after the war, being almost completely reconstructed during the nineteen thirties with large C type hangars replacing most of the original aeroplane sheds, in fact very few of the old aerodrome buildings survived the reconstruction programme. This was fine and produced a well equipped airfield with just one snag – the surveyors seem not to have realised that the land on the airfield was unstable and was unable to support permanent runways so a steel mesh runway was put down and even this was so prone to damage that night flying was forbidden except in the most exceptional circumstances and flying couldn't start each morning until this runway had been inspected, and repaired as necessary, by AMWD engineers.

On 29 June two Thunderbolts reported sighting a dinghy in position 5200N 0340E and two Hudsons, H/279 flown by Canadian F/O Carmichael and W/279 captained by F/O Myatt, were scrambled with an escort of two more Thunderbolts to the area. The two Hudson became separated but F/O Myatt sighted smoke floats and then the dinghy and managed to home Carmichael to the scene. At 1204 hours Myatt dropped his airborne lifeboat, which landed 50 yards from the survivor, F/O Colleary of 455 Beaufighter Sqn based at Langham. Colleary made no attempt to board the lifeboat so Carmichael dropped a Lindholme dinghy, which unfortunately did not inflate. W/279 managed to contact an HSL a short time later and this was homed to the dinghy and Colleary was picked up.

This was not the end of Colleary's ordeal, however. Later that afternoon the HSL came under attack from enemy aircraft and was left on fire. Two Hudsons, F/Lt Welply L/279 and F/O Reade X/279, were scrambled to assist. On arrival at the scene they found fighters already circling to protect the survivors. The launch had sunk leaving only an oil patch and six dinghies containing the crew and the unfortunate Colleary. The Hudson crews orbited overhead as two HSLs arrived and picked up at least thirteen survivors. Welply and Reade continued to search the area for more survivors before setting course for base.

July 1944 opened with no operations for the first four days, a welcome rest for the crews after a busy period. Operations re-commenced on the 5th and two days later Lt Coale, flying W/279, experienced the frustration of being unable to help a group of ditched aircrew. Airborne from Bircham Newton at 1022 hours he sighted a circling Thunderbolt and flew towards it. Arriving over an area of well-dispersed wreckage the crew observed four aircrew in lifejackets floating alongside their unopened and awash dinghy. They believed that only two were still alive. Coale remained over the wreckage until two more Hudsons, X and F/279, arrived to relieve him. By now only two bodies could be seen in the water. The relieving Hudsons homed HSLs to the scene but they picked up only one, unrecognizable, body.

The 7th saw the award of the DFC to S/Ldr DT Downer 'in recognition of gallantry and devotion to duty in the execution of air operations'.

En route to target in Germany on 28 July two 100th BG B-17s collided 26 miles east of Lowestoft. The two aircraft involved were B-17 42-32009 *Black Cat 13* flown by 2nd Lt Albert S. Spear and B-17 42-9762, captained by Lt W.G. Stansbury. An eyewitness report from another crew stated:

> *At 1231 hours near 5238N 1057E while the formation was flying just above undercast at 9,000ft A/C #009 was flying #7 in the low squadron. It pulled up climbing and struck A/C #621 with its vertical stabilizer. A/C #009 broke in half at the waist and fell through the undercast. Two bodies were seen to come from #009 but no open chutes were seen. A/C #621 had its left aileron torn off and the aircraft went into a steep dive, disappearing into the undercast with pieces of wreckage falling off. No chutes were seen to come from this A/C. Aircraft #903 was sent back to patrol the area and assist Air Sea Rescue. However, observers on that aircraft failed to find any trace of the crew members.*

B-17 42-32009 *Black Cat 13* was ditched by 2nd Lt Albert S. Spear after a mid-air collision on 28 July 1944. Sgt Robbie L. Gill was the only survivor. (The crew shown with *Black Cat 13* is not the Spear crew). (100th Bomb Group Photo Archives via Michael Faley)

P/O Curtis was scrambled in K/279 to the position and found oil, debris and one empty dinghy. One airman in a Mae West was then sighted in a patch of flourescine dye. This was Sgt Robbie Gill, the only survivor of the twenty men of the two bomber crews. Curtis then dropped a smoke float with great accuracy, which landed 5 yards from Gill. A sighting report was sent and Curtis flew his Hudson in on another run, this time dropping a Lindholme dinghy. Gill made no attempt to reach it and Curtis continued to circle him. As a launch approached Curtis fired off Very cartridges to mark the location and Gill was taken on board at 1420 hours. He later made a statement about the collision and rescue.

> #009 struck #621 and I was thrown forward in the ship between the ammunition boxes. There was quite a bit of noise and the ship seemed to be thrown around a lot. I pulled the door off the tail and baled out. By the time my chute opened I was below the clouds. I saw the tail from which I had baled out spiraling slowly down to the sea. That was all there was left of the ship. Directly below me was a large fire and there were numerous small pieces of aircraft floating in the air. I saw no other chutes before or after landing in the sea. I was picked up by Air Sea Rescue approximately one and one half hours after landing in the water.

The following day was another frustrating one for the squadron. Several searches were carried out. On one of them, K/279, flown by F/O Hollebone, was scrambled to a point between Cromer and Haisborough after reports of two aircraft colliding. These were two 44th BG B-24's from Shipdham. The day's mission was to the shipyards in Bremen and they despatched thirty-two aircraft. 2nd Lt William F. Green of the 67th Sqn was flying B-24 42-109820:N-Bar named *The Wasp's Nest*, when he collided with 506th Sqn B-24 42-95309:Bar-V piloted by 2nd Lt Bernard J. Eberhardt Jr. Green was flying in the number 3 position of the lower left element of the formation and whilst the formation was in a turn this element slid under the centre section of the formation. Eberhardt's B-24 descended and its No. 2 propeller chewed off the tail of Green's B-24. *The Wasp's Nest* went into an immediate dive whilst Eberhardt's went into a flat spin.

Crew members from both aircraft baled out, four parachutes

F/Lt Hollebone's logbook for July 1944 showing the ASR search on the 29th for the survivors of the mid-air collision. (B Palmer)

being seen to leave both aircraft. Two of those baling out were seen to be caught by debris. When Hollebone arrived there were already several USAAF aircraft circling and a small motor vessel and three minesweepers were also searching. Hollebone homed an HSL to the area and the motor vessel reported that it had picked up three dead aircrew, Mortensen, Kenner and Landry. A minesweeper had picked up the only survivor, Sgt Alva F. Favors and along with the three dead bodies he was transferred to the HSL. Favors reported later that he had seen the collision coming, had his parachute on and was attempting to escape when it occurred. He stated that an ammunition box fell on him as he tried to get out but apart for that he only suffered shock and exposure. K/279 was then diverted to search a few miles further offshore and spotted further wreckage and a small white object, which sunk before the HSL could be brought to the scene. Hollebone continued to search but nothing further was found. The sea had claimed seventeen men from the two bombers.

In August 1944 F/Lt William Clark, a Canadian member of the Squadron was awarded the DFC for his efforts in a rescue in February 1944 and another more recent rescue. The citation read:

F/Lt B.P. Hollebone. (B Palmer)

Flight Lieutenant Clark has taken part in numerous operational sorties, many of which have been of a difficult and dangerous nature and have called for a high degree of airmanship. He has also participated in a number of air/sea rescues. In February 1944, while on patrol and during a snowstorm, this officer sighted a dinghy. He laid a line of flame floats and guided the high speed launch to the dinghy and despite the adverse weather which was rapidly deteriorating he stayed with the launch until all the occupants of the dinghy had been rescued. More recently this year Flight Lieutenant Clark participated in a successful rescue whereby the complete crew of a Fortress were saved.

The first successful search of the month occurred on the 10th. Reports were received of a sighting of a dinghy from a crashed Fortress in position 5240N 0210E. Hudsons L and K/279 piloted by WO Oakes and F/O Aggett were sent to investigate. On reaching position 5235N 0238E they sighted pyrotechnics being fired and were soon over two dinghies containing nine men. The survivors were from a B-17, 42-107087 *Big Barn Smell* of the 728th BS 452nd BG based at Deopham Green, which had ditched on the 9th returning from a target in south-east Germany. The Hudsons dropped marine markers followed by a Lindholme dinghy and

A blurred photo taken from F/Lt Hollebone's Hudson on 29 July 1944. (B Palmer)

the B-17 crew reached and successfully boarded it. A launch was then homed to the scene and 2nd Lt Paul N. Gilbert and his crew were taken on board.

By this time the Squadron was carrying out ASR support sorties for the Beaufighter, and later Mosquito, strike wings. This would become a regular feature and over the next year many searches and some successful rescue would be made during the extremely risky campaign against coastal shipping along the Scandinavian and Dutch coasts.

On 16 August WO Johnson and crew were scrambled in Hudson L/279 to position 5320N 0135E after a report of nine aircrew having baled out of an aircraft and who were being circled by a Thunderbolt. The ditched B-24J was 42-50580 of the 467th BG 788th BS based at Rackheath. WO Johnson provided a comprehensive report of the incident on his return.

Airborne at 1657 hours and set course immediately for the position. At 1715 hours a Thunderbolt and Liberator were sighted ahead at a distance of approximately one mile. A moment later three bodies in Mae Wests were seen in the water and a Marine Marker dropped. A mile further on another body was sighted and a second Marine Marker dropped. Both markers operated success-fully. At 1723 hours a Lindholme was dropped to the three survivors and fell within 30 yards of the target. However, they made no attempt to board the dinghy, but, instead, climbed into another 'H' Type dinghy presumably dropped by the Liberator. After climbing to 1,500 feet an attempt was made to contact 'Colgate' on Button 'C', but 'Colgate's' reply was unintelligible, whereupon 'Largetype' was contacted on Button 'D' and a message passed giving details of the bodies together with the position and a launch requested. 'Largetype' replied and stated that Seagull 18 was on the way.

A W/T fix was obtained and a message sent to Pulham 'Am over live bodies in the water, Lindholme dropped'. After the three survivors had climbed into the dinghy another message was sent 'Am over dinghy containing three bods' and IFF was switched to 'Distress'. Base replied 'Launch arriving 1900. Remain PLE'. Efforts to contact Seagull 18 [an HSL] were unsuccessful so it was decided to carry out a search in the area for any more survivors. Two more dinghies were found, both of which appeared to be empty and a marker was dropped. At 1846 hours Seagull 18 appeared approximately 8 miles distant and was homed onto the dinghy containing the 3 bods. Following this, the launch picked up Lindholme gear. Unable to locate the further survivor previously found, A/C 'L' requested two accompanying Thunderbolts to assist in search. Body was located again and launch picked him up at 1937 hours. Launch was then directed to two other dinghies and one more survivor was found clinging to the side of one of these. At 1947 hours Seagull 18 requested 'L' to obtain a fix for their use. Climbing to 1,000 feet this was obtained and passed to the launch. While fix was being obtained, Thunderbolt a/c homed launch onto another body clad in Mae West and floating in the water. The body was picked up but found to be dead.

A W/T message was sent informing that the launch had arrived and five bods rescued. Another message was sent immediately afterwards to the effect that a dead bod had also been picked up.

At 2032 hours Seagull 18 informed 'L' that they were returning to base with survivors and Seagull 38 arrived to relieve Seagull 18 also informed 'L' that survivors had stated that all the crew had been accounted for as the pilot and co-pilot had not been able to get out of the distressed aircraft.

Aircraft 'L' then carried out a general search of the area together with two Thunderbolts and after checking on small amounts of scattered wreckage, pilot decided to return to base.

W/T Messages were sent informing of intention and ETA base given. 'Colgate' was also informed on Button 'C'. Set course for base at 2032 hours and landed at 2055 hours. Weather in general was good, visibility 8–10 miles lowering in haze and the sea was calm.

The following day it was the turn of F/O Elliot and his crew to pull off a successful rescue. Piloting Hudson B/279, Elliot was scrambled to position 5413N 0034E to aircraft reported to be circling a dinghy. Elliot's report tells the story.

Airborne 1142 hours and set course from Brancaster for above position at 1146 hours. At 1209 hours three Halifaxes were seen circling in the area, whereupon we altered course to investigate and immediately found a 'J' type dinghy in position 5410N 0034E. Smoke floats were dropped followed by a Flame Float and at 1223 hours 'General Call' on 500Kcs, 'Am over dinghy containing 7 bodies' was sent out.

We then prepared to drop our Lindholme, making a 'dummy run' and at 1230 hours the Lindholme was successfully dropped. It dropped within a very short distance of the distressed crew, who, however, made no attempt to paddle towards it. At 1230 hours W/T message was sent to Pulham – 'am over dinghy containing 7 bodies – my IFF is on distress' and at the same time a fix was obtained. Homing transmissions were then begun on 500Kcs. HSL 45 being eventually contacted. At the same time continuous efforts were made to contact 'Largetype' on VHF and after climbing to Angels 5.5 we were able to pass our message, as above – 1300 hours. They came back advising us that HSL 38 was on its way and would be with us in an hour. They also suggested we called 'Midas' for better reception. This we did and contacted them at 1315 hours.

It was decided to drop a message to the dinghy and we descended to Angels 0 at 1345, a message container was successfully dropped containing the following message – 'HSL on its way, will be with you in 45 mins. – Try and paddle to Lindholme Dinghy if you can – we will stay with you until HSL arrives. Best of luck. 1335 hours, 17.8.44.'

We continued circling dinghy and at 1400 a second Flame Float was dropped, after which we again climbed to Angels 5 calling Seagull 38 on VHF, whom we eventually contacted – strength one.

At 1415 hours a second class fix was obtained from Pulham – a first class fix being obtained from Bircham. A 'General Call' was sent out on 500Kcs giving new position – 5434N 0039E. During this time we were unable to contact HSL 38 on W/T, but we had him on VHF his transmissions becoming stronger all the time. He requested Homing Transmissions on W/T and these were re-commended on 500Kcs at 1432 hours. We were unable to contact

*circling Halifaxes on VHF so signalled by Aldis to them 'Go home',
2 went, 1 stayed.*

*1540 hours, HSL was sighted in company with one Halifax. We
then joined the HSL flew over it and dropped a stick of smoke floats
to occupied dinghy.*

*1557 hours, Survivors were picked up and HSL reported by
VHF that they were all unhurt.*

*1557 hours, message passed to Pulham – '7 aircrew safe, picked
up by HSL 38 – ops completed, returning to base'.*

*HSL picked up Lindholme and second u/s dinghy and requested
a fix. 1606 Fix obtained from Pulham and passed to HSL. 5418N
0040E. 1612 set course for base. 1620 Pulham informed – 'my IFF
off distress'. 1650 landed.*

On 19 August 1944 after nine months without loss the
squadron suffered another tragedy when Hudson Mk III
AE513:P, flown by F/O Blake, was lost. Blake was flying at 100
feet when the Hudson stalled, turned over onto its back and spun
into the sea 20 miles east of Great Yarmouth. Seconds later a
partially inflated dinghy appeared and one man was seen, in-
credibly, swimming towards it. A lifeboat from a nearby ship
rescued him and picked up one dead body in a Mae West. Despite
a search by and HSL and squadron Hudson no other survivors
were found. Dougie Whittaker, flying in Z/279, recalls the incident. 'We were on patrol with F/O Drake, who was flying P/279.
It crashed into the water and only WO Howell survived. Sad day.'

Minor accidents were inevitable during operations and busy
airfields, tired crews and worn-out aircraft could result in crashes
and collisions in the air and on the ground. Hudson Mk III V9161
sustained category B damage in a crash on 22 August 1944 but
was repaired and returned to service, and Hudson Mk III V8982
sustained similar damage the next day.

F/Lt Radford was airborne from Bircham Newton on a search
at 0550 hours on the 26th. On reaching the search area, escorted
by three Mustangs, he sighted a dinghy with a single occupant.
Smoke floats were dropped to mark the position, but despite
these, contact was lost. A short while later an RML was sighted
and radio contact made with it. The RML reported that the
survivor had been successfully rescued. The lucky pilot, Lt R.F.
Semon, was from the Mustang-equipped, Bodney-based 328th
FS, 352nd FG. He had baled out 80 miles from the English coast-

line the previous day. Accurate fixes had been obtained but a swift rescue was hampered by mist. His fellow squadron pilots did everything possible to keep watch over him in his dinghy until the late hours of the day and he suffered no ill effects from his night in the dinghy.

The following day saw another success for the squadron when three Hudsons carried out a search for a ditched crew. At 5420N 0410E a dinghy was sighted with seven occupants and F/O Gaze in H/279 dropped an airborne lifeboat to them. Unfortunately it drifted away from the survivors, F/Lt Goldsmith and crew of Lancaster B/156 Sqn. (listed in the squadron ORB as a Halifax). Goldsmith had lifted from the runway at Upwood at 2021 hours in PB302: GT-B. During the operation they were attacked by a JU 88 and badly shot up, causing them to ditch. P/O Curtis in L/279 then ran in and dropped a Lindholme dinghy, which was boarded by four of the survivors. Attempts were made to contact HSLs, but with no success, and the Hudsons continued to circle until relief arrived. This came in the form of F/O Lambert in J/279, who remained overhead until he was relieved by F/O Carmichael in L/279. Carmichael's Hudson developed engine trouble and he was forced to make an early return to base, leaving the Lancaster crew adrift in the dinghies.

The next crew to arrive was that of F/O Myatt in B/279 accompanied by V/279 flown by F/O Brown. The dinghies were located after the survivors fired pyrotechnics and Brown dropped his airborne lifeboat within 30 yards of them illuminated by the Hudson's landing lights. Low cloud and poor visibility hampered the Hudsons' ability to maintain contact with the survivors and they had to depart. The rescue attempt would continue the next day.

Meanwhile on the night of 27th/28th August the RAF pounded the Ruhr refineries and WO Hill and crew in Hudson K/279 were tasked with a search for a missing crew in the early hours of the morning off the Dutch coast. It resulted in the rescue of only one survivor as WO Hill's report relates.

We were scrambled from Docking at 0123 hours and set course for position 5228N 0253E. Coltishall was contacted on VHF and the position was changed to 5254N 0207E where an aircraft with navigation lights burning was circling a dinghy containing one aircrew.

We arrived in position at 0157 where the circling aircraft was seen and contacted on VHF. We were plotted by Happisburgh RDF which informed us when we were immediately over the position where the aircraft, a Mosquito, had ditched. This position was slightly west of a flashing buoy, which was used to maintain position.

Upon instructions from Coltishall, Seagull 18 was contacted on VHF at 0250, identifying himself upon request by a green Very light. He was informed that he was right in position and a flare was dropped at 0255. Seagull 18 was unable to see anything upon the sea by this means and commenced to search using a searchlight.

At 0305 a dinghy was reported in the launch's searchlight and a pilot picked up at 0307, a second flare having been dropped for assistance.

The following information was obtained from the rescued pilot and passed to Coltishall by aircraft 'K' at 0320. The pilot had set course from the Dutch coast 4 miles south of Egmond IAS 140MPH course 268 degrees magnetic and the navigator had baled out at about 50 miles from the Dutch coast.

At 0328 Happisburgh RDF ordered us to climb to 800 feet and vectored us to position 5242N 0340E when a CLA search was commenced northwards, to find the navigator. Having sighted nothing at the end of the search we set course base at 0445 and landed at Docking at 0600 hours.

The surviving pilot was F/Lt HM Huggins of 515 Sqn, which flew Mosquitoes.

WO Johnson was airborne early, at 0428 hours, to recommence the rescue effort for the 156 Sqn crew. Just as he reached the lifeboat containing the survivors a Ju 88 appeared. After a few tense moments it turned away and Johnson was able to turn his attention back to the lifeboat. The survivors appeared to have some trouble with the engines, which stopped, but they managed to get them going again after an hour and Johnson remained overhead until low fuel forced him to return to base. F/O Gaze in W/279, who made unsuccessful attempts to raise an HSL, relieved him.

A Danish fishing vessel was spotted making for the lifeboat and a warning shot was fired across its bows, but it transpired that the Danes were friendly and the survivors were taken on board. S/Ldr Downer and F/O Lambert arrived at this point and

The trawler which picked up the crew of Lancaster PB302 0f 156 Sqn.
(M Barnard)

F/Lt Welply and F/O Hollebone, who were out on the same search tried to contact an HSL to take the survivors on board, but without success. By now the rescue was turning into an operation involving almost every crew on the squadron. F/O Nicholson on O/279 was next to arrive, relieving the others and in turn he was relieved by Lt Coale in B/279, who circled in drizzle and poor visibility over the fishing vessel. F/Lt Goff continued the vigil, following the lights of the fishing vessel through the night until the bad weather made him lose contact.

The following day Dougie Whittaker's crew (P/O Curtis in K/279) was out on the same search, but initially not in the right place. 'We searched for a fishing vessel containing 8 bods and found it 130 miles south of the given position! All safe.'

The fishing boat was heading for the Humber. Curtis was relieved by F/O Bedford in X/279 and he was able to contact an HSL and pass details of the vessel before engine trouble forced him to leave. The squadron later received a message that the survivors had been successfully picked up.

Throughout the summer of 1944 the satellite airfield of

Docking was in regular use by the aircraft of 279 Sqn and Ken Border recalls the daily routine there.

The stand-by aircraft had to take off each day before dark and fly the short distance to the Docking satellite where the squadron had its own dispersal on the edge of the airfield near the railway. If the aircraft were called out during the night they would sometimes return direct to Bircham Newton the next morning leaving the ground crew to return by bus but otherwise each morning everyone would fly back to base in time for breakfast. On these overnight detachments the ground crew were issued with basic rations of bread, marg, jam, tea etc. It wasn't unknown for one of the ground crew to get over the fence and have a short walk along the railway track to a nearby cottage where a friendly farmer would always sell them a few fresh eggs (and often throw in some potatoes) and soon the smell of a supper of fried eggs and chips would waft over the dispersal; rather more appetising than jam sandwiches.

September 1944 saw a slight improvement in the weather over the previous month and this allowed the squadron to complete 144 sorties. Forty-nine of these were searches, with a further eighty-four patrols awaiting the return of US, Bomber Command and Coastal Command forces from operations. Eleven more patrols were carried out checking the ASR buoys and floats in the North Sea.

Although the month generally saw an improvement in the weather, this was not the case on 2 September when a Hudson was sent to investigate a sighting of Very lights. F/Lt Radford was airborne at 0219 hours in Hudson K/279 to search for the lone survivor of a ditched 524 Sqn Wellington. Despite having to search in the dark and in poor visibility Radford's crew sighted the dinghy. To try and maintain contact Radford dropped flame floats but they did not have the desired effect. Radford continued to search but was forced to depart the scene as he ran low on fuel. S/Ldr Downer in Hudson B/279 relieved him, struggling through extremely poor weather to reach the search area. As he searched, Downer's crew picked up a faint message that four survivors in a dinghy had been picked up. Downer continued his search of the area between Skegness and the Wash for the remaining crew members. At 1050 hours F/O Brown and F/O

Carmichael, in N and X/279 respectively, flew out to relieve Downer. They found the ditched Wellington, still afloat but with no sign of life. The four survivors were F/O Paterson, F/Sgt Moffatt, F/Sgt Pearson and WO Hurtick.

WO Hill was on patrol in Hudson L/279 awaiting the return of US bombers from targets in Germany, when the crew sighted a ditched Liberator from the 392nd BG 40 miles east of Great Yarmouth. Close to the bomber was an upturned Lindholme dinghy and a further two aircraft dinghies containing eight survivors. The survivors were picked up by an MTB, which had a Fortress circling above it. Hill also remained overhead until the rescue was successfully achieved.

On the night of 15/16 September 1944 Bomber Command carried out a heavy attack on Kiel with 490 aircraft. Eleven aircraft were lost, including the 420 Sqn RCAF Halifax of F/Lt V. Motherwell which ditched. A Mk III, NA629:PT-W, it had left Tholthorpe at 2156 hours. They bombed the target at 0119 hours from 18,000 feet before turning for home. On the return journey the hydraulic system failed, probably holed by flak. The loss of hydraulics caused the flaps to lower followed by the under-carriage and then the bomb doors. The wireless operator put out an SOS and despite attempts by the crew to rectify this situation, Motherwell was forced to ditch in this highly dangerous con-figuration at 0405 hours. They were 70 miles off the East Anglian coast.

At times a search scene could resemble flies around a honeypot and this was the case during the search for Motherwell and his crew. S/Ldr Simpson in L/279 and F/O Garven in U/2279 were scrambled at 1801 and 1823 hours respectively. On arrival at the search area they discovered three Lancasters and two Halifaxes, one of which was another 420 Sqn aircraft flown by F/Lt E.S. Heimpel RCAF, circling two dinghies containing the seven survivors. The Hudsons dropped smoke floats to help mark the position and shortly afterwards a Walrus amphibian arrived and picked up the survivors. Some time later an RML was homed to the area and the survivors were transferred to this from the Walrus. The RML then took the Walrus under tow and headed for home.

On 17 September Operation Market Garden commenced with a huge airlift of paratroops and glider combinations taking off for Arnhem in a bid to capture the bridges over the Rhine. Of 321 gliders towed aloft on that day twenty-six parted company with their tugs, either over England, in the sea or over Holland, due to broken tow ropes or other malfunctions. The following day 257 out of 275 gliders made it to the battle, whilst on the third lift 36 gliders failed to make it with several coming down in the North Sea. F/O Brown in K/279 and F/Lt Radford in W/279 were airborne on the morning of the 17th to cover the glider train. In position 5153N 0215E they sighted a Dakota circling three ditched gliders. There were also three HSLs in the vicinity and one of them, Seagull 36, reported that all the survivors had been picked up.

During this series of airlifts 279 Sqn provided ASR cover. A report made on 19 September gives an account of the Squadron's part in the rescue of some of the unfortunate glider crews and troops. It covers the activities of F/O Gaze and crew in Hudson V/279 and P/O Curtis and crew in K/279.

Both Hudsons got airborne at 1200 hours to cover the Airborne troop movements. At 1352 hours a glider was sighted in the sea in position 5122N 0210E, and Gaze sent off a sighting report and got a fix. Shortly afterward he and Curtis lost sight of each other. Curtis dropped his Lindholme dinghy to the survivors and switched his IFF to distress to assist in fixing the position. K/279 then attempted to contact any launches on the area.

At 1415 hours Gaze sighted another ditched glider with five survivors in position 5120N 0203E and flew towards them. K/279 meanwhile set off in search of any launches in the area. Five minutes later K/279 found yet another glider, this time with eighteen survivors. V/279 was ordered to circle and was informed that two launches were on the way. Thirty minutes later Gaze discovered a fourth glider on the water with four survivors. He was ordered to drop its dinghy to these survivors. By 1621 hours the survivors of all four glider ditchings had been picked up by the launches and two minutes later both Hudsons resumed patrolling. K/279 then set course for base landing at 1720 hours. Meanwhile, at 1715 hours Gaze had sighted a dinghy with ten survivors. He sent a sighting report, but then discovered that a Warwick was already on the scene and had begun homing a launch to the dinghy. Gaze then turned for base, landing at 1810 hours. It had been a highly successful day for the crews with four gliders, a dinghy and thirty-seven survivors found and rescued.

Patrols covering the glider trains and troop transports heading for Arnhem with reinforcements continued over the days that followed with no incidents requiring the assistance of the squadron. The loss of airborne lifeboats due to inadvertent drops was a problem which seemed to be unresolved and, once again, on 30 September the squadron lost another one when it fell away from E/279 flown by F/Lt Piprell with no apparent reason for its release.

On 3 October F/Lt Thomas O'Gorman received a Bar to his DFC. This was the same O'Gorman who had to navigate F/O Clark's Hudson from the cabin after a birdstrike shattered the nose perspex on 13 November 1943. The squadron had another success on this day when F/Lt Goff in Hudson U/279 was scrambled to search for a dinghy containing one survivor. Setting out with an escort of Mustangs to 5319N 0508E they found it and Goff released his airborne lifeboat from 700 feet. The lifeboat landed 100 yards downwind of the dinghy and fifteen minutes later the survivor had climbed on board. Goff returned to base leaving three Thunderbolts circling the dinghy

On 8 October two Hudsons, F/279, a Mk III flown by F/Lt Pederson, and D/279, a Mk VI captained by F/O Carmichael, were carrying out an ASR search when they came under attack from an enemy aircraft identified as either an Me 210 or 410. The fighter was first sighted at a range of 800 yards as it swept round in a wide circle to come in on D/279's starboard beam opening fire at 400 yards and closing to 150 yards before breaking off. While Pederson observed the attack and his gunner fired 50 to 60 rounds at extreme range at the fighter, Carmichael turned steeply to starboard into the enemy fighter with both turret and side gunners returning fire. Several hits were observed on the fighter and D/279 was also damaged in the exchange of fire. While the fighter turned to make another attack on D/279 from low on the port quarter Pederson made his escape into a thin layer of cloud. Before the fighter could get into an attacking position Carmichael also slipped into the cloud. The fighter was determined, however, and was next sighted attacking from a range of 800 yards dead ahead. Carmichael quickly dived to port and into thicker cloud, where he lost the fighter. It was a lucky escape.

On 14 October 1944 the squadron finally made the long-awaited move to Thornaby and began re-equipping with Vickers Warwick ASR aircraft. A rear party left behind at Bircham Newton followed on at the end of the month. The Hudsons would

An airborne shot of a Vickers Warwick ASR Mk I Stage C carrying an airborne lifeboat.

gradually be phased out over the coming months as crews converted to the new type. The Warwick had originally been conceived as a bomber type but its performance and handling were disappointing and it was not taken into service in this role. Instead it would become a general reconnaissance, transport and ASR aircraft. Coastal Command urgently needed an ASR type capable of carrying Lindholme gear and an airborne lifeboat and

Vickers Warwick ASR Stage A BV301 was used as an airborne lifeboat trials aircraft. (S Gifford)

Vickers Warwick ASR Stage A BV301, which had a modified bomb bay and doors to allow the carriage of two sets of Lindholme gear and a Mk 1 Lifeboat. (S Gifford)

in July 1943 the Warwick ASR Mk I was accepted. In its fully developed Stage C version it was equipped with ASV radar and additional fuel tanks and could carry the heavier (1,633 kg) Mk II airborne lifeboat. It was also better armed than the Hudson, with nose, tail and dorsal gun turrets. The squadron would operate several versions of the Warwick; the Warwick Bomber/ASR, The Warwick ASR Stage C (also known in service circles as the ASR Mk I), the Warwick ASR Mk I and the Warwick ASR Mk VI, which was equipped with more powerful Pratt & Whitney R-2800-47 engines. To confuse the issue further squadron records note all of these Warwick marks as Mk Is!

Ken Border moved to Thornaby with the squadron and recalls the period of re-equipment:

The squadron was posted to Thornaby and the Hudsons flew up there following the coastline but taking care to avoid any coastal convoys who always welcomed any opportunity for a bit of target practice! Thornaby was another pre-war airfield with permanent hangars and concrete runways but the accommodation was in rows of wooden huts. Almost opposite the main gates was a pub

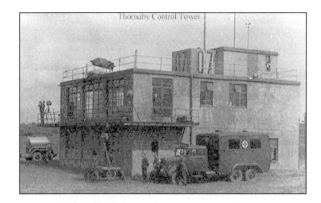

Thornaby control tower. (via Carl James/HAiB)

and the town of Stockton on Tees was within walking distance but perhaps the most welcome feature was the friendliness of the local population, it was unusual to walk back from town at night without someone along the way inviting you in for a 'cuppa', very different from the far more reserved East Anglians. The downside of the move was the fact that the Hudsons were withdrawn and 279 was issued with Warwick Mk 1 aircraft in their place, plus a few

A post-war photo of the town of Wick with the aerodrome in the background. (Blair Bartholomew)

Sea Otter amphibians and Hurricane fighters. The Warwick was effectively an enlarged version of the Wellington with a mid-upper turret as well as the nose and tail turrets but it was not popular with the squadron. I recall some USAF aircrew, diverted into Thornaby, looking round one of the Warwicks and just not believing that the RAF actually flew 'canvas-covered trelliswork framed airplanes in combat' –I can't imagine what they would have said if they had flown in one and seen the wingtips flexing up and down!

From October 1944 the squadron crews would find themselves spread all over the north of England and Scotland providing ASR support to the strike wings of Coastal Command. Detachments to Reykjavik in Iceland, Tain, Fraserburgh, Wick and Banff were maintained and the Warwicks and Hudsons would often start a patrol or search at one base to end it at another. The detachment of Hudsons arrived at Banff on 31 October.

On 18 October F/Sgt Wood and his crew narrowly missed being shot down by friendly fire. Airborne in Hudson L/279 they were searching for an aircraft reported ditched just off Chapel St Leonards. An HSL was sighted firing a smoke signal and Wood attempted to contact it using VHF and TR9 radios, with no success. Descending to a lower altitude the Hudson crew then tried to make contact by Aldis lamp, but this only resulted in the HSL sending a burst of machine-gun fire ahead of and below the Hudson. Discretion being the better part of valour, Wood turned away and continued the search, but unfortunately found nothing. The remainder of the month was filled with unsuccessful sorties; the only incident of note was that Warwick BV233 sustained category AC damage on 28 October 1944 during conversion to the type.

CHAPTER SEVEN

November 1944
– April 1945

T he first five days of November saw no operational flying, as the squadron was busy converting to the Warwick. Detachments were now being maintained at Banff and Wick, which completed nineteen of the total of twenty-nine operational sorties flown during the month. Whilst the conversion was in progress No. 280 Sqn (Det) covered any ASR sorties from Thornaby.

On 8 November F/O Hollebone and F/Sgt Wood were airborne in Hudsons K and W/279 to cover the return of US bombers. At 1406 hours Hollebone's crew were witnesses as a tragic event unfolded. The crew sighted an empty J-Type dinghy with a dead body alongside and two smaller yellow objects, possibly bodies. On the chance that they might still be alive Hollebone ran in and dropped a Lindholme dinghy, which landed 50 yards from the two possible survivors. One was seen to grasp it but appeared to be too weak to enter it. A while later two P-47s appeared in the area and at 1510 hours a Walrus arrived and landed. Hollebone's crew watched as it motored around and examined both dinghies but it did not pick up any survivors. Help had arrived too late for this crew.

The following day two Hudsons from Thornaby, J/279 and W/279 flown by F/Os Carmichael and Elliott, carried out a search for a Swordfish missing from the Royal Naval Air

Vickers Warwick fitted with an airborne lifeboat slung underneath the bomb bay. (Air Historical Branch (RAF)

Station at Arbroath, but they found no trace of it or its crew.

The Banff detachment commenced on 18 November when two Hudsons were detailed to move there. Both set off, but one arrived unserviceable. As soon as the other, W/279 flown by F/O Elliott, arrived it was tasked to search for a missing Liberator between Rattray Head and Sumburgh Head. This first sortie of the detachment was unsuccessful.

The Squadron's first operational Warwick sortie was carried out on 18 November with F/O Grimston taking off from Wick at 1421 hours for a search. Perhaps it was a portent of the engine problems to come, but take off was delayed by forty minutes due

A closer view of the airborne lifeboat which was dropped by
Warwicks of the squadron and was instrumental in saving many
aircrew lives. (Air Historical Branch (RAF))

to engine trouble. Grimston landed at Banff at the end of the
sortie.

One of the squadron's main duties from now would be
providing ASR cover to the Banff and Dallachy strike wings as
they set about enemy shipping off the Scandinavian coast. The
first Warwick sortie to carry out this duty was flown by S/Ldr
Levin-Raw in RL-J on 20 November. Meeting up with the strike
wing at 0951 hours he escorted them until he developed a generator problem, after which he kept within visual range. He set
course for home at 1144 hours and landed safely at Wick.

The early days of Warwick operations were not without their
problems. The squadron was tragically to lose a crew on 20
November 1944. F/Lt D. Welply and crew took off from
Thornaby in Warwick ASR Mk VI HG210/RL-Q at 1742 hours for
a navigation exercise. At 1830 hours they signalled that they were
in position 5415N 0100E and were returning with engine trouble.
Welply was passed a position fix six minutes later, after which
nothing further was heard. The radar plot of the Warwick faded

F/Lt Hollebone's logbook entry showing the search on 8 November 1944. (B Palmer)

from the screen 22 miles south-east of Flamborough Head, suggesting that it had ditched or crashed. Hudson N/279 carried out a search on the 20th, but that and a search by five aircraft on the 21st and a further eighteen on the 22nd found no trace of the Warwick or its crew.

On 21 November the squadron's Warwicks had a busy day. Three aircraft, RL-N, L and F, flown by Lt Shanks, F/O Grimston and F/Lt Moreton respectively, were tasked to provide ASR cover to the Banff and Dallachy strike wings. They covered them to position 6230N 0545E, where they circled, awaiting the return of the Mosquitoes and Beaufighters. RL-N returned and landed at Banff, whilst F/O Grimston in RL-L escorted a damaged aircraft from the strike to Sumburgh and was then diverted onto an unsuccessful search for a dinghy before landing at Banff. F/Lt Moreton developed engine trouble and diverted to Wick, landing safely.

As these three were landing S/Ldr Levin-Raw was getting airborne from Wick in Warwick RL-T for a search, but twenty minutes later he was recalled. As he approached the airfield he found that he could not lower the undercarriage and it took a further hour and a quarter to resolve the hydraulic problem before he too landed safely. Four Hudsons from Thornaby were also involved in an unsuccessful search for the missing Warwick.

Two Hudsons, W/279 flown by F/Sgt Wood and C/279 captained by F/O Gaze carried out a search for a ditched Mosquito on the 23rd. Nothing was sighted and the two aircraft had to return early due to adverse weather conditions, diverting for a landing at Skitten.

The remainder of the month saw the Squadron busily escorting the strike wings. There was little activity until the penultimate day of the month when F/O Grimston in Warwick RL-N – his second aircraft of the task as the first had become unserviceable – and F/O Richards in RL-G, provided ASR cover to the Dallachy strike wing. Richards was unable to contact the strike wing due to an unserviceable radio. Grimston provided an escort to one of the returning aircraft for part of the return trip, before both aircraft landed at Banff.

By December the squadron was operating detachments from Wick, Banff, Fraserburgh and Sumburgh as well as maintaining aircraft and HQ at Thornaby. Warwicks were now flying the majority of the sorties and the Hudson strength was gradually being run down. Most of the sorties were in support of the Coastal Command strike wings.

The squadron's first successful operational rescue with the Warwick was achieved on 5 December by F/O Garven in Warlock RL-H. Scrambled from Sumburgh at 1617 hours he made for position 6038N 0021W, where he found a Beaufighter circling a dinghy. Dropping a marine marker, he saw a steady light 100 yards from it. Garven continued to search but his crew could not see any sign of the dinghy. Attempts to contact the circling Beaufighter were frustrated by equipment failure and to make matters worse, shortly afterward all the lights on the Warwick failed. Luck was with the ditched crew, however, and red Very lights fired from the surface were spotted by the Warwick crew and they were able to signal base that they were over live bodies in the water. After a while a launch was seen to approach and pick up the aircrew. Garven then set course for home, landing at Banff at 1950 hours.

Also on 5 December, Lt Shanks was airborne in Warwick RL-L with F/O Grimston in RL-G, covering an anti-shipping strike off the Norwegian coast, when Beaufighter M/144 Sqn reported engine trouble. Shanks and Grimston escorted it back to Sumburgh and then went on to land at Banff.

The Dallachy Strike Wing were out in force again on 6 December escorted by Warwicks RL-N and RL-G, flown by F/O O'Reilly and Lt Shanks. As they patrolled they picked up a message from one of the Beaufighters that it was circling a dinghy in position 6200N 0510E. As they turned towards this position they received a further message that the survivors were being picked up by a rowing boat! The two Warwicks returned to Banff. Two Hudsons from Thornaby carried out a search for a Desborough-based Wellington of No. 84 OTU which had ditched off Flamborough but they had no success.

On 7 December the Banff Strike Wing was carrying out a strike off the coast of Norway near Gossen when German fighters attacked them. Amongst those lost was a 489 Sqn Beaufighter crewed by F/Sgt Graham and WO Clarke. The aircraft, LZ448:X, was hit in the starboard engine and ditched in flames. Both crewmembers managed to reach the aircraft dinghy and climb aboard. An aircraft from the Banff Wing was quickly sent out to search but had no luck. Three Warwicks from the squadron were providing ASR cover for the strike. At 1514 hours RL-N, flown by F/O O'Reilly, began to experience engine trouble and immediately set course for Wick, escorted by S/Ldr Simpson and P/O Horsburgh in RL-G and RL-N. As they approached Sumburgh Head they picked up a message from a callsign 'RWD12' advising that he was over a dinghy containing live bodies but the position was uncertain. Forty-five minutes later another message from the same callsign advised that he had lost sight of the survivors and had seen nothing for almost thirty minutes. O'Reilly landed at Wick and the other two Warwicks continued on to Fraserburgh. The search the following day also failed in poor weather. Another Mosquito lost on the same day on a flight from Northolt to Charterhall was also searched for by a Thornaby Hudson, but it was not located.

Warwick RL-U flown by P/O Richards carried out the continuing search for the dinghy with no result and two further Warwicks from Wick provided ASR cover for Operation Urbane during which the rear gunner of one aircraft reported a dinghy sighting, but on closer examination it turned out to be two round mine-like objects.

On the 9th Warwick G/279, captained by 1st Lt Shanks USAAF, joined the search. Forty-five miles east of Fetlar in the Shetlands the crew sighted Graham and Clarke in their dinghy. Shanks dropped marker flares over their position then ran in and dropped his airborne lifeboat, which deployed correctly, and the survivors were able to board it at 1600 hours on the third day of their ordeal. Shanks was relieved by F/Lt Hansen-Lester in Hudson N/279 from Thornaby and he was in turn relieved by P/O Hill in K/279 from Sumburgh, who then carried out a search for surface vessels to assist and found the fishing vessel *Molde*. He homed the trawler to the lifeboat position and at 2050 hours the Beaufighter crew were taken on board. They were landed at Lerwick the following day. Three days later Shanks carried out an ASR patrol between Ytterdene and Storholm but was forced to return to base with engine trouble.

Don Mabey was WOp/AG on F/O O'Reilly's crew and recalls the type of ASR support the squadron provided to the strike wings during the winter of 1944/45.

The groundcrew look on in this posed wartime publicity photo of F/O Paddy O'Reilly and crew approaching their Warwick for another sortie. (D Mabey)

Part of the Banff Strike Wing was a Norwegian squadron, whose main job was to take off, timed to arrive off the Norwegian coast at first light, and send a sighting report if any German shipping was on the move. The Beaufighters and Mosquitoes standing by, as were 279 Sqn Warwicks, then took off to attack the German shipping.

Our job was to take off immediately and we were airborne before the strike aircraft. We then flew to a prearranged position, flew very low over the sea and dropped smoke floats in a circle, a mile in diameter, and timed to ignite around the time the strike commenced. Thus, the strike aircraft had a position to make for if they were in trouble and hoping to ditch. The Warwick would be orbiting within the circle of smoke floats so that there was help if they ditched.

Sadly, the weather, state of the sea etc. was often against us and the lifeboat drops were not always successful. These times were quite traumatic in many ways for we were pretty exposed and on one occasion a whole squadron of FW 190s flew directly over us without spotting us.

The detachment at Banff was visited by an official photographer late in 1944 and as part of the visit he was taken flying in a Warwick flown by F/O O'Reilly, as Don Mabey recalls.

The photographer was a big man and very much wanted a trip in a Warwick, so we took him up. When airborne he said he would like to sit in the rear turret, so I was told by the Skipper, Paddy, to help him into the turret. This I did and remained in the rear of the fuselage. I must tell you that he didn't stay in the turret very long! He turned the turret a few times then asked to come out! I had explained the operation of the controls and when I told him to centralize the turret I had to take over by using the 'dead man's handle' because he was going to open the turret doors whilst the turret was facing the beam. Thank God, I remained outside the turret, because we would have lost photographer, turret doors and all! I must say a very shaken and pale photographer was most relieved to exit the turret and aircraft. He couldn't wait to get his feet back on the deck.

On 13 December F/Lt Hanson-Lester in Hudson N/279 and P/O Hill in U/279 had a timely reminder that not all the danger of wartime flying came from the enemy when they were bracketed by three light flak bursts on the outward leg of a search from Thornaby. They were looking for a dinghy containing three aircrew, but all they sighted was a small naval force, an RML and two trawlers in the search area.

On 16 December the Mosquitoes of the Banff Strike Wing carried out an attack on a disabled vessel, the SS *Ferndale*, aground at Kraklellesund. During the attack Mosquito R/248 was hit in the port engine. The pilot, F/Lt J. Kennedy, turned away and with the aircraft on fire managed to make a controlled ditching at 6059N 0409E. He and his navigator F/O F. Rolls managed to get out and climbed into the dinghy. They were briefly circled by two Mosquitoes from the strike force and soon afterward S/Ldr Levin-Raw arrived on scene. An airborne lifeboat was dropped, but unfortunately the parachutes failed to release and it was dragged away before being destroyed in the heavy swell. Warwick F1/279 then appeared, flown by F/O O'Reilly. O'Reilly dropped a second lifeboat, but once again the equipment failed, the parachute release gear activated in mid-

Don Mabey's logbook for December 1944 showing the rescue attempt
on 16 December. (D Mabey)

air and the lifeboat crashed to the sea, braking up on impact.

Disappointed but undeterred O'Reilly next dropped a Lind-holme dinghy close to the survivors, but they made no attempt to reach it. They were observed to be sitting upright and clinging to the dinghy handling rope. The Warwick crew then observed one of them entering the Lindholme dinghy and the Warwick ran in and dropped a second. The second survivor meanwhile had paddled to the swamped airborne lifeboat and attached a line to it. O'Reilly remained overhead until fuel shortage forced his departure. Another Warwick, RL-P flown by WO Bolton, relieved him dropping yet another lifeboat. This time the parachutes failed to release and the lifeboat capsized and was dragged for over a mile before righting itself, too far for the Mosquito aircrew to have any hope of reaching it. Bolton attempted to drop Lindholme dinghies but these drops were also unsuccessful due to the high seas.

F/O Garven in Warwick RL-U relieved Bolton and on arriving in the area found a Wellington orbiting the dinghies. He dropped further markers and continued to circle. At 2156 hours an uniden-tified enemy aircraft was spotted approaching from the east at 500 feet and showing a light. It spotted Garven and immediately extinguished the light before closing to about 700 yards. Garven took evasive action and lost it in the dark, it was not seen again. A further marine marker was dropped before Garven turned for Sumburgh. A grim night for Kennedy and Rolls followed, but they were shadowed by a Liberator through the hours of

An airborne lifeboat dropping away from the relief Warwick RL-P during the rescue attempt of 16 December 1944. (D Mabey)

F/O Paddy O'Reilly pictured at Banff in 1944. (D Mabey)

darkness. Next morning the Warwicks took up the cover and at 1200 hours Warwicks RL-E and RL-C arrived, to find Mosquito K of 235 Sqn circling. They found only one dinghy with one person on board, who was apparently dead. With nothing further sighted they returned to base.

O'Reilly and his crew almost came to grief on returning to base. Having landed at Sumburgh and stayed overnight they set of for Banff the next morning. As they were taking off a van was driven across the runway directly in front of them. Having barely reached take-off speed O'Reilly hauled the Warwick up and over it, bounced back onto the runway and finally climbed laboriously away from the runway.

F/Lt Ashby was airborne in Warwick RL-R from Thornaby on the 21st searching for a Beaufighter dinghy at 5528N 0218W. A naval launch, two Beaufighters and a Mosquito were also searching but nothing was found except aircraft wreckage and an oil patch.

F/Lt Carmichael was airborne from Banff in Warwick RL-E on the 23rd to provide ASR cover to the Dallachy Strike Wing. Whilst circling at the ASR rendezvous an unidentified aircraft showing

Three members of F/O Paddy O'Reilly's crew at Banff in 1944. L to R: Australian WOp/AG Ray Cooper, WOp/AG 'Taffy' Hendra and WOp/AG Don Mabey. (D Mabey)

a light was spotted on a westerly coast. A while later a distress blip was picked up on the radar and Carmichael attempted to home onto it, finding two Hurricanes which showed no signs of distress. The Warwick then picked up another distress call, thought to have originated with the Polish leader of the strike

Canadian 'Red' Marvin was rear gunner on F/O Paddy O'Reilly's crew at Banff in 1944. (D Mabey)

F/O Paddy O'Reilly and crew pose for a pre-sortie briefing at Banff in 1944. L to R: Navigator Johnny Drinkwater, Pilot Paddy O'Reilly, Rear Gunner 'Red' Marvin, First WOp/AG Don Mabey, second WOp/AG 'Taffy' Hendra, third WOp/AG Ray Cooper. (D Mabey)

force. Carmichael carried out a search but found nothing. Meanwhile F/O Elliot in Warwick RL-P was airborne from Sumburgh on a dinghy search. The downed aircraft was a Mustang and two other Mustangs were seen circling. The Warwick rear gunner reported sighting an empty K-type dinghy and Elliot dropped markers over the position. Unfortunately, both markers and dinghy were soon lost in the white caps and were not seen again. The search continued the next day without success.

(Text continues on page 156)

F/O O'Reilly checks the airborne lifeboat slung beneath his Warwick at Banff in 1944. Note the 'invasion stripes' on the fuselage. (D Mabey)

Another view of the same Warwick from a slightly different angle showing some of the airfield buildings behind. (J Hughes)

Crew debrief at Banff in 1944. L to R: Rear gunner 'Red' Marvin, pilot Paddy O'Reilly, WAAF Joyce Sherlock and debriefing officer F/Lt Mills. (D Mabey)

A Liberator, similar to the one shown, relieved F/O O'Reilly's Warwick during the hours of darkness during the search for a ditched Mosquito crew on 16 December 1944. (Via A Rodgers)

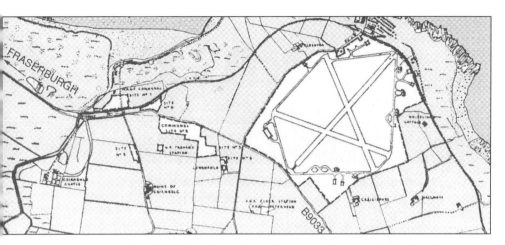

A map showing RAF Fraserburgh and the associated technical and accommodation sites around the airfield. (J Hughes)

No. 24 Wellington Torpedo Course, X Sqn, No. 6 OTU, Silloth, 9 June 1943. Front row 3rd and 4th from left are Sgt Acton and Sgt Russell of F/O Murray's crew. (CA Evans)

Another view of the Vickers Warwick ASR Mk I Stage C equipped
with an airborne lifeboat.

A vertical view of RAF Fraserburgh in 1946. (J Hughes)

F/O Murray's crew whilst serving with 281 Sqn at Wick in 1944. Rear L to R: F/O Haywood, Sgt Russell, Sgt C. A. Evans, Sgt Acton. Front L to R: F/O Murray, Sgt Bath, F/O Bartholomew. (C. A. Evans)

Wick 1944, L to R: Ted Russell, Jack Murray and Colin Acton. The three young ladies are relatives of Jack Murray. (E Russell)

F/Lt Murray and his crew standing in front of a 281 Sqn Warwick.
The Warwick carries the code B4, which was the code carried by
aircraft of No. 282 Sqn until it amalgamated with 281 Sqn in January
1944. Murray and his crew served with 281 Sqn until joining 279 Sqn
in November 1944. L to R: John 'Bart' Bartholomew, navigator, Bert
Bath, 2nd pilot, Ted Russell, W/Op, Jack Murray, pilot, Cledwyn
'Taffy' Evans, 2nd WOp/Radar operator (left crew before joining 279
Sqn), Colin 'Joe' Acton, MUG, Happy Haywood, RG. (Blair
Bartholomew)

On 26 December fourteen Mosquitoes of 143, 235 and 248
squadrons laid on a strike against shipping in Leirvik harbour.
German fighters came up to counter the attack and one of the
Mosquitoes was shot down. Three more were damaged, one of
which returned to Banff on one engine, escorted by a Warwick of
279 Sqn captained by F/Lt Murray. The Mosquito was LA-N
of No. 235 Sqn, flown by F/Lt W Clayton-Graham and his navigator F/O Webster. The navigator contacted the Warwick 20
miles off the coast and it joined the Mosquito, which was firing
red, green and yellow Very cartridges in an effort to pinpoint its
location. At one point Clayton-Graham, flying with the port
engine feathered, asked if he was flying too fast for the Warwick;
the reply was not a polite one!

At the end of 1944 Ted Russell was flying operations in F/Lt Murray's crew and recalls this period.

We were involved in strike cover patrols. We took off ahead of the strike force, usually Mosquitoes and Beaufighters. They would catch us up near the target and we would follow them home in case any were in trouble.

On 26 December 1944 we escorted a Mosquito back to base with our port engine u/s. All went OK and we landed after 4 hours and 30 mins. On New Year's Eve we spent 7 hours and 10 mins over a dinghy.

We also did 24hr standby where the engines were kept warm and Jack [Murray] interrupted our card games with crash and ditching drills, which were a bind at the time, but stood us in good stead.

The squadron detachment, which had been based at Banff supporting the activities of the Banff Strike Wing, moved out to a new base at Fraserburgh on 27 December, from where it would continue to provide ASR cover for both Banff and Dallachy strike wings and the escorting fighters.

F/Lt Carmichael, flying Warwick RL-L from Fraserburgh was covering the Dallachy Strike Wing on 29 December. The sortie passed without incident until, arriving back at base, Carmichael discovered that he could not lower the undercarriage or flaps due to hydraulic failure. Carmichael circled the airfield for some time before the undercarriage was finally pumped down manually. The flaps refused to budge, however, and the Warwick made a faster than normal landing but still landed safely.

Carmichael was not the only one having problems with the temperamental Warwick that day. Earlier that morning F/Sgt Wood had taken off in Warwick RL-S from Thornaby to search for a missing 38 Group Halifax. In the search area the pilot and rear gunner both spotted a black tubular object in the water, but this quickly disappeared from sight before it could be identified. With nothing sighted and the search complete Wood turned for home. On the way back the Warwick developed engine trouble and twenty minutes later the starboard engine cut completely. Wood jettisoned the lifeboat immediately. In order to stay airborne, however, more weight had to be lost and the lifeboat was quickly followed by the four machine-guns from the rear turret and the flame floats and ammunition. W/Cdr Cox in

Warwick RL-K scrambled from Thornaby to assist him and sighted him off Sunderland limping home. The two Warwicks met off Seaham and Wood set course for Usworth, hoping to land there. He was unable to find the airfield in poor visibility and continued on to Thornaby, where a safe landing was made. Meanwhile, W/Cdr Cox was having troubles of his own, having developed an oil leak just north of Sunderland. He too set course for Thornaby and landed safely.

On New Year's Eve 1944 twenty Mosquitoes from the Banff Strike Wing made an attack on shipping in the Flekkefjord. HP922:U of 248 Sqn, flown by F/Lt J. Lown, was hit by flak. Lown turned his crippled aircraft for home and a message was sent out scrambling a Warwick of 279 Sqn. The Mosquito lost height steadily and Lown was forced to ditch, the Mosquito breaking up on impact, 110 miles south-west of Stavanger. Lown scrambled out of the cockpit and into the dinghy, but Dayton, the navigator did not escape.

The last day of 1944 turned out to be a very busy one for the Warwick crews. First off at 0949 hours was RL-D from Thornaby, flown by F/Lt Burgess. He carried out an unsuccessful search for a dinghy before returning to base. The next off was P/O Duthie from Wick at 1232 hours in RL-G for an ASR patrol. He was followed from Wick an hour and a half later by F/Lt Murray in RL-T, also on an ASR patrol. Fraserburgh launched RL-B, flown by F/O Grimston, at 1409 hours to cover Dallachy Strike Wing operations. All three had been on patrol for some time when Grimston in RL-B picked up two IFF distress signals at 1523 hours. He homed onto them and found two groups of Mosquitoes, in each of which one was flying on one engine. He fell into a position to follow the second formation back to base. P/O Duthie also picked up a distress signal followed by another indicating that an aircraft was circling a dinghy in position 5754N 0310E. He turned to make for this position.

Meanwhile F/O Grimston had received a message from the formation leader of the strike force that a Mosquito had ditched. On reaching the scene a dinghy and single survivor was sighted at 1558 hours. At 1616 hours he dropped his airborne lifeboat, observed by Duthie, who was closing on the position. The lifeboat landed 200 yards to starboard and downwind of the survivor's dinghy, which was floating close to the still visible tail of the Mosquito, but the parachutes failed to release. Duthie in RL-G then swept in and dropped a second lifeboat, which dropped 50 yards from the dinghy. Once again the parachutes failed to release, although the rocket lines did fire. Grimston then attempted to drop a pair of Lindholme dinghies, one of which landed close to the survivor whilst the other failed to release.

While Grimston was busy dropping the dinghy Duthie and the circling Mosquito attempted to cut the lifeboat parachutes loose with machine-gun fire, but had no luck. The helpless Warwick and Mosquito aircrew watched as the survivor in his dinghy overtook the lifeboat, passing within 30 feet of it, but making no attempt to reach it. Duthie dropped a delayed timing marine marker before departing for base. RL-B continued to circle until a relief aircraft, RL-K arrived from Thornaby. F/Lt Ashby continued to circle over the survivor until 2155 hours when a Catalina relieved him.

While all this activity over the Mosquito survivor was taking place F/Lt Murray also picked up an IFF distress signal. Homing onto this he arrived at position 5747N 0323E to find a dinghy with a single occupant who was flashing a torch. He reported the sighting and was ordered to drop his airborne lifeboat, but before he could do so the crew lost sight of the dinghy and could not relocate it. Marine markers were dropped to mark the area before Murray set course for base.

Warwicks took up the first two days of January with a series of searches from Thornaby and Fraserburgh for the Mosquito survivor. Several empty dinghies were located, but no survivors.

By now squadron Warwicks were operating from Thornaby, Fraserburgh and Wick and many unsuccessful searches were carried out during the early days of the month, until, on the 6th, F/Lt Butt, flying Warwick RL-K, was scrambled to reports of a Spitfire pilot having baled out in position 5327N 0132E. It looked like the first success of the year, but it was not to be. On arrival at the search area Butt's crew sighted a rocket projectile but was unable to find the pilot.

That same afternoon F/Lt Carmichael was providing ASR cover for the Dallachy Strike Wing, taking off in Warwick RL-S from Fraserburgh at 1337 hours. Eleven minutes later smoke was seen inside the aircraft and Carmichael immediately turned for base. Fortunately the cause of the smoke was quickly found – the wiring beneath a radio set had fused and when the current to the radio was switched off Carmichael resumed the sortie.

F/Lt Butt and crew at Thornaby with a Warwick in background. L to
R: WO Dicky Vere, WO Pat Kelly, F/Lt Denny Butt, F/O Harry
Jackson, WO Tommy Ansell, WO Paddy Watt. (Lee Kelly)

The squadron suffered a tragic loss during a training sortie on
7 January. Warwick BV233:RL-J, captained by F/Lt H.S. Luck,
took off from Thornaby at 1050 hours to take part in a homing and
flare dropping exercise. At 1310hr two of the squadron's
Hurricanes, PZ814 and PZ829, flown by F/O Bromley and F/O
Massey, bounced it over County Durham. Luck took evasive
action, but during a second attack over Dinsdale, near
Darlington, he lost control, entering a high-speed stall, and dived
vertically into the ground from 500 feet. There were no survivors.

Losses were always tragic, but sometimes a crew could avoid
being shot down, even when they seemed to be doing their best
to attract trouble, as WOp/AG Don Mabey recalls.

*On one occasion over the North Sea I was on the wireless and
listening out. On the half-hour we received any messages from
base. We did not broadcast, by order, unless in emergency and I
received an instruction to switch off RT. I told Paddy [F/O
O'Reilly] to switch off his RT, only to be told it was 'so and so'
switched off! Three or four times more the same signal came
through with the same answer from the Skipper. The RT, being a
crystal job, couldn't be interfered with, but the Skipper told me to
have a look at it anyway. In the meantime we were told to return*

to base. This, of course, was reported to the Skipper and I went down to the RT transmitter, which seemed to be OK, however I told Paddy I would give it a '**&!!**' good kick, which I did and it appeared to be OK afterwards, because we went on to finish the job. Looking back we realized how fortunate we were, because we had been broadcasting our intercom chat nearly to Norway. How the German DF didn't pick us up we never knew.

What we did know was we were nearly charged when we returned to base for not obeying orders, and me for damaging air force property, not to mention the fact that the WAAFs on radio duty were relieved by airmen because of the lurid intercom chat! It was all forgiven though because we completed the job! From then on we were known as 'Blimey O'Reilly's Crew'.

F/Lt Murray was to have a frustrating day on 8 January. Taking off from Wick in Warwick BV413:RL-C for an ASR patrol at 1242 hours he was forced to turn round and land a few minutes later due to an over-revving starboard engine. The problem was quickly rectified and Murray was off again at 1350 hours, but, eight minutes later the mid-upper turret was found to be unserviceable. The gunner checked the hydraulic system and found a severe leak, which was flowing through the fuselage and into the airborne lifeboat below. Murray had no option but to return to base. Ted Russell recalls this incident.

The 'Blimey O'Reilly' crew at Fraserburgh in 1945. Standing, L to R: 'Taffy' Hendra 'Goldie' Goldstone, Paddy O'Reilly, 'Red' Marvin. Kneeling, L to R: Ray Cooper, Don Mabey. (D Mabey)

On 8 January 1945 our starboard engine was u/s 10 minutes after getting airborne in BV413 C Charlie and we returned to base and got airborne in BV401 T Tommy, which was the replacement aircraft. After 25 minutes we had a hydraulic leak and returned to base. The op was strike cover – maybe we were not meant to go on that one!

Squadron Warwicks provided ASR cover for the Banff Strike Wing and its escort of Mustangs from Peterhead on 9 January. At 1100 hours one of the escorting Mustangs sent out a distress call and F/Lt Moreton in Warwick RL-S attempted to home in on it, but was unable to do so as it was not equipped with IFF and the Mustang pilot did not make any VHF transmissions. Eventually Moreton was able to close to within 8 miles and

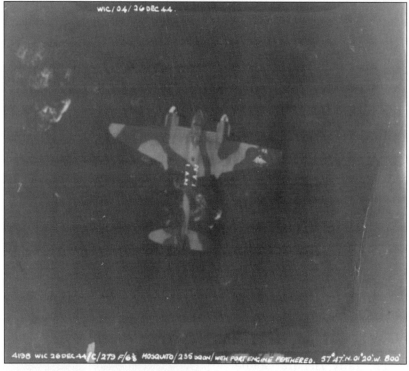

Mosquito LA-N of 235 Sqn returning from the raid on Leirvik harbour on Boxing Day 1944. The Mosquito had its port engine feathered and this remarkable photo was taken from the escorting 279 Sqn Warwick, flown by F/Lt Murray. (Blair Bartholomew)

followed it to Peterhead, where it made a safe landing.

The number of Warwick losses continued to mount. On 11 January F/Lt Moreton and his crew, in Warwick HG209:RL-B failed to return. They had taken off from Fraserburgh at 1230 hours to support strike operations by the Banff and Dallachy wings. They were last seen by a Beaufighter orbiting a ditched Mosquito in position 5813N 0630E at 1447 hours. The Beaufighter crew believed the Warwick was being chased by an Me 109. This report was followed by another Beaufighter which reported seeing an unidentified aircraft crash into the seas at 1446 hours approximately 20 miles off the Norwegian coast. That evening the squadron sent F/Lt Carmichael out in Warwick RL-F to search for Moreton and his crew but no trace was found.

Bomber Command went after the U-boat pens in Bergen on 12 January sending thirty-two Tallboy-equipped Lancasters of 9 and 617 sqns. They were escorted by Mosquitoes and Mustangs and ASR cover was provided by Warwick RL-F, flown by S/Ldr Simpson. Four of the Lancasters were lost on this raid. P/O Duthie, in Warwick RL-G was airborne from Sumburgh on an ASR search for one of them at 1443 hours. The crew sighted a patch of oil in position 5958N 0415E and as they closed on it they were greeted by the sight of an almost submerged Lancaster, with the seven-man crew standing on the fuselage.

The Lancaster was NF992 of 617 Sqn, flown by pilot Ian Ross. As he reached the target area Ross was attacked by two Focke Wulf FW 190s and two of the engines were put out of action, forcing the Lancaster to ditch. The crew braced for the ditching as the pilot made a copybook effort and another Lancaster crew observed all seven of the crew escape through the hatches onto the wing. The observing Lancaster noted that the ditched aircraft's dinghy had failed to appear from its stowage. Two more Lancasters radioed the ditched aircraft's position, setting in motion Duthie's rescue effort.

Duthie dropped his airborne lifeboat to the survivors at 1605 hours, by which time the Lancaster had sunk. The boat landed 200 yards upwind so Duthie dropped a Lindholme dinghy between it and three of the survivors who were seen to be treading water. Unfortunately this dinghy failed to inflate. After fifteen minutes of struggle one of the survivors reached and boarded the lifeboat, and the remaining six were nearing it. Duthie was unable to observe their activities any further as an enemy fighter approached from the north-east at 500 feet and he decided to turn away and make for base.

That night a Leigh light-equipped Coastal Command aircraft searched the area for signs of the survivors, but nothing was found and no radio signals were picked up, nor were any flares sighted. Three Warwicks continued the search through the daylight hours with no luck. It was hoped that the Germans had picked up the crew, but nothing more was heard of the crew until two months later when the body of the wireless operator, P/O R. Ellwood, was found in the sea on 13 March, by a fisherman near the island of Slyngen – 300 miles north in the Arctic Circle.

While the Lancasters were striking the U-boat pens the strike

F/Sgt Don Mabey at the wireless operator station of a 279 Sqn Vickers Warwick, Fraserburgh 1945. (D Mabey)

wings were also active and Warwicks RL-C, flown by WO Spargo from Wick, and RL-S captained by WO Williamson from Fraserburgh, provided ASR cover. Williamson's crew spotted red flares in position 6108N 0205E at 1725 hours and sighted two aircraft in the area. On investigation they found a dinghy in position 6100N 0203E and dropped the airborne lifeboat close to the flares. However, no more flares were seen and darkness swallowed up the dinghy and lifeboat. Williamson had attempted to drop another Lindholme dinghy on the position before it was lost in the dark but the bomb door release handle had jammed.

At 2010 hours F/Lt Carmichael was airborne from Fraserburgh in Warwick RL-E to continue searching in the area. Green flares were sighted but nothing could be seen on the surface, even with the help of a parachute flare. Searches of the area continued the following day with S/Ldr Levin-Raw in RL-T and F/Lt Garven in RL-C getting airborne from Wick. Garven's Warwick was in trouble almost immediately due to a hydraulic fault causing the undercarriage to retract fully. The crew had to pump the gear down again and landed back at Wick safely ten minutes later. Garven quickly changed aircraft and was off again in RL-G by 0845 hours to join in the search. On reaching the search area the

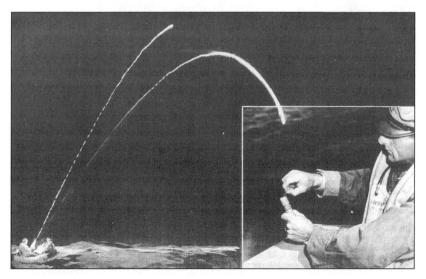

Signal flares were particularly useful in attracting the attention of searching aircraft at night. (USAAF via A McLeod)

only encounter the Warwicks had was with an HSL escorted by two Mosquitoes, no dinghies or lifeboats were seen. Four more sorties were flown searching for dinghies by the Squadron Warwick's, including a search by S/Ldr Simpson in RL-F, on the return track of the Dallachy Strike Wing's route that day for the dinghy reported on the 12th. Once again the crews had no luck.

Over the next four days many unsuccessful searches were carried out from Thornaby and the detached bases and then on 18 January the weather closed in and no sorties were flown for a week. They recommenced on the 25th with flights in support of the strike wings. The following day the weather turned with a vengeance and Lt Shanks in Warwick RL-E, who had taken off from Fraserburgh to cover the Dallachy Strike Wing was recalled in a snowstorm forty minutes after take-off. He was forced to orbit the airfield for twenty minutes before a gap in the storm allowed him to land. F/Lt Murray in Warwick RL-O was also recalled due to the weather. Once again operations came to a halt.

F/Sgt Douglas Wells and crew in front of a 279 Sqn Warwick. Rear, L to R: F/Sgt Victor Woolford RAAF, WOp/AG, F/Sgt Mike Taylor RAAF, navigator, F/Sgt Douglas Wells, pilot. Front, L to R: F/Sgt David Wylie RAAF, WOp/AG, Sgt Jack Aston, rear gunner, F/Sgt Joe Sawyer RAAF, WOp/AG. The Warwick serial number is BV3?? and the code letter may be B, P or S. No. 279 Sqn had several Warwicks with serials in the BV range including BV305, BV310, BV316 and BV392. (David Wylie)

This view of the Warwick nose is thought to have been taken at the same time as the photo of Well's crew. A very faint code letter is visible just left of centre on the nose below the turret, possibly a 'P'.
(David Wylie)

WOp/AG Don Mabey recalls the atrocious weather conditions encountered at Fraserburgh during the winter of 1944/45.

It was really grim, bitterly cold, deep snow and freezing winds. We had three attempts to take off on one occasion, being blown off course by the crosswind. We did make it eventually and I thanked God that we never had to ditch. Seeing Fraserburgh after a long trip over the North Sea to Norway and back was always a most welcome sight.

The aircrew at Fraserburgh, our crew included, went off to Dyce in lorries to collect salt, which they proceeded to lay on the runway in use so that operations could continue.

The weather was little better at Thornaby but WOp/AG F/Sgt David Wylie recalls that no flying did not mean no work for the aircrews.

In January 1945, with snow thick on the ground, the tannoy system came to life early one morning with an instruction to all personnel not on duty to get out and help clear the runway of snow.

My two Australian crewmates and I decided it was far too comfortable in bed so there we stayed. Everything was fine until the Station Warrant Officer, who was responsible for discipline, came bursting into the hut with his offsider tagging along. 'What are you men doing in bed!' he screamed. As spokesman and a smart arse to boot I said 'We Australians don't do manual labour.' I think his blood pressure must have climbed 50 points and he shouted 'You'se are all on a charge!'

The next morning the three of us fronted the CO expecting the book thrown at us but we got off relatively lightly – half a day clearing the runway and loss of a day's pay. However it flew right back in my face, for when I applied for a commission at war's end the CO said that because of the charge he couldn't recommend it.

By this stage of the war a great many of 279 Sqn's aircrew personnel were tour expired types from Bomber and Coastal Commands. Several of them were unusual characters and Don Mabey recalls a couple.

One was a rear gunner we called 'Tapper'. He had been a gunner on Bomber Command and during a fighter attack his turret had been badly shot up and his feet were badly wounded by cannon fire. After being discharged from hospital he was posted to 279 Sqn. He had springs on his special boots to enable him to walk and whilst walking he tapped his feet, hence his nickname. He was well liked and well known for the weight of his parachute bag. Why? – he carried with him a piece of armour plate steel, which just fitted the rear turret seat; this he sat on every time he flew. He said after one go he was not prepared to have his 'wedding equipment' shot off!

Another chap, also from Bomber Command, was 'Tiger' Teague. Once again a rear gunner and like 'Tapper' a warrant officer. He was shot down over France, rescued by Frenchmen and worked with the Maquis until he was repatriated.

He was the biggest scrounger and 'bullshitter' you ever met. Somehow at Fraserburgh he got in with the local laird, never would say how, but he would come back from visits with one or two lovely salmon.

During this period the Warwick crew stood many standbys waiting for the inevitable scramble to search for a ditched crew. David Wylie recalls the routine at Thornaby.

This Warwick seen crash landing may be RL-T flown by F/L Butt, which crash-landed on 8 February 1945. It lost an engine just after take-off and did one circuit of the base at very low level, before crash landing and catching fire. (David Wylie)

Once or twice a week the crews at Thornaby were rostered to man the 'Standby Hut', which was located near the dispersal area. The idea was that when the operations room received a call that required some action the standby crew was supposed to be airborne within three minutes. Warwick's were notoriously hard to start when cold so the ground crew had to start the engines every half hour or so throughout the day. It wasn't a real chore to spend the day in the standby hut as it was warm and comfortable and there were plenty of games and a small, well worn, pool table.

Sorties recommenced on the 29th with F/O Grimston getting airborne from Fraserburgh, flying Warwick RL-E, in the early hours of the morning. Grimston was tasked with searching for two dinghies from a pair of Dallachy Beaufighters which were reported overdue. A search was carried out parallel to the Norwegian coast but nothing was found. Then, on the return trip, the crew sighted three red flares fired in quick succession in position 5831N 0119E. Grimston circled the area until daylight with his navigation lights on and dropping flares to illuminate the scene. Four marine markers were also dropped, but after an extensive search, and having reached the limit of his endurance, Grimston was forced to turn for home. S/Ldr Levin-Raw took his place on the search, getting airborne from Wick in Warwick RL-O at 0905 hours. Levin-Raw had no more success than Grimston.

F/O Elliot and crew in Warwick BV358:RL-H had an altogether more exciting sortie. They were airborne from Wick at 1401 hours to provide ASR cover for a Dallachy Rover patrol, which went off without incident; however, on returning to Wick the Warwick crashed, luckily with no injuries to the crew.

Once again the weather closed in and there were no sorties for the next three days. The bad weather continued in February, stopping any operational sorties from being flown for almost one third of the month. The squadron managed forty-four sorties, five of them being flown by the newly introduced Hurricanes. The Warwick crews had a change of environment for the next successful search and rescue. Rather than finding their survivors floating in a dinghy they were found on land in Caithness. Warwicks O/279 and G/279, captained by S/Ldr Levin-Raw and F/Lt Elliot respectively, were launched from Wick to search for the crew of a missing Fortress on 2 February. The Fortress, FL455, had gone missing the previous day and had crashed near Westerdale, killing four of the crew and injuring two others who died later. The remaining three crew members were unhurt. The aircraft was sighted by F/Lt Elliot's crew at 1025 hours in position 5823N 0327W with three survivors visible, walking around the wreckage. Elliot's wireless operator sent out a sighting report, which was intercepted by Levin-Raw, who made for the scene. F/Lt Elliot located the nearest farmhouse and dropped a message container asking for assistance and then returned to circle the Fortress. Shortly afterward two men were sighted approaching the wreckage from another farm and Elliot dropped a message to the survivors to the effect that help was on the way. Meanwhile, Levin-Raw had arrived and dropped a first-aid kit pack, chocolate and cigarettes. Shortly afterward a Dominie arrived on the scene and a Hudson appeared and dropped supplies near the wreckage.

The winter weather continued to play its part in frustrating searches, and on the 7th it hampered the search for a missing Hudson crew. Warwicks O/279 from Wick, piloted by F/O Elliot and R/279 from Fraserburgh, captained by Lt Shanks, were both airborne that morning to search for the missing crew. Elliot was forced to return to Wick due to the extremely poor visibility in his search area, but Shanks was able to search on. His rear gunner reported seeing a yellow, unevenly shaped, object in the sea, which was believed to be a dinghy with a person on board. Unfortunately in the rough seas, low cloud and showers, it was lost and not relocated. Later in the day P/O Bolton continued the search from Wick, as did WO Palmer from Fraserburgh, but with no success.

Whilst the detached crews at Wick and Fraserburgh were busy supporting the Banff and Dallachy Strike Wing operations, those crews remaining at Thornaby were equally busy. A major search for a missing Mustang pilot commenced on the 7th when F/Lt Burgess in B/279 got airborne in the late afternoon. The pilot had been reported to have baled out 10 miles north-east of Filey Bay and the search was concentrated in the bay. B/279 carried out a search of the area and observed a rescue launch and a lifeboat making for the area too, but the pilot was not found. On return to Thornaby Burgess discovered that he had failed to receive radio instructions to remain in the search area, so twenty minutes later B/279 was airborne again to return to the search. The bay was covered three times in the darkness and Burgess dropped eight flame floats to help illuminate the area, but still nothing was found.

At 0849 hours on the 8th Warwick B/279 lifted off from Thornaby once more, this time with F/Sgt Wells at the controls. On reaching the area Wells found several surface vessels, a Mosquito, a Wellington and two Hurricanes searching the area. The Hurricanes were B/279 and C/279 from Thornaby. Flown by F/O Gill and F/O Coppack, they were making their debut operational sorties with the squadron. The missing Mustang pilot was not found.

Serviceability problems continued to plague the Warwicks and were highlighted by those encountered by two aircraft operating from Wick on the 8th providing ASR cover to anti-shipping sorties that day. F/Lt Murray in P/279 and F/Lt Butt in T/279 were airborne that morning to cover the operation. About an hour after take-off Murray, who had also been tasked with continuing the search for the missing Hudson from the previous day, had problems with his rear turret. He decided to continue with the search, hoping to use cloud cover, but when no cloud was found he abandoned the search and made for the area of the anti-shipping operation. Flying the Warwick was not made any easier by the fact that the throttles began to give trouble and had to be held in position for the remainder of the sortie. F/Lt Butt meanwhile had some compass trouble, which caused him too to abandon the sortie. On returning to Wick the undercarriage collapsed on landing, luckily with no injuries to the crew.

Sighting a U-boat was rare for Coastal Command crews, never mind ASR crews, but F/O O'Reilly's crew did just that on 15 February, as Don Mabey recalls.

> *Covering a Beaufighter strike off Norway, I was on the radar and picked up a signal which I first reported as whales, but as the signal remained constant, I suggested we had a look at it. A blip from a single whale was intermittent. Getting nearer we discovered that it was a U-boat below the surface using its Snorkel. Having no bombs or depth charges, only our lifeboat and Lindholmes, we dived on it, but before we could use our guns it went down very steeply. The sighting was, of course, reported to base immediately the U-boat was spotted.*

F/Lt Butt seemed to have poor luck with his aircraft around this period. On 21 February he was airborne on a sortie in Warwick C/279, covering anti-shipping operations off the Norwegian coast, when a fuel cover came loose and jammed the starboard aileron. Despite this handicap he skilfully flew back to a safe landing at Wick.

F/Lt Burgess was scrambled from Thornaby at 2328 hours on the 22nd to search for a Wellington which had been sending out SOS signals. It was believed to have ditched in position 5527N 0010W, but despite searching for an hour nothing was found.

Two days later two of the squadron Hurricanes carried out another search from Thornaby. A/279, F/O Fer, and B/279, F/O Gill, were airborne at 1455 hours on a training sortie when they were diverted to a position 18 miles east of Berwick to search for a ditched Spitfire pilot. On arrival in the search area they found a Beaufighter whose crew informed them that they had sighted then lost an object in the water, possibly a dinghy. The Hurricanes remained in the area for several hours, but had no more luck than the Beaufighter. Warwick B/279, flown by WO Williamson was also tasked to assist and got airborne at 1554 hours. Reaching the

| 279 SQDN DET FRASERBURGH. | | | | | | Time carried forward | 447.30 | 45.00 |
Date	Hour	Aircraft Type and No.	Pilot	Duty	Remarks (including results of bombing, gunnery, exercises, etc.)		Day	Night
		WARWICK.						
4.2.45	12.25	R.RL.	F/o O'REILLY.	WOP/AIR.	PHOTOGRAPHY WITH MOSQUITOES.		3.00	
7.2.45	16.00	R.RL.	F/O GRIMSTONE	WOP/AIR.	TRANSIT TO BANFF.		0.20	
7.2.45	15.00	A.RL.	F/O O'REILLY.	WOP/AIR.	BANFF TO BASE.		0.20	
10.2.45	10.20	R.RL	F/O O'REILLY.	WOP/AIR.	ASR. PATROL OFF NORWAY. R.T.B. WEATHER.		3.30	
12.2.45	13.05	S.RL	F/O O'REILLY.	WOP/AIR.	ASR. PATROL COVERING MOSQUITO STRIKE OFF NORWEGIAN COAST. LANDED DALLACHY.		5.40	
13.2.45	11.45	S.RL.	F/o O'REILLY.	WOP/AIR.	DALLACHY TO BASE.		0.30	
15.2.45	12.25	R.RL.	F/O O'REILLY	WOP/AIR.	A.S.R. PATROL COVERING BEAUFIGHTER STRIKE OFF NORWAY. SIGHTED & REPORTED U-BOAT SCHNORKEL. WHICH CRASH-DIVED.		5.30	
20.2.45	11.40	F.RL.	F/O O'REILLY.	WOP, AIR.	TRANSIT - BASE TO SCATSTA.		1.20	
23.2.45	10.30	F.RL.	F/O O'REILLY.	WOP/AIR.	TRANSIT - SCATSTA TO BASE.		1.30	
27.2.45	10.10	M.RL.	F/O O'REILLY.	WOP/AIR.	PRACTICE QGH - WALTER & VHF HOMING.		1.30	

SUMMARY FOR FEBRUARY 1945   UNIT 279. SQDN.
SIGNATURE D.Mabey F/S. DATE 28:2:1945.
TOTAL TIME FLOWN —
TYPE OF A/c FLOWN WARWICK.
CERTIFIED CORRECT. O.C DET. S/L
NON-OPS - 8.30
OPS. 14.40

TOTAL TIME ... 442.10 | 45.00

Don Mabey's logbook for February 1945 records the U-boat sighting on the 15th. (D Mabey)

search area they found Fer and Gill in their Hurricanes, two Beaufighters and a rescue launch all searching. Williamson also saw nothing of the Spitfire or its unfortunate pilot.

For many Germans the writing was now clearly on the wall and it was not unknown for troops to surrender or defect during the last months of the war. Whilst based at Fraserburgh, Don Mabey recalls, there was one incident which caused quite a stir.

One incident I remember at Fraserburgh was a Ju 88 coming straight in over the sea. He landed immediately, taxied to the end of the runway and exited the aircraft only to be held up by the controller from the caravan with his Very pistol. The pilot had had enough and gave himself up. He was taken to the Officers' Mess and given a hearty welcome.

We were allowed to have a good look at the Ju 88 and were quite shocked to see the condition it was in. The tyres were threadbare and the Perspex around the cockpit and also the fuselage had been patched in places. Obviously it had well and truly been peppered at some stage in air combat.

On 27 February F/Lt Carmichael in Warwick D/279 and F/Sgt Grady, flying Hurricane G/279 on the type's first operational sortie from Fraserburgh, carried out a search between Buchan Ness and Rattray Head for a crashed Dallachy Strike Wing Beaufighter. They were advised at 1314 hours that the aircraft had been found crashed on land in position 5734N 0250W, but continued the search for the pilot in the sea in conjunction with an HSL without result. The following day Warwicks D/279 and F/279, S/Ldr Simpson and Lt Shanks, continued the search and covered all the beaches and inlets in the hope that the pilot had made it to shore, but again had no success.

March saw an increase in the sortie rate and although the majority were searches and cover for the strike wings the squadron still found itself tasked to support ASR cover for returning US and Bomber Command forces in the 16 Group area of responsibility on seven occasions.

It found its services 'not required' during another successful rescue, however. On 3 March when F/Lt Hanson-Lester took off from Thornaby in Warwick V/279 to search for an aircraft, reported as a Beaufighter, crashed off St Abbs Head. He arrived to find two HSLs, two RNLI lifeboats, four Beaufighters and a Mosquito all searching already. The Beaufighter crew reported that three survivors had already been picked up and taken to port and that there might be further survivors in the water. The incident was unusual in that the Beaufighter, KV976 of No. 54 OTU had four crew on board. During the flight the aircraft's gyros and altitude indicator (AI) failed at 500 feet and the pilot lost control turning the Beaufighter upside down before crashing into the sea 3 miles north of Berwick. The two pilots, WO P.J. O'Malley and F/O J.A. Paterson escaped with shock and slight injuries. The two navigators on board, F/O F.E. Larkman and F/Sgt R.M. Wedgewood were not so fortunate, both being killed. Hanson-Lester carried out a search and found oil and wreckage 3 miles off Burnmouth, which he circled for an hour dropping marine markers. An HSL was guided to the spot and a Mae West was sighted 400 yards south of the marine markers. The HSL approached the survivor, P/O F.E. Larkman, and he was picked up and given immediate first aid. Hanson-Lester turned the Warwick for home and on the way back began to suspect a problem with his engines, but it turned out to be faulty instruments.

The next day a 38 Group Halifax went missing and the squadron was tasked to search for the crew. F/O O'Reilly got airborne from Fraserburgh at 0845 hours in Warwick D/279, making his way to the search area. At 1040 hours a dinghy with three survivors was sighted in position 5632N 0532E. The men were not well equipped to survive in the icy conditions of the North Sea in March, wearing only battledress. As the Warwick approached they waved a yellow flag and O'Reilly dropped an airborne lifeboat to them, which landed 150 feet upwind. It did not drift onto the dinghy, however, and the survivors made no attempt to reach it before it began to drift rapidly away. Thirty minutes later three Halifaxes arrived on the scene and five minutes later two Lindholme dinghies, one of which failed to open, were dropped to the survivors. The second Lindholme also drifted away.

A second Warwick arrived to assist at 1345 hours. This was Y/279 from Thornaby flown by S/Ldr Burge. It dropped a second airborne lifeboat at 1417 hours, which landed 300 yards downwind of the dinghy, but unfortunately one of the parachutes remained attached for twenty minutes before detaching and, once again, the lifeboat drifted away. At 1545 hours contact was lost with the dinghy containing the survivors in the rough seas. Burge, now short of fuel, was forced to head for Thornaby, O'Reilly having left some time before. Warwick K/279, captained by WO Williamson, was airborne from Thornaby at 1440 hours to relieve the others and at 1709 hours the dinghy and two airborne lifeboats were sighted. The dinghy was by now observed to contain only one, apparently lifeless, body lying in the bottom. Williamson remained in the area until 1838 hours when he set course for base, only to be diverted to Acklington in the steadily worsening weather. The search to relocate the

279. SQDN. DET. FRASERBURGH.					Time carried forward :—	442·10	45·00.
Date	Hour	Aircraft Type and No.	Pilot	Duty	Remarks (including results of bombing, gunnery, exercises, etc.)	Flying Times Day	Night
4·3·45	0845	WARWICK. D·R·	F.O. O'REILLY	W.OP/AIR.	A.S.R. SEARCH FOR HALIFAX CREW OFF DENMARK. DINGHY FOUND WITH THREE SURVIVORS. DROPPED A/B LIFEBOAT AND TWO LINDHOLMES. - REMAINED ORBITTING AREA UNTIL RELIEVED.　*	7·25	

Don Mabey's logbook entry recording the search for the 38 Group Halifax crew on 4 March 1945. (D Mabey)

survivors was continued by Warwick V/279 flown by F/Lt Ashby, who took off from Thornaby at 1705 hours. Although a radar contact was found in the area, which faded quickly, no sign of either dinghies or lifeboats was found.

The search continued on the 5th with the squadron making a major effort to locate and rescue the Halifax crew. Four aircraft from Thornaby and one from Fraserburgh took part. H/279 and Y/279 were first off at 0450 hours and 0641 hours respectively but searched without success. F/O Grimston was next away in Warwick E/279 at 1100 hours from Fraserburgh, but he found only two empty airborne lifeboats. The final attempt was made by WO Williamson in K/279, who took off from Thornaby at 1456 hours, but was back at base less than an hour later due to the rapidly deteriorating weather. F/Sgt Wells in RL-V developed engine trouble and was forced to jettison his airborne lifeboat and pyrotechnics before turning for home. Australian David Wylie was the WOp/AG on F/Sgt Wells Warwick crew and recalls this sortie.

> *We were on our way to search for a ditched aircraft in the North Sea and our starboard engine cut out completely. As we were at very low level at the time it was necessary to reduce weight quickly so the skipper dropped the lifeboat, but this was not enough so he told us to toss out flares, ammunition belts and everything that wasn't nailed down. We got back to Thornaby without further incident. The CO was not happy about the equipment we lost!*

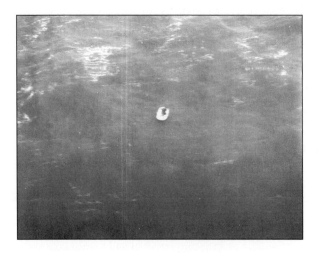

Two survivors from the ditched 38 Group Halifax found on 4 March 1945. (D Mabey)

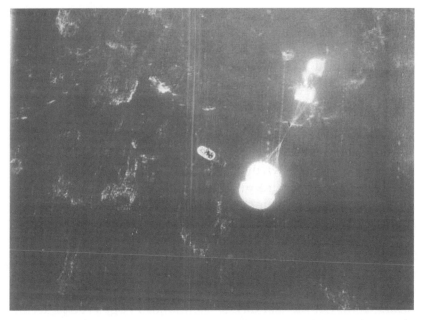

The Halifax survivors, still in their dinghy, next to the parachutes of the airborne lifeboat which had broken up. (D Mabey)

Several searches were made on the 8th and 9th for a dinghy from a ditched bomber and F/Sgt Wells in Y/279, taking part in the second day's search, had a difficult sortie once more. The Warwick's starboard engine cut out twice and he decided to turn for home. On the homeward leg the engine cut out three more times and a distress message was sent out. The 'Expound' radar station made contact with him and vectored him to a rendezvous with one of the squadron's Hurricanes, H/279 flown by F/O Massey, who shepherded him to a safe landing at base. F/Sgt Wylie recalls this sortie. 'The engine failure on 9th March I remember because I sent the "SOS" signal, which was the second in my short career, the first being on a night navigation exercise out of OTU Turnberry. The same old problem – engine failure'.

Several uneventful ASR cover sorties were flown over the next few days in support of the strike wings and several searches were also completed, with nothing to report. Then, on 14 March a Sunderland, DP178:B-A, on a training sortie from Alness, went missing. The next day WO Palmer was first away to commence a search in D/279 at 0711 hours from Fraserburgh, followed by

F/O Coppack in Hurricane G/279, covering the area of the Moray Firth out to Tarbet Ness. Neither aircraft had any success. Warwicks E/279 and F/279 were next away, flown by F/Lt Carmichael and F/Sgt Wood. At 1440 hours Carmichael's crew sighted the wreckage of a partially submerged aircraft, but unfortunately it was lost during a turn and could not be located. The rear gunner of F/279 also caught a fleeting glimpse of the wreckage in position 5945N 0020W.

The next day a Liberator of the 567th BS ditched and Warwick's K/279 and B/279, flown by W/Cdr Cox and F/Sgt Wells, carried out the search for it. Unfortunately the search area was covered in sea fog, severely hampering their efforts, and nothing was found.

The routine of searches and ASR cover for the strike wings continued throughout March, with little to break the monotony. One break from the norm was an unsuccessful search for a missing fishing boat by F/Lt Shanks operating from Fraserburgh on the 28th. On the last day of the month F/Sgt Woods, flying Warwick F/279, was covering the Banff Strike Wing and its Mustang escort in company with S/Ldr Simpson in D/279. Just over an hour into the sortie Woods' port engine failed and he turned for base. Simpson asked if he required assistance, but Woods declined any help. On learning of F/279's problem F/O Coppack was dispatched from Fraserburgh in Hurricane D/279 to escort the limping Warwick home. In the meantime Woods had jettisoned his airborne lifeboat and the crew threw out all the ammunition and pyrotechnics to lighten the aircraft. The Hurricane met the Warwick and escorted it back to Banff, where Woods made a safe single-engined landing.

Operations began in April with an uneventful ASR cover for the Banff Strike Wing on the 2nd, followed by an unsuccessful search from midday to midnight on the 3rd by Warwicks from Wick and Fraserburgh for a missing Catalina. Amongst the searchers were F/Sgt Wells and crew, who had flown up to Wick from Thornaby. F/Sgt Wyllie, the WOp/AG remembers the search.

Bad weather was one of the worst problems confronting the squadron. You couldn't choose not to fly because there was a storm blowing in – if there was a kite in the drink you had to go and look for it. One day we flew to Wick, had a meal while the Warwick was

*being refuelled, and then flew out into the Arctic Circle to look for
a ditched Catalina. The weather was foul. Icy cold, a cloud base of
less than 1,000 feet and very, very dark. We saw nothing and
neither the plane nor a dinghy could have survived in those
tumultuous seas. It was not a happy experience!*

The Dallachy Strike Wing and its escorting Mustangs were also
given ASR cover on the 3rd by Warwicks E/279 and Z/279 flown
by S/Ldr Simpson and F/Lt Carmichael. At 1906 hours in
position 5800N 0450E they intercepted a message from one of the
strike Beaufighters that another aircraft had ditched. Homing to
the Beaufighter IFF they reached the scene only to find aircraft
wreckage, an empty, upturned dinghy and no sign of life. The
Beaufighter was asked to sink the dinghy and the Warwicks
returned to ASR cover for the returning wing.

On 5 April four of the squadron's Hurricanes, two each from
Wick and Fraserburgh, set out to search the area around
Duncansby Head for a ditched Halifax. The Fraserburgh pair,
C/279 flown by F/O Coppack and D/279 flown by F/Sgt Grady,
were vectored to a point 10 miles off Tarbet Ness, where a
Dominie was circling wreckage in the water. They remained on

The Beaufighters of the strike wings and their Mustang escorts were
frequent customers of the ASR Warwicks of No. 279 Sqn. This pair is
Beaufighter P6-S of 489 Sqn RNZAF based at Banff and PK coded
Mustang of No. 315 (Polish) Sqn. (via A Rodgers)

station until relieved by Warwicks G/279 and Y/279 from Wick. The Warwicks located two bodies, a parachute and numerous pieces of debris, which were later retrieved by HSL Seagull 19. The Warwick crews continued to search for survivors until fuel shortage forced their return to Wick. Another search was carried out that day for a missing Mustang pilot in the North Sea by F/O O'Reilly in Warwick RL-Z.

The next week was the usual mix of ASR cover and searches. Many of the strike wing operations resulting in the Warwick's escorting crippled Mosquitoes, Beaufighters and Mustangs safely back to base. Then, on 14 April, S/Ldr Levin-Raw was providing ASR cover to the Dallachy Strike Wing in Warwick G/279 from Wick, as they struck at shipping off the Norwegian coast, when he received a message from a strike aircraft that it was circling a dinghy with two survivors on board in position 5810N 0530E. Levin-Raw made his way to the position and dropped an airborne lifeboat, which landed about 30 yards upwind of the dinghy. Though it had landed in an almost perfect position, however, it had descended on only three parachutes, the rest failing to open, and on landing the parachutes failed to release,

A fine portrait of Warwick ASR Mk I BV403 carrying an airborne lifeboat. BV403 served with the A&AEE for initial service trials and is representative of the many Warwicks operated by 279 Sqn. (Via A Rodgers)

Whilst operating from bases in the north of Scotland crews carried a silk cloth in a celluloid packet with the Union Flag and instructions in English and Russian marked on it in the event of having to ditch and being picked up by Russian vessels. (D Mabey)

Я англичанин

" Ya Anglicháhnin " *(Pronounced as spelt)*

Пожалуйста сообщите сведения обо мне в Британскую Военную Миссию в Москве

Please communicate my particulars to British Military Mission Moscow

dragging the lifeboat 200 yards away from the survivors in the dinghy. In quick succession, as darkness approached, Levin-Raw dropped two Lindholme dinghies and marine markers to mark the position set for two, four and six hours respectively. The Warwick circled the survivors, who appeared to be well, until fuel forced a return to Fraserburgh, the weather being unfit for landing at Wick.

The relieving Warwick, V/279 flown by F/Lt Ashby from Thornaby, arrived on scene and sighted the marine markers dropped by Levin-Raw at 2127 hours. Ashby dropped three more markers, the last of which landed very close to the dinghy, whose occupants had been firing pyrotechnics. Using the marine marker as an aiming point he dropped the airborne lifeboat and this time the gear operated correctly. Dropping another marine marker set to ignite a few hours later Ashby circled the dinghy before setting course for base. On the way back the starboard engine failed and

Ashby sent out an SOS. Twenty minutes later he cancelled this and landed safely at Thornaby ten minutes later.

The search to relocate the dinghy resumed the next afternoon when Warwick U/279 took off from Wick escorted by four Beaufighters. At 1735 hours they sighted an empty lifeboat and a partially deflated Lindholme. They also found an empty dinghy, but no survivors. At this point German fighters put in a rare appearance. The Beaufighters sighted four Me 109s and instructed P/O Bolton to run for cover and return to base, which he duly did, landing at 2034 hours.

The remainder of April was taken up with the usual round of searches and ASR cover interspersed with requests to cover crippled aircraft returning from strikes, all of which made safe havens in various states of repair. The Warwicks continued to have their share of engine problems and several returned to their bases from sorties on one engine including F/O O'Reilly in Warwick RL-E, which returned to Fraserburgh with engine trouble whilst covering a Beaufighter strike in the Skaggerak on the 26th.

CHAPTER EIGHT

May – October 1945

In May 1945 the German resistance was rapidly collapsing and the Strike Wings of Coastal Command were able to range far and wide in the search for targets. Ably supported by Mustang escort fighters they began to attack shipping in the Baltic and, as always, 279 Sqn was there to provide ASR cover. On 3 May the Dallachy Strike Wing made the long flight to Kiel to hit shipping in the area. Three of the Warwicks covered this raid, S/279, M/279 and A/279. F/Lt Ashby in S/279 intercepted a message from the strike force that one of the escorting Mustangs, callsign 'Presto Yellow 4' was in trouble and making for a landfall. Ashby's crew quickly worked out an estimated position and attempted to rendezvous with it but they were unsuccessful. While Ashby was trying to find the Mustang, Hurricane F/279 flown by F/Sgt Jewitt was launched from Thornaby in an attempt to intercept and escort the damaged fighter home. Like Ashby, Jewitt had no luck. Twenty minutes after he had left Thornaby WO Lintott lifted Warwick V/279 off and headed out to the last known position of the Mustang. At 2019 hours his crew sighted a dinghy with the pilot on board and just over five minutes later began homing a searching HSL to it. The HSL picked up the pilot, F/O Lucas of No. 65 Sqn, twenty minutes later.

While this frantic activity was taking place Warwicks A/279 and M/279 continued to provide cover for the Beaufighters and escort Mustangs. At 1946 hours A/279, flown by F/Lt Burgess picked up a distress message form one of the Beaufighters.

Warwick BV301 is an ASR Stage A version. This version had a
modified bomb bay and bomb-bay doors to enable it to carry two sets
of Lindholme gear and a Mk I lifeboat. (Via A Rodgers)

Burgess requested the position and then learned that it had an
engine on fire and was about to ditch. He altered course to search
around 5432N 0551E and his W/Op sent out a message,
'Searching for Beaufighter. Need assistance. Rooster [IFF] on.'
F/O Price in Warwick M/279 responded and joined A/279 in the
search. M/279 dropped marine markers around the position for
some time, but had no success in finding the ditched aircraft. At
2056 hours Warwick Q/279 lifted from Thornaby to continue the
search, but only succeeded in finding numerous fishing vessels
and the delayed marine markers dropped by M/279. F/O
Clasper eventually returned to Thornaby at 0214 hours after a
fruitless five-hour search.

The search continued the following day with F/Lt Burgess
getting airborne from Thornaby in A/279 at 1253 hours. He
completed six search legs, each 53 miles long, before being forced
to return to Thornaby with an unserviceable intercom and VHF
radio. Within a few minutes of him taking off, a further three
Warwicks, V/279, J/279 and Q/279, were also airborne to assist
in the search. Each completed ten search legs with no luck. In
addition to the large force of aircraft from Thornaby, S/Ldr
Levin-Raw from Wick was tasked to search in Y/279, but like the
others he found no trace of the hapless Beaufighter crew. The
search continued into the night with F/O Price in Warwick
M/279 but until 0343 hours on the 5th with no success. In the
early afternoon of the 5th the squadron launched another four
aircraft to continue the search, followed on the 6th by sorties by
W/Cdr Cox in Q/279 and F/O Price in L/279. None was
successful. W/Cdr Cox, landing back at Thornaby at 1607 hours

completed the Squadron's last operational sortie of the war in Europe, which ended two days later.

F/Lt 'Squibs' Pinnell's crew arrived on posting to the squadron at Thornaby in May 1945 from Turnberry in Scotland and carried out their first operational flight on 5 May. WOp/AG F/Sgt Bob McGill recalls their first sortie.

On 30th April 1945, as the Russian Army encircled Berlin, Hitler committed suicide in his bunker. The people of Occupied Europe realised that WW2 was coming to an end and started to take advantage of the loosening of German control of their countries. Thus, the Danish fishermen who, during the occupation, had been banned from their traditional fishing grounds in the North Sea, prepared to go to sea and then set sail. The movement of the Danish fishing fleet was noted by the Allies, who realised that there was a danger of the fleet entering the minefields, with the resultant loss of vessels and lives.

On 5th May 1945 I was a member of the crew of a Warwick aircraft of 279 Sqn based at Thornaby and we were briefed to fly towards the Danish coast and intercept the Danish fleet. When intercepted we were to guide, by use of our radio, an RAF HSL to the fleet. The launch would be carrying staff and would be able to advise the fishermen of areas to avoid.

We located the fishing boats and by using our radio 'homed' the HSL to a position where it could communicate with the fleet. On completion of our task we flew over some Danish coastal villages where I remember the lines of washing and the people waving excitedly to us as they celebrated the prospect of the end of WW2. After some six hours we landed back at RAF Thornaby.

The end of the war in Europe did not, however, bring an end to the squadron's operational activity. With the occupation of Germany, the repatriation of prisoners of war, constant movement of squadrons to and from the UK, and the reoccupation of territories such as Norway, as well as the constant flow of aircraft and crews to the Far East in the continuing struggle against the Japanese, it would be kept busy in the search for missing crews.

The first operational sorties after the German surrender came on 10 May. F/Sgt Wells got airborne from Thornaby in Warwick A/279 to intercept a bomber which had sent out a distress message in position 5434N 0345E. Getting off at 1046 hours the

F/Lt 'Squibs' Pinnell and crew at Thornaby in May 1945. Rear L to R:
WOp/AG George Kaufman, WOp/AG Bob McGill, WOp/AG Len
Cockerill. Front L to R: Navigator 'Sixty' Hill, Pilot 'Squibs' Pinnell,
AG Mark Goddard. (RS McGill)

crew picked up another distress indication from IFF at 1119
hours. At 1155 hours the radar operator plotted the distressed
bomber overland and it was not until over an hour later that Wells
was informed that it had landed safely.

The second sortie of the day was by WO Lintott in V/279 from
Thornaby to search for a dinghy in position 5428N 0050E.
Arriving at the position, he discovered a Halifax circling the
survivors. Radioing for instructions he was ordered to remain
with the dinghy and to home an HSL to the location. He was also
told to drop his airborne lifeboat if this became necessary.
Lintott's W/Op was successful in raising an HSL and it was
homed to the seven survivors, who were picked up at 1953 hours,
three hours after Lintott had lifted from Thornaby.

From 11 May the squadron became involved in a major search
for three Stirlings which had gone missing. Two were from
No. 190 Sqn at Great Dunmow, and were involved in the move
of troops to Norway in Operation Doomsday. Stirling Mk IV
LK297:L9-G was flown by S/Ldr D.R. Robertson DFC CG RCAF.

It was carrying AVM Sir James Rowland Scarlett-Streatfield CBE CDG of No. 38 Group. Also on board were a Norwegian liaison officer and sixteen paratroopers. All, including the five crew, were killed when the Stirling crashed in Norway.

The second loss was Mk IV LJ899, also from Great Dunmow. The aircraft was brought down in an emergency landing on a lake in Norway. The crew all survived but four troops being carried were killed. The third loss was Mk IV LK147:ZO-Q of 196 Sqn, which crashed just short of the runway at Gardermoen, killing the six crew and thirteen troops on board.

At the time the ASR crews were scrambled this information was not known. The first Warwick airborne was L/279 from Thornaby, flown by F/Lt Pinnell, followed a few minutes later by X/280 flown by F/Lt Burgess, operating from Beccles. Pinnell followed the track of the Stirlings from Cromer to Kristiansand, but all that was found was a floating red aircraft ladder and some pieces of fabric wreckage. Pinnell circled the wreckage three times in the hope of locating survivors but nothing was seen. The WOp/AG on F/Lt Pinnell's crew, F/Sgt Bob McGill shed some light on the reasons for the massive search for these missing aircraft.

During the last weeks of World War 2, Hitler, in his Berlin bunker, contemplated the idea of going to Norway for a last desperate stand. This could have prolonged the war for several weeks or months. The existence of 'Milorg', the best organised and armed underground army in German occupied Europe (with the exception of Yugoslavia) must have thwarted this notion, just as it persuaded General Von Falkenhorst to capitulate on 8th May 1945, even though his troops with heavy artillery and tanks, and with a fairly strong air force, outnumbered by ten times the armed Norwegian patriots.

It will be realised that Norway was the only occupied country in western Europe which liberated itself from the Nazi invaders. In addition to over 400,000 men in the German forces there were 85,000 Russian, 2,000 Yugoslav and 4,000 British, Danish, French and Belgian POWs. The Germans in Norway had established 12 fortresses – Alta, Bergen, Bodde, Gossen, Harstad, Kjevtik, Kristiansand, Lakselv, Lista, Narvik, Orlan Det and Stavanger.

'Operation Doomsday' was organised to assist 'Milorg' in

dealing with the capitulating Germans and a maximum effort was asked for to carry the 1st Airborne Division to Gardermoen airfield in southern Norway. Twenty-five aircraft of No. 38 Group were detailed, of which only one did not take off. Unfortunately, there was a front lying across the North Sea and Norway covering Gardermoen, consequently successes were low, only 15 aircraft landed. The remaining aircraft were either diverted to various continental or UK airfields. At least two Stirling aircraft (possibly three) crashed. The crashed aircraft were from No. 190 Sqn at RAF Great Dunmow.

On 11th May 1945 I was a crewmember of Warwick 'L' of 279 Sqn, RAF Thornaby, briefed to cover the track of three missing Stirlings from Cromer to Kristiansand. Before setting course from Cromer lighthouse we refuelled at RAF Beccles.

At 1430 hours in position 5518N 0515E a red aircraft ladder and two small pieces of aircraft fabric were seen. 'L' circled three times – no survivors were seen. We were subsequently told that the wreckage had nothing to do with the missing Stirlings, which had crashed in Scandinavia. Stirling LJ899, flown by F/O Atkinson, ditched in Sweden owing to technical trouble. S/Ldr Robertson, flying Stirling LK566, crashed in Norway. Eleven lives were lost in these incidents. The third missing Stirling may have been LK297, for which our search was carried out on 11th May.

It is interesting to note that Stirling LK566 carried a crew of three Canadian officers and AVM Scarlett-Streatfield as second pilot. The AVM was the AOC No. 38 Gp. At briefing we were told that a senior Norwegian officer was a passenger in this aircraft. As we were briefed to search for three missing Stirlings I now assume

Vickers Warwick ASR Mk VI, believed to be HG173 coded RL-P of 279 Sqn in 1945. (R.S. McGill)

that at 0600 hours on 11th May 1945 news that one had crashed in Norway (killing all on board) and one in Sweden had not reached Thornaby, thus my conclusion that we were really only looking for one of the three missing aircraft. We had been told that these aircraft took off for Gardermoen on 10th May and this is confirmed by the operations record book of No. 38 Gp, which gives the start of 'Doomsday' as 10th May 1945, whilst No. 190 Sqn's ORB gives 9th may 1945 – one must assume that in these hectic days after VE Day not all records were entirely accurate.

The following day the search effort was increased with Warwicks F/279 and Z/279 getting airborne at 0338 hours from Fraserburgh to search, with no success. They were followed by four Warwicks, Y, V, W and J/279 flown by S/Ldr Levin-Raw, F/Lt Stevens, F/Lt Butt and F/Sgt Wells, airborne from Thornaby just after lunchtime. Despite flying eighteen 25 mile legs they also found no trace of the Stirling crews. At 1954 hours F/O Price in Warwick L/279 took over the search again with no luck.

While the search for the missing Stirlings was being carried out on the 12th another search commenced for a missing Sunderland with Warwick G/279, commanded by P/O Bolton, lifting from Wick at 1045 hours to head for position 6201N 0649W. *En route* Bolton was passed a new position of 6108N 0844W and made for that, finding the Sunderland down on the sea with the eleven crew standing on the wing. Bolton circled until an approaching fishing vessel was within 800 yards of the survivors. Three hours later Warwick X/279, also took off from Wick to assist. F/Lt Elliot arrived to find the Sunderland crew on board the trawler, which was attempting to take the Sunderland under tow. Shortly afterwards a Catalina arrived and Elliot turned for base.

The search to locate the missing Stirling crews had not yet been abandoned and WO Lintott was airborne from Thornaby at 0123 hours in J/279 searching in very poor weather with visibility of only 400 yards. At 0342 hours on the 13th Lt Shanks lifted Warwick F/279 off the Fraserburgh runway to search off the Danish coast. Five hours later S/Ldr Simpson took off from Fraserburgh in Z/279 to relieve Shanks, who had been unsuccessful in his search. Simpson was airborne for five and a half hours in very poor weather searching for dinghies, but had no more luck than his predecessors. By now the chances of finding survivors were slipping away and a major effort to locate them was launched with a force of Mosquitoes and Mustangs searching off the Danish coast covered by Warwick G/279, flown by F/O Richards, providing ASR cover and an airborne lifeboat if required. F/O O'Reilly in Warwick P/279 and a force of Beaufighters were also involved in the inconclusive search.

The following day three Warwick sorties were flown from Thornaby and Wick alongside Mosquitoes from Banff, all to no avail. On the 15th Mosquitoes from Banff searched again, covered by Warwick Y/279, flown by F/O Richards and W/279, captained by F/Lt Elliott. A force of Beaufighters from Dallachy also went out with ASR cover provided by WO Jervis in P/279 from Fraserburgh. None of the searchers was successful. An hour after take off Y/279 developed engine trouble and turned for home escorted by F/Lt Elliott, who returned to the search after Y/279 had landed safely.

While the major search for the missing Stirlings was going on a smaller-scale search for a missing Wellington was being carried out by F/Lt Gill in Hurricane G/279 at 5740N 0345W. Although other Wellingtons were seen searching, there was no sign of any survivors.

On the afternoon of 16 May Lt Shanks and F/Sgt Wood, airborne from Fraserburgh in Z/279 and P/279 respectively, carried out a search for a missing MGB in very poor weather. Earlier that morning S/Ldr Levin-Raw had been out from Wick to search in Y/279. The MGB was not found but the search would continue with a further seven Warwick sorties from Fraserburgh and Thornaby until the 19th. Later that night F/Sgt Wood was airborne again to search an area off Montrose in Warwick F/279. At 1920 hours he sent a message that he was returning to Fraserburgh with engine trouble. On the return trip the port engine caught fire and Wood quickly feathered it before making an attempt to land at Dyce. Unfortunately the Warwick crashed in the attempt and F/Sgt Wood and F/Lt Wheelock were killed. F/Sgt Clarke, the second pilot, was injured, but the rest of the crew escaped unharmed. F/Lt Coppack in Hurricane C/279 also searched off Montrose without success in rain and cloud down to the deck.

Late on the night of the 17th May F/Lt Gill carried out a search off Bell Rock in Hurricane C/279 for a crashed aircraft. He flew five 10 mile legs before being recalled. The search was continued the next morning by F/Lt Coppack in Hurricane D/279. Coppack found two yellow planks and a yellow petrol tin, but no sign of survivors.

On 20 May the Squadron began a series of ASR cover sorties for formations of aircraft transiting the Atlantic and the North Sea. The first was cover by Y/279 and G/279 from Wick for a formation of American Fortresses flying from Prestwick to Iceland and passed without incident. The next, on 22 May was cover for a formation of Spitfires flying from Dyce to Stavanger. This was covered by two Wick aircraft, W/279 and M/279, and also passed quietly, the crew of W/279 sighting three captured U-boats in Stavanger harbour.

The Americans lost a B-17 on 26 May. It was believed to have ditched and 279 Sqn were tasked to search for survivors. F/Lt Hayes in V/279 from Thornaby was the first aircraft off. At 1215 hours he located a dinghy containing six survivors in position 5518N 0229E and dropped the airborne lifeboat to them from 700 feet. Unfortunately the parachutes failed to deploy and the boat was smashed to pieces on the surface. Just over three hours later W/Cdr Cox followed Hayes out to the scene in Warwick Z/279 equipped with another airborne lifeboat. This time the drop went well as Cox released the boat at 500 feet. It came to rest 50 yards downwind of the survivors, who quickly made their way to it and boarded. W/Cdr Cox's crew then sighted a launch about 6 miles away and homed it to the lifeboat, where it picked up the survivors and was underway for port with the lifeboat in tow at 1716 hours.

Another Wick Warwick was launched on the 27th to attempt an interception of a Catalina in difficulties. It had been heading

WOp/AG Bob McGill poses in front of a Lend-Lease Catalina bound for Russia at Reykjavik in 1945. (RS McGill)

for Sullom Voe with engine trouble. F/Lt Garven in G/279 took off at 0940 hours. Just over an hour later he was informed that the Catalina had put down on the sea and he returned to base.

Whilst the search for the missing B-17 was being carried out another of the Squadron's crews was preparing to fly to Iceland to establish a detachment there, as Bob McGill recalls.

On 26th May we were ordered to fly to Reykjavik, Iceland to form a detached flight of 279 Sqn to provide ASR cover for the with-drawal of the USAAF from the UK to the USA to take part in the Pacific war against Japan. The flight to Iceland was a series of mishaps and despite leaving Thornaby on 26th May we did not arrive in Reykjavik until late afternoon on 31st May.

We flew first to RAF Fraserburgh to pick up a de Havilland civilian engineer as a passenger. His arrival delayed us until 30th May when we left for Reykjavik. We were about a third of our way to our destination when one engine packed up – I had to send an urgent signal that we were returning to the nearest airfield in Scotland, which was Wick. After repairs we were ready to depart to Reykjavik on 31st May, but the de Havilland engineer declined to join us and was picked up by a Mosquito, which arrived before

Three 279 Sqn WOp/AG's in Iceland, 1945. L to R: George Kaufman, Bob McGill and Len Cockerill. (RS McGill)

*us in Reykjavik. We eventually landed in late afternoon on 31st
May.*

Ken Border also travelled on this Warwick, but recalls the
engineer was from Rolls Royce, rather than de Havilland.

*In May 1945 one Warwick was detached to Iceland and flew from
Thornaby to Fraserburgh where the aircraft was refuelled. A
couple of days later the aircraft took off from Fraserburgh with a
full air and ground crew plus all their kit, tools and some spares
plus a rather large Rolls Royce engineer for whom it had been
waiting and who was going to sort out a problem on a Mosquito
grounded at Reykjavik. Just before the point of no return the starboard engine stopped, later found to have been caused by some
de-icer paste blocking the carburettor, and the pilot was instructed
to try and get back to Wick in the north of Scotland. Another
Warwick was scrambled, complete with airborne lifeboat, and
escorted us for the last few miles into Wick where the pilot made a
good single-engine landing and then we had to wait several days
while a replacement aircraft was flown up from Thornaby.*

*Finally we took off once again for Iceland (minus the Rolls Royce
engineer who had made no secret of his opinion of the Warwick!)
and had a good trip up to Reykjavik where we were billeted in
Nissen huts not very far from the fjord in which were several flying
boats (there were also masses of fish which were easy to catch and
provided a welcome change to our diet).*

The last day of May 1945 saw the detachments at Wick and
Fraserburgh providing two Warwicks and three Hurricanes,
along with another Hurricane from Thornaby, to search for a
missing B-17 Fortress. The first pilot airborne was F/Lt Gill in
Hurricane D/279 from Fraserburgh at 0832 hours to search
between Aberdeen and Flamborough Head. Twenty-five
minutes later Hurricane H/279 took off from Thornaby and
covered the area from the Tay estuary to Flamborough Head. The
two Warwicks, W/279 and B/279, flown by F/Lt Elliott and F/Lt
Butt lifted from Wick just before 1000 hours and searched for over
six hours from Aberdeen out to 5600N 0300E. Mid-afternoon saw
two more Hurricanes, E/279 and B/279, also from Wick, join the
search. F/Lt Fer and WO Hopkins, like all the others, were unsuccessful in their search.

Three 279 Sqn WOp/AG's and an AG at Reykjavik, 1945. Rear :
George Kaufman. Front L to R: Bob McGill, WO 'Tiger' Teague and
Len Cockerill. According to Bob McGill Teague was a great character
who, having bombed Berlin and Rome, had the ambition to bomb
Tokyo and was very upset when Japan surrendered. (R.S. McGill)

Ken Border remembers that the squadron's main task during
this period was providing ASR cover for the many formations of
USAAF bombers returning to the USA.

The squadron's task was to provide air cover to USAF aircraft
returning to the States and at one stage there were strong rumours
that we were to move across the Atlantic to Canada but they proved

Vickers Warwick ASR Mk VI, HG214:RL-H of 279 Sqn at Reykjavik,
Iceland in July 1945. (via R.S. McGill)

to be nothing more than rumours. There were not many RAF personnel in Iceland and we received our rations from USAF stores but they were not very good, vastly different from the food served on USAF stations in England. Kit was also a problem and it wasn't long before most of us were wearing hybrid uniforms comprising whatever was available in the stores. I still have the RCAF cap with which I was issued but the khaki trousers are long gone!

The Icelandic detachment was reinforced by F/O O'Reilly and Warwick RL-C on 8 June. A week later he took Warwick RL-A into new territory with a navigation exercise above the Arctic Circle. The 279 Sqn detachment to Reykjavik continued throughout June, but had little to do, as Bob McGill recalls. 'The month of June in Iceland means virtually 24-hour daylight and, although we flew on some five occasions none were on operations as the deployment of the USAAF proceeded without incident in good weather.'

'In fact, during June the squadron saw a marked reduction in operational sorties. This was a reflection of the number of sorties being flown by all of the various commands now that the war had ended and in total only twelve operational sorties were flown in the month. Eight were searches and four ASR cover to aircraft flying to Norwegian bases'.

A group of 279 Sqn detachment aircrew at Reykjavik in 1945. (D. Mabey)

The first two weeks of July were filled with fruitless searches for amongst others a Mustang, a Wellington and a Seafire. On the 8th F/Lt Elliot in Warwick Y/279 provided ASR cover for the Mosquitoes of No. 334 (Norwegian) Sqn as they made their way home to their new base at Oslo/Gardemoen. The sortie passed without incident and the courageous Norwegians returned safely to their homeland. This sortie was followed by a similar one on the 20th when another formation, this time Spitfires, made for Kristiansand escorted by F/Lt Elliott in Warwick D/279 and P/O Spargo flying Warwick Y/279. All went well until the formation was 19 miles west of Trondheim. Then one of the Spitfires crash-landed, but the pilot escaped unhurt. The following day it was the turn of F/O Duthie, who lifted from Wick in Warwick X/279 to escort a Spitfire formation from Sumburgh to Trondheim without incident.

The Reykjavik detachment continued to fly sorties and on 7 July F/Lt Pinnell's crew had a lucky escape, as Bob McGill recalls.

Our first flight in July to carry out air to sea firing ended in disaster as we crashed on landing. The runway in use ended near the edge of a Fjord and one of our wheels hit the edge, with the result that the oleo leg collapsed. The Warwick did a spectacular ground loop ending up facing the wrong way on the runway with the airborne lifeboat wedged between the engine nacelle and the fuselage. We evacuated the aircraft in some haste. The aircraft was a complete write-off and was taken to the station dump.

The days of the 279 Sqn detachment in Iceland were numbered and Bob McGill recalls some of his flights during the final period before the detachment became a part of No. 281 Sqn.

On 18th July we flew back to Thornaby – a seven hour flight without incident. I believe that Thornaby was the major base for Warwick maintenance and that was the reason for this flight. Whilst at Thornaby we went on leave and did not fly back to Reykjavik until 22nd August – another seven hour flight.

Whilst at Thornaby we said good-bye to our Skipper, F/Lt Pinnell, and were given a new Skipper – F/Lt Bob Hayes. We went back to Thornaby on 30th August carrying mail to the UK – back to Reykjavik on 3rd September via RAF Ballykelly. Sometime in

No. 279 Sqn detachment at Reykjavik in 1945. Rear row 7th from right 'Tiger' Teague, 6th from right Don Mabey, 2nd from right 'Tapper'. (D. Mabey)

September we were told that we had become part of No. 281 Sqn based at Ballykelly. We left Reykjavik for Ballykelly for the last time on 16th September.

Ken Border was amongst those who remained in the final days of the Reykjavik detachment and recalls its end and absorption into 281 Sqn.

We managed to have a good look round Iceland, both on the ground and from the air, and it was a fascinating country. The paved road ended a short distance outside Reykjavik, other roads being what I think was compacted lava so land travel was not particularly comfortable while some of the bridges had severe height and weight restrictions. We were confined to camp on VJ day as there had apparently been some problems in the town on VE day; the local inhabitants were, to put it mildly, not particularly friendly so the authorities would not risk any further confrontation! So we stopped on camp, drank quantities of the locally brewed 'Polar Beer' and had a contest with the other squadron with Very pistols, I don't remember the exact details which is probably as well! Shortly after VJ day the camp held an open day and numbers of locals came to look over the aircraft, for most of them it was their first close-up view of an aircraft and I doubt if any of them had been inside one before so they were very interested and the event was a big success.

Eventually there was no longer any need for an Iceland detachment but 279 Squadron had moved from Thornaby to Beccles on 3rd September 1945, so the detachment was transferred to 281 Squadron and not very long afterwards we flew down to their base at Ballykelly in Northern Ireland, were sent home for a spot of leave and then posted to other units as 281 disbanded in October 1945.

The final sorties of the month were flown on the 24th when F/Lt Stevens and WO Lintott, in Warwicks O/279 and C/279, searched for a missing Anson off Holy Island. Nothing was found and the search was called off when the Anson was found crashed in Perthshire.

July was only two days old when the Warwick engine problems reared their head again. F/Sgt Carter had taken off from Thornaby in Warwick L/279 to search for a Firefly missing from Drem and had barely completed a circuit of the airfield when the port engine began to give trouble. Completing the circuit he landed seven minutes after he had taken off. The engine cut completely after landing and Carter and his crew had had a lucky escape.

F/Sgt David Wylie recalls the weather and serviceability of the Warwick hampering operations on occasion.

Returning to Thornaby one day in clear weather we found that Middlesborough's industrial smoke had completely covered the aerodrome right to the ground. We flew back out to sea and then

Two No. 279 Sqn Warwicks carried out a search for an Anson similar to this one on 34 August 1945. (Via A. Rodgers)

up to Leuchars where we spent the night. The weather was fine the next morning except for a belt of fog about 50 miles wide south of St Andrews. We flew through the fog and back to Thornaby without incident. However, an aircraft that took off from Leuchars just after us was not so lucky. The pilot, for some unaccountable reason, turned towards the land at low level and crashed into the cliffs killing all on board.

One day when coming in to land at Thornaby the 'horn' sounded a warning when the skipper closed the throttles, even though the green lights indicated that the undercarriage was down and locked. He tried the emergency hydraulic pump but this had no effect. At this stage the skipper was making noises about baling out and heading the aircraft out into the North Sea. The rest of us thought this was a rotten idea and voted to take our chances in a crash landing. By this time, having been circling the drome for a considerable time, every one on the station was out to watch the fun. The control tower suggested we come in at flying speed and bounce on the runway and take off again. We did this and the wheels didn't collapse so we took up ditching stations and came in for a perfect landing. It was just an electrical fault.

The pace of operations began to reduce now that the European war was over and the numbers of aircraft in use by the Allies reduced as American, Commonwealth and other air forces returned home, disbanded and demobilized. During July the squadron began to add Supermarine Sea Otter amphibians to its strength and to detach them around the country at Thornaby, Banff and Tain. The first operation for the Sea Otters commenced on 26 July when F/O Fuller and F/Lt Smith carried out a search from Thornaby in A/279 and E/279. They searched in the Filey Bay area for a parachute, in conjunction with an HSL, but had no luck. Sea Otter sorties from Banff began on the 28th with a search around 5723N 0103W by WO Granger in F/279, which located an out of control fishing vessel. The next Sea Otter sorties from Banff were on the 31st, when F/O Fuller in F/279 and H/279 flown by WO Granger took off in the late afternoon to search for an aircraft reported to have crashed 10 miles east of Arbroath. The search produced nothing.

The Squadron provided the Fleet Air Arm with assistance on 1 August when a Hellcat and a Barracuda went missing off the coast near Drem airfield. F/Lt Hayes took off from Thornaby in

Warwick N/279 at 0610 hours and searched the area in company with an HSL. Nothing was found and at 1055 hours Warwick L/279, also from Thornaby, joined the search with F/Lt Forbes at the controls. The rear gunner sighted an object coloured yellow, black and red, which might have been a dinghy but it was soon lost. At midday on the 2nd the Sea Otters from Banff joined the search and WO Campbell and F/O Fuller in F/279 and Z/279 sighted numerous pieces of wreckage in the area but no survivors.

The Warwicks from Thornaby were back in Filey Bay on the 5th searching for a ditched Mosquito. P/O Wells in N/279 took off at 0255 followed by F/Lt Forbes in L/279 at 0500 hours to cover the area. Wells, working with HSL Seagull 52, found a 25 gallon tank, wood and fabric wreckage. The wreckage had the RAF roundel on it. N/279 found no sign of the crew and L/279 took up the search. Forbes directed the HSL to the wreckage, which also included both the Mosquito wingtips and a dinghy. The crew was not found.

The Fleet Air Arm appeared to be having the lion's share of losses during August and on the 8th another two aircraft went missing. The first, a Hellcat, drew the services of Warwick L/279 from Thornaby, flown by P/O Wells. Wells searched the coastline as far north as Arbroath with no success and it was later reported that the Hellcat had crashed in the hills of Midlothian. The second aircraft was a Firefly searched for by W/Cdr Cox in

As well as searching for and rescuing ditched Mosquito crews the Warwicks of No. 279 Sqn also provided ASR escort to the Mosquitoes of the Banff and North Coates Strike Wings. This Mosquito is a Mk XVIII of No. 254 Sqn based at North Coates in June 1945. (Via A. Rodgers)

EXERCISE NEWCASTLE FIGHTER OPS.

1. Exercise with destroyer at 10-00hrs. on 11/7/45 weather permitting.

2. Warwick to rendevous with D.R. which will be cruising about 10mls. E of Tyne on a N-S line between 20. C. Buoy (8mls. E.S.E. of Tyne entrance) and 20.R. Buoy (8mls. E.N.E of Tyne entrance)
Destroyer is of latest type with single funnel.

3. A/C. to carry out passing runs at 3000' N&S, nearest point of run to be 2½ mls. to Eastward of ship.

4. Listen out on 12 OF. GD.I, 6570kcs. A/C. to be handed over to D.R. for control.
Speed of A/C. as slow as possible.

5. Ship will ask pilot for "Canary", and the pilot on receipt of this will switch on M.K.III. I.F.

    D.R. C/Sign "DRILLGROUND".

EXERCISE NEWCASTLE FIGHTER OPS.

1. Exercise with destroyer at 13-30hrs. in Same Position as the Morning Exercise, weather permitting. Viz-

2. Warwick to rendevous with D.R. which will be cruising about 10mls.E of Tyne on a N-S line between 20 C. buoy (8mls. E.S.E. of Tyne entrance) and 20.R. buoy (8mls. E.N.E. of Tyne entrance)
Destroyer is of latest type with single funnel.

3. A/C to fly at 5000' and to proceed due E for a distance of 25mls., then return and approach ship from E'Ward.

4. A/C to make two approach runs at each of following heights-
(a) 5000' (b) 1500' (c) 500' (d) 50' (at pilot's discretion)

5. If time permits, a 3rd.Exercise.-
Same A/C to carry out two runs at 10,000' from a distance of 45mls. due East returning on reciprocal.

6. If ship asks pilot for "Canary" M.K.III. I.F. to be switched on.

7. D.R. C/Sign "DRILLGROUND". Listen out on 12 G.P. G.D.I. 6570kcs.

The two naval cooperation exercises flown by the squadron in July 1945 were controlled by the Fighter Sector Operations Room at Newcastle. (Author's collection)

Warwick N/279 without success. Two Sea Otters from Banff, flown by WO Granger and WO Campbell, also searched down the coast in bad weather, with cloud down to sea level, eventually landing at Drem.

The squadron then went through a quiet spell. The next operational sortie was not until 27 August when F/Lt Elliott provided ASR cover to an exercise involving a Lancaster and Spitfires. Elliot operated from Tain in Warwick Y/279 without incident. The first day of September brought searches for the Tain Sea Otters when H/279 and F/279 covered an area between Tain and Dyce with no luck.

These were the last sorties by the squadron before it moved its main base from Thornaby to Beccles on 3 September. Following a period of settling in at the new base WO Jervis carried out the first patrol from Beccles in a borrowed 280 Sqn Warwick, A2/280. The first sortie by a 279 Sqn aircraft was that afternoon when F/Sgt Carter got airborne in Warwick Q/279, but he landed just over fifteen minutes later with compass and starboard generator trouble.

WO Jervis in G/279 flew the final Warwick sortie on 13 September before the Squadron stood down to convert to the Lancaster ASR Mk III. It received a Lancaster Mk I, ME371:RL-C, for type familiarization, and during September a steady stream

The general reconnaissance version of the Lancaster, the GR Mk III, shown here in service with No. 120 Sqn. Second in line is RE222 an ASR/GR Mk III. (Via A. Rodgers)

of ASR Mk III's began to arrive. Most of them were converted from the bomber role and had seen service with the squadrons of Bomber Command before being transferred.

The Lancaster was a great improvement on the Warwick in terms of range, payload and engine reliability. It also had the advantage of commonality of spares with the other squadrons of Bomber Command and Coastal Command, which was in the process of returning its Lend-Lease Liberators, Catalinas and Fortresses and re-equipping with the general reconnaissance version of the Lancaster.

Gerald Austin was posted in October 1945 from No. 280 Sqn at Beccles to the 279 Sqn detachment at Thornaby to convert to the Lancaster. He recalls this period.

As far as I can ascertain 279 was the first squadron to be equipped with lifeboat carrying Lancasters. Some of the crewmembers came from Bomber Command, whilst others like myself, a WOp/AG, came from Coastal Command. My first flight with the squadron was in November 1945 and the last in February 1946. These were all training flights. I was in 'D' Flight and I am sure it was 'A' Flight that flew out to Pegu and was renumbered 1348 Flt.

I had my embarkation leave in January 1946, but for some reason the transfer of the three remaining flights was cancelled and the squadron disbanded at Thornaby. No Lancasters went to Beccles.

CHAPTER NINE

November 1945
– March 1946

N o. 279 Sqn flew its first Lancaster operational sorties on
8 November 1945 with F/O Davis the first to get airborne
at 0205 hours in RL-O from Thornaby to search for a 279
Sqn Lancaster, that had gone missing the previous night on a
navigational exercise. The missing aircraft was PB431:RL-F.
Davis was followed by F/O Witchell in RL-E at 0249 hours. A
second pair, RL-M and RL-B, captained by F/Lt Barrington and
F/Lt Moon were off at dawn followed by F/O Scholey and F/O
Thompson in RL-H and RL-L. Liberators of No. 111 OTU also
assisted in the search. Nothing was sighted by any of these crews.

Avro Lancaster
GR Mk III, RL-K
of 279 Sqn at
Thornaby in
November 1945.
(G. Austin)

No. 279 Squadron personnel in front of one of the squadron's
Lancaster's in 1945. F/Sgt Goodman is 6th from the right in the front
row. (J. Burden)

Throughout the day another eight Lancaster sorties were flown
without success. The next two days saw another fourteen
Lancaster sorties flown from Thornaby but nothing was found.

In January 1946 F/Lt Jack Murray was awarded the AFC. The
citation gave an excellent description of the trials and tribulations
of an ASR crew and could equally be linked to many other
aircrew members of 279 Sqn who endured similar hardships and
difficulties.

*This officer served in No. 281 Squadron from November 1943 until
November 1944, when he joined 279 Squadron. He has to his credit
150 hours operational flying. For the past eight months he has
served as deputy flight commander and his loyalty, perseverance
and initiative have been outstanding.*

*He has proved to be an excellent pilot and has carried out
numerous searches over enemy waters in adverse weather. On
one occasion, Flight Lieutenant Murray was returning from a
search in June 1944, when off Scapa Flow at about midnight and*

in conditions of 10/10 cloud, both engines of his aircraft failed. Nevertheless Flight Lieutenant Murray brought the aircraft down on the water without incurring any damage. The ditching drill was carried out in an exemplary way and no casualties occurred.

On another occasion, after taking off at Sumburgh in adverse weather, an engine failed completely. Flight Lieutenant Murray returned to base on one engine and owing to strong wind, low cloud and local topography, was forced to land across and slight down wind. The aircraft ran off the end of the runway, into the sea and caught fire. Flight Lieutenant Murray remained on top of the burning aircraft until all the occupants had got clear. He then jumped into the water and went to the assistance of an airman, a non-swimmer, in danger of drowning. This officer is an excellent captain of aircraft and has displayed the highest standard of devotion to duty.

(Right) F/Sgt Goodman, a Lancaster crewmember of 279 Sqn. (J. Burden)

(Left) Three 279 Sqn aircrew. F/Sgt Goodman at rear. (J. Burden)

The remaining flight of Lancasters and their crews left Thornaby in January 1946 for Pegu in Burma and on arrival there the flight became No. 1348 Flight providing ASR cover for the area. The story of No. 279 Sqn had come to an end. They had operated from bases all around the coast of the United Kingdom and searching for downed crews from Norway to Denmark, to the coast of France and the English Channel, to the Bay of Biscay and the South West Approaches, the Irish Sea, the North Sea and North Atlantic, off Iceland and into the Arctic Circle. 279 Squadron can truly say they went anywhere for a dinghy.

APPENDIX I

Squadron Commanders

29 November 1941 – 22 January 1943	S/Ldr (later W/Cdr) V.H.P. Lynham DSO
22 January 1943 – 10 February 1944	W/Cdr B.G. Corry DFC
10 February 1944 – 1944	W/Cdr N.W.C. Bindloss
1944 – 1946	W/Cdr H.F. Cox

APPENDIX II

Bases

16 November 1941 – 14 October 1944	Bircham Newton
14 October 1944 – 3 September 1945	Thornaby
3 September 1945 – 10 March 1946	Beccles

Detachments

28 April 1942 – 29 May 1942	Sumburgh
29 June 1942 – 1942	Benbecula
15 July 1942 – 1942	Leuchars
26 July 1942 – 15 August 1942	Reykjavik, Iceland
14 August 1942 – 15 August 1942	Thorney Island
15 August 1942 – 19 August 1942	Chivenor
23 August 1942 – 5 February 1943	St Eval
25 September 1942 – 1942	Beaulieu
5 February 1943 – 9 June 1943	Davidstow Moor
9 June 1943 – 14 December 1943	Harrowbeer
28 September 1943 – 1945	Wick
1 January 1944 – 1 August 1944	Reykjavik
1 October 1944 – September 1945	Tain
1 October 1944 – September 1945	Wick
31 October 1944 – 27 December 44	Banff
27 December 1944 – September 1945	Fraserburgh
26 May 1945 – September 1945	Reykjavik
July 1945 – September 1945	Banff
August 1945 – September 1945	Tain

Appendix III

Aircraft Operated

Armstrong Whitworth Albemarle Mk I
P1409

Lockheed Hudson Mk I
T9284

Lockheed Hudson Mk III

The code letters OS were used by the Squadron on Hudson Mk IIIs.

T9024	T	Allocated to 279 1 December 41.
T9394	B later C	Allocated to 279 22 November 41. SOC 11 December 44.
T9398	E later S	Allocated to 279 24 November 41. To 269 Sqn.
T9399	M later R	Allocated to 279 26 November 41. Crashed in sea 24 August 43.
T9400	O later B	Allocated to 279 26 November 41. To 48 Sqn.
T9401	G later D	Allocated to 279 25 November 41. To 139 Sqn.
T9402	J later Q	Allocated to 279 26 November 41. SOC 23 August 42.
T9405	Q later U	Allocated to 279 1 December 41. To 269 Sqn.
T9406		From 6 OTU. Transferred 23 December 44. SOC 5 March 45.
T9407	Z	From 6 OTU. Crashed on take-off, Bircham Newton, 27 November 42.
T9408	D later H	Allocated to 279 24 November 41. Crashed in forced landing, Docking, 24 December 43.
T9411		From 6 OTU. Transferred 28 December 44. SOC 31 March 46.
T9414	V, P	Allocated to 279 8 December 41. Abandoned when lost 6 miles north west of Kinross, 5 February 43.

T9415	K	Allocated to 279 10 December 41. SOC 19 April 45.
T9420		From 1407 Flt. Transferred 23 October 44. SOC 25 April 46.
T9422		From A&AEE. To 500 Sqn.
T9433		From 206 Sqn. To RAE.
T9441		From ATA. Transferred 6 January 45. SOC28 March 46.
T9443	J	From 206 Sqn. Crashed on take-off from Bircham Newton and damaged by fire, 28 February 43.
T9451		From 206 Sqn. To 233 Sqn 7 January 45.
V8974	W	Allocated to 279 8 December 41.
V8976		From 269Sqn. Transferred 28 October 44. SOC 31 March 46.
V8979		Allocated to 279 Sqn 24 August 44. To RAE 28 December 44.
V8982		From 320 Sqn. To 1407 Flt 24 August 44.
V8987	Y	From 269 Sqn. Hit hill in cloud 1 mile east of St Eval, 8 September 42.
V8988		6 OTU. To Bircham Newton.
V8993	L later J	Allocated to 279 26 November 41. Missing from ASR Search 13 February 42.
V8996	X	Allocated to 279 12 December 41. Crashed in forced landing 3 miles west of Docking, 13 April 42.
V8988		Transferred as surplus 5 August 44.
V8999	A later N	Allocated to 279 17 November 41. To 251 Sqn 5 August 44.
V9024	J	Allocated to 279 Sqn. Crashed on landing at Stornoway, 16 July 42.
V9031	P later A	Allocated to 279 30 November 41. Missing from ASR sortie, 7 January 43.
V9033		From 320 Sqn. To 269 Sqn.
V9042	H later P	Allocated to 279 26 November 41. Ran out of fuel and abandoned 4 miles north of Bodmin, 22 January 43.
V9044	F later E	Allocated to 279 25 November 41. Missing from ASR search, 4 February 43.
V9046	C later F	Allocated to 279 23 November 41. Abandoned in bad weather near Swansea, 21 January 43.
V9047		From 233 Sqn. To 269 Sqn.
V9057		From 269 Sqn 28 August 44. Transferred 2 January 45. SOC 31 March 46.
V9058		From 269 Sqn. To 520 Sqn 17 January 45.

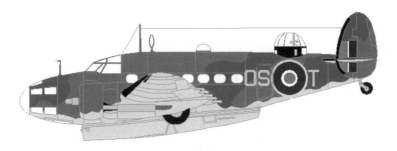

Lockheed Hudson Mk I V9158:OS-T was used to carry out trials of the airborne lifeboat designed by Uffa Fox. (M. Barrass)

V9113		From 608 Sqn. To 500 Sqn.
V9118		From 269 Sqn. To 519 Sqn 9 October 44.
V9158	OS-T	From 289 Sqn. To 269 Sqn.
V9161		From 269 Sqn. Crashed at Bircham Newton, 23 August 44.
AE513 P		From 301 FTU 6 July 44. Stalled at low altitude and crashed in sea 20 miles east of Great Yarmouth, 19 August 44.
AE514	C	Allocated to 279 11 June 42.
AE519	S	From 1428 Flt. Allocated to 279 11 June 42. Crashed in sea off St Ives, 29 March 43.
AE531	B	From 1406 Flt. Missing on navigation exercise (navex), 13 November 43.
AE534		From 1406 Flt. To 519 Sqn 9 October 44.
AE559		From 287 Sqn. To 161 Sqn.
AE564		From 1428 Flt. Transferred 17 January 45. SOC 24 April 46.
AE585		From 1406 Flt. Engine caught fire and crashed in forced landing at Horplay, Norfolk, 6 May 44.
AE594	C	From 1428 Flt. Crashed 4 November 42.
FH419		Transferred battle damaged Category B 10 September 44
FH433		Transferred 17 January 45.
FK748		Transferred 18 October 44.
FK752		Transferred as surplus 10 July 44.
FK757		Transferred 27 October 44.

LOCKHEED HUDSON MK V

The codes OS were used on the Squadron's Hudson Mk Vs.

AM554 E   From 320 Sqn. Crashed on take-off from Bircham
                Newton and damaged by fire, 26 March 44.
AM641   From 407 Sqn. To USAAF, 4 February 44.
AM681   From 1 OTU. To 5 OTU 24 August 44.
AM686   From 320 Sqn. To ATA.
AM700   From 6 OTU. To 5 OTU 1 August 44.
AM702   From 224 Sqn. To 6 OTU.
AM848   From 407 Sqn. To 5 OTU 26 July 44.

LOCKHEED HUDSON MK VI

The codes OS were used on the Hudson Mk VIs used by the Squadron.

EW914   Transferred 5 November 44.
EW922   Transferred 10 December 44.
FK402
FK450   Transferred 30 October 44.

HAWKER HURRICANE MK IIC

KZ383 RL-N
LD843   Received 28 December 44.
LF583   Received 11 January 45.
LF773   Received 8 December 44.
PG490   Received 3 December 44.
PZ814   Received 7 December 44.
PZ829   Received 6 December 44.
PZ830   Received 6 December 44.
PZ831   Received 28 December 44.

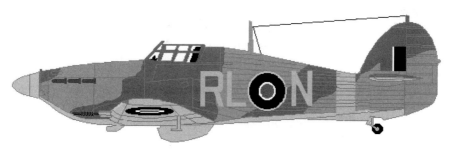

Hawker Hurricane KZ383:RL-N of 279 Sqn in 1945. (M. Barrass)

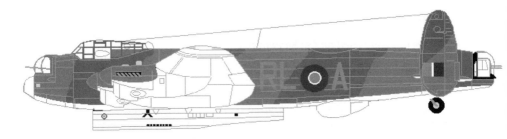

Avro Lancaster ASR Mk III RF310:RL-A. (M. Barrass)

AVRO LANCASTER ASR MK III

The Lancasters continued the use of the RL coding.

ME371 (Mk I)	RL-C	Received August 45. To MU September 45. SOC 15 May 47.
NE180		From 106 Sqn. To 160 Sqn.
PB431	RL-F	Missing on navex 7 November 45.
PB529		From 106 Sqn, converted to ASR Mk III. To 6 OTU.
RE120		From 514 Sqn, converted to ASR Mk III. To 38 Sqn.
RE129		From 97 Sqn, converted to ASR Mk III. To Middle East.
RE158		From 514 Sqn, converted to ASR Mk III. To 120 Sqn as GR MkIII.
RF272	RL-A	Received December 45. To 37 Sqn.
RF292		To 179 Sqn.
RF310	RL-A and G	From 46 MU. To 1348 Flt. Crashed in Burma 4 March 46.
RF313	RL-F	Received December 45. To 38 Sqn.
RF320	RL-N	To 621 Sqn.
RF322	RL-J	To 38 Sqn.
RF324		To 179 Sqn.
RF325		To ASWDU.
SW283		To 179 Sqn.
SW288	RL-G	To 38 Sqn.
SW294		To 179 Sqn.
SW295	RL-C	To 38 Sqn.
SW373		To 179 Sqn.
TX269	RL-N	

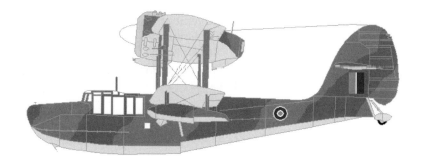

Supermarine Sea Otter Mk I. (M. Barrass)

SUPERMARINE SEA OTTER MK I

JM861

VICKERS WARWICK BOMBER / ASR

When the Squadron re-equipped with the Warwick the codes RL were adopted.

BV233 RL-J	Received 14 October 44. Category AC in accident 28 October 44. Returned 6 December 44. Crashed 3 ½ miles SE of Darlington 7 January 45.
BV287	
BV305	
BV310	
BV316	

VICKERS WARWICK ASR STAGE C (LATER REDESIGNATED ASR MK I)

BV358	RL-H	Received 18 November 44. Crashed on landing at Wick 29 January 45.
BV392		Received 17 November 44.
BV400	P	Received 17 November 44. *(Code not confirmed as used whilst with 279 Sqn but noted whilst aircraft were with No. 281 Sqn which operated a detached flight with 279 Sqn.)*
BV401	RL-T	Received 18 November 44.

BV404		Received 15 November 44.
BV413	RL-C	Received 19 November 44.
BV419		Received 16 November 44.
BV440	RL-U	Received 19 November 44. Lost 20 December 44.
BV516		Received 15 November 44
BV518		Received 12 October 44.

VICKERS WARWICK ASR MK I

HF948	
HF961	Received 30 October 44.
HF963	
HF964	Received 4 November 44.
HF978	
HF981	Received 16 November 44.

VICKERS WARWICK ASR MK VI

HF983	
HF985	
HF986		Received 31 January 45.
HG118	
HG142	
HG144	
HG151		Received 19 January 45.
HG169	
HG170	RL-R
HG171	
HG173	RL-P

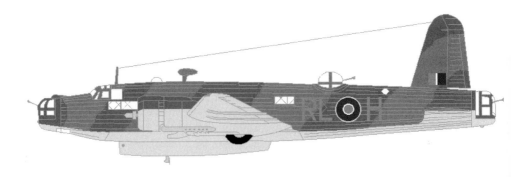

Vickers Warwick ASR Mk VI HG214:RL-H flown from Reykjavik,
Iceland in July 1945. (M. Barrass)

HG176		
HG177		Received 19 January 45.
HG180		
HG181		
IIG189		Received 27 October 44.
HG193		Received 24 October 44.
HG207		Received 24 October 44.
HG209	RL-B	Received 14 October 44. Missing 11 January 45.
HG210	RL-Q	Received 30 October 44. Missing 22nm south-east of Flamborough Head, 20 November 44.
HG212	RL-G	Received 14 October 44.
HG214	RL-H	

Appendix IV

Aircrew Losses

13 February 42	Hudson Mk III V8993:J	Sgt Garrard
		Sgt Redhead
		Sgt Schulty
		Sgt Logan
8 September 42	Hudson Mk III V8987:Y	Sgt Farrar
		Sgt Granger
		P/O Waters
		P/O Holloman
7 January 43	Hudson Mk III V9031:A	Sgt Arnold
		Sgt Sclater
		Sgt Bannister
		Sgt Paradise
5 February 1943	Hudson Mk III T9414:V	Sgt Pertus
29 March 1943	Hudson Mk III AE519:S	F/O Gibbs
		F/Sgt Long
		F/Sgt Povey
		F/Sgt Bacon
		F/Sgt Fletcher
15 May 1943	Hudson Mk III V8974:W	F/Sgt Rusby
17 August 1943	Hudson Mk III T9405:U	F/Sgt Flanagan
24 August 1943	Hudson Mk III T9399:R	F/Sgt Neil
		F/O Whapham
		F/Sgt Pennington
		F/Sgt Gourlay
13 November 1943	Hudson Mk III AE531:B	M/Sgt Courson USAAF
		F/O Carpenter
		Sgt Franks
		Sgt Chapman
		1st Lt Dooley USAAF

19 August 1944	Hudson Mk III AE513: P	F/O Blake
		F/Sgt Anderson
		Sgt Hunt
20 November 1944	Warwick ASR Mk VI	F/Lt D. Welply
	HG210:RL-Q	?
		?
		?
		WO S.H. Burrow
		WO A.D. Grant
7 January 1945	Warwick Bomber/ASR	F/Lt H.S. Luck
	BV233:RL-J	?
		?
		F/O F.W. Ritchie
		F/O D.C. Holland
		F/O R.P. Woolfield
11 January 1945	Warwick ASR Mk VI	F/Lt J.H. Moreton
	HG209:RL-B	P/O F. Bentley
		F/O G.C. Galloway
		WO A.E. Goodall
		WO G. Mansfield
		F/Sgt W. Bryan
		WO W.J. Sandercock
16 May 1945	Warwick RL-F	F/Sgt Wood
		F/Lt Wheelock
7 November 1945	Lancaster ASR Mk III	F/Sgt Anderson
	PB431:RL-F	F/Sgt Blake
		F/Sgt King
		Sgt MacLean
		F/Sgt Mortimer
		F/O Parmenter
		WO Robinson
		F/Sgt Vickers

Appendix V

Contents of the
Lindholme Dinghy System

CONTAINER No. 1

Water cans	6	Milk cans	2
ERF Mk 2	1	Waterproof suit	1
Torches	1	Everhot Bags	2
Bailers	1	Cards	1
Sponges	1	Whistles	1
Waterproof apron	1		

CONTAINER No. 2

Water cans	6	Milk cans	2
EFR Mk 2	1	Waterproof suit	1
Torches	1	Everhot bags	2
Bailers	1	Sponges	1
Whistles	1		

CONTAINER No. 4

Water cans	6	Milk cans	2
EFR Mk 2	1	Matches	2
Cigarettes	2	Everhot bags	2

CONTAINER No. 5

Water cans	6	Milk cans	2
EFR Mk 2	1	Waterproof suit	1
Torches	1	Everhot bags	2
Bailers	1	Sponges	1
Whistles	1		

SPECIAL CONTAINER S6

Signal distress marine	2	Torches electric 5a/426	2
Signal pistol 1½ in signal	1	Cartridges white/white	8
Cartridges red 1½ in	8	Cartridges green	8

Report on Medical Aspect of Short Experimental Trips in a Hudson Dinghy

Information was wanted by W/Cdr Linham [sic], Officer Commanding 279 Squadron about the relative effects of wind and current on the travels of a loaded dinghy in the sea. He arranged on three occasions for a Hudson dinghy with four men on board to be left drifting under observation from a seaplane tender about 10 miles off the coast of Norfolk. This experiment presented an opportunity for a limited observation of life in a dinghy from the Medical aspect. S/Ldr Mandow and F/O Maile each made one trip.

DESCRIPTION OF TRIPS

(1) S/Ldr Mandow

The inflated dinghy and nine passengers went on board the seaplane tender at Wells-next-the-Sea at 0845 hours; the tender went to buoy 11A about five miles off the coast and eight miles from Wells. The dinghy was put in the sea and four men entered it direct from the tender without first getting into the sea. S/Ldr Mandow remained in the dinghy for six hours, the remainder of the passengers changing over at two hourly intervals.

The weather was overclouded and slight rain fell for about half the time; the wind was about 20 miles an hour; the sea was slightly rough with short waves travelling in fairly rapid succession but there were no 'white horses'. The dinghy was pumped up a little once although this was not necessary.

Clothing worn was flying boots, oil wool socks, sidcut [sic] flying suit outer and inner over grey flannel trousers, shirt and pullover, flying helmet and waterproof cap designed by W/Cdr Winfield, and fleece lined leather gloves.

(2) F/O Maile

A similar party assembled at Wells but the dinghy was dropped two miles off the coast. The weather was clear with bright sunshine. There was a wind of 40 miles per hour with a definite rough sea; high waves in rapid succession, many 'white horses'. The dinghy remained at sea for four hours and then had to be hauled on board owing to an approaching squall.

Clothing was the same with the exception of sheepskin gloves and an experiment was made of wearing oiled anti-gas gloves, the head was uncovered.

EFFECTS ON INDIVIDUALS

(1) Sea Sickness

Of the eighteen people who occupied the dinghy during these two trips, 15 were seasick; in most cases the seasickness was of a very severe character with repeated nausea and vomiting and very marked tiredness and apathy. Most people lay completely relaxed with closed eyes and very green complexion. In some cases vomiting appeared to produce temporarily a diminution in the apathy which, however, rapidly recurred. F/O Maile had taken Phenobarbitone, grains one, after a light breakfast at 0730 hours. This had no effect whatsoever on his seasickness. No experiments were made with Chlorotone. The seasickness was of about the same severity in the dinghy and in the tender.

(2) Cold

No ill effects were noticed from cold during these short excursions. The temperature in the dinghy on the first trip was six degrees Centigrade; in the water three and a half degrees Centigrade. Unfortunately the thermometer had been broken before the second trip. Some people were not wearing gloves and in spite of this their fingers did not become numb. S/Ldr Mandow whose fingers are exceptionally easily affected by cold, found that when his gloves had become wet that his fingers rapidly became numb and white. When the gloves were removed and the hands held beneath the outer sidcut, [sic], the fingers soon warmed up. The anti-gas gloves give good protection against wet but not against cold.

(3) Wet

Practically no water is shipped by the dinghy even in a rough sea so all occupants remained comparatively dry. It is hoped to do a further experiment in which the occupant starts off in the sea and therefore enters the dinghy in a thoroughly moistened condition.

CONCLUSION

The Hudson dinghy when fully inflated is a most stable craft. It rides big waves with the utmost ease, ships no water, is comfortable and roomy, gives excellent protection against the wind, is almost impossible to fall out of and can be easily pumped up with the pump supplied. Providing it remains inflatable life could be maintained in this dinghy for a very long time. The main causes of death in dinghy life are exposure due to cold and wet and aggravated by sea sickness; thirst and starvation. It would seem therefore, that the supplies provided in dinghies should be chosen entirely to counteract these causes of death combined with devices for attracting attention of rescuers. The following comments are made on the existing equipment:

The pump is excellent. It is considered that a small compass might be fixed on to the cover which holds the pump in position on the floor of the dinghy. The emergency ration of chocolate is considered to be excellent but although the tins are meant to be opened with a coin, no coin is supplied nor is it likely that the aircrews would be carrying coins. It is possible to open these tins with the tin opener supplied with the RAF flying rations. The tins of tomato juice or apple juice have no stoppers. They are opened by puncturing the top with a sharp implement. This might be very difficult to accomplish and once opened could not be stopped after a small amount had been drunk. It is considered that a screw stopper controlled by a large butterfly nut would be an improvement. The amount of fluid supplied is considered sufficient.

The RAF flying ration tins are considered to be very bad indeed; they contain a few very dry biscuits, the food value of which is not known, chewing gum, malted milk tablets and chlorinating tablets. There is a considerable amount of waste space inside these tins; chewing gum could have no effect on prolonging life; there is no water in which to use the chlorinating tablets and they are not considered necessary in any case. The malted milk tablets are individually wrapped in oiled paper which it is impossible to unwrap with numb fingers. The space occupied by this tin would be better employed in other ways. It is thought that four ounces of barley sugar per man would be more useful than the tin of flying rations and would take up very much less space.

There are four marine distress signals which occupy a considerable amount of space but only make it possible to signal four times. It is considered that a Verey [sic] pistol and cartridges would give much more scope for distress signals.

The first aid kit which takes up a lot of room is considered to be fatuous to the last degree. The impedimenta in these outfits consisting of such things as compressed bandages and compressed wool would not be manipulated by cold hands nor would they have any effect on prolonging life. It is considered that no first aid kit should be placed in the dinghy but if this displeases too many people's sensibilities, two first field dressings and two tubunic ampoules of Morphia are the maximum.

It is thought that the space gained by deleting the first aid kit should be employed in supplying silk gloves, then woollen gloves, and waterproof outer gloves, stored in watertight tins. If sufficient space could be found, the same series for feet should be supplied. It is of the greatest importance that the hands should be protected as much as possible from the numbing effects of cold and wet not only because of the ultimate danger of frostbite but because of the immediate possibility of doing such simple things as opening tins of food when the fingers are thoroughly numb.

The two paddles supplied are satisfactory; the bungs supplied were not tested but are presumably satisfactory. It is considered that the addition of a sponge and collapsible baler would be of the greatest assistance. Water is bound to get on the floor of the dinghy when people climb into it; rainwater collects on the floor and in a very rough sea a little spray sometimes enters the dinghy. This means that people are sitting in a small pool of water which could be easily controlled by a sponge.

The waterproof cap designed by W/Cdr Winfield was not found to be of any advantage in this type of dinghy as the flying clothing helmet is amply sufficient to prevent rain or spray from pouring down the neck. The cap fits snugly over the flying helmet and the cape can easily be tightened round the upturned collar of the sidcut. It is thought that the tape which tightens the cape should be much thicker and stronger in order to be more easily handled by numbed fingers. The Flurescin signals were not tested but it is understood that W/Cdr Linham intends to carry out a practical test.

It is suggested that a waterproof bag containing an inflated tube sufficient to keep the bag floating should be carried in the aircraft. This bag should contain a few essentials for dinghy life. It would be additional to those carried in the dinghy. It would have a thin rope which could be instantaneously attached to a clip on a specified man's tunic and would be thrown into the sea at the time he jumped from the aircraft; it could then be hauled on board the dinghy. This would seem to be a more certain method of ensuring that the accessories which the crew are now supposed to gather and put in the dinghy. A telescopic pole and flag were going to be suggested but it is observed that these have already been introduced in AMO N448/42.

The Lindholme rescue outfit has been examined and it is generally considered to be very excellent. The packing of the tins of apple juice is not very satisfactory and it is suggested that similar stoppers to those described above should be introduced. Cigarettes, matches, playing cards and first aid kit are not considered essential. Rum is considered a risk because the effect of rum on a cold person who is remaining in cold surroundings would be definitely harmful because it creates a loss of heat. The emergency flying ration provided is the same as that which was adversely criticised in the dinghy outfit. The waterproof sleeping suit is considered to be a magnificent piece of equipment; here again there is no provision for warm gloves which are considered to be very important.

Signed
S/Ldr
Officer in Medical Charge
RAF Station Bircham Newton

Appendix VII

Airborne Lifeboat Diagrams

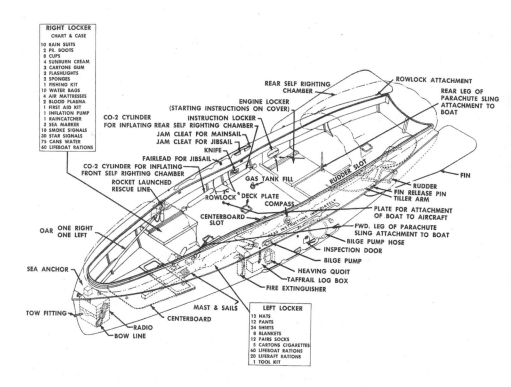

Diagram of the airborne lifeboat showing stowage positions for
equipment. (USAAF via A. McLeod)

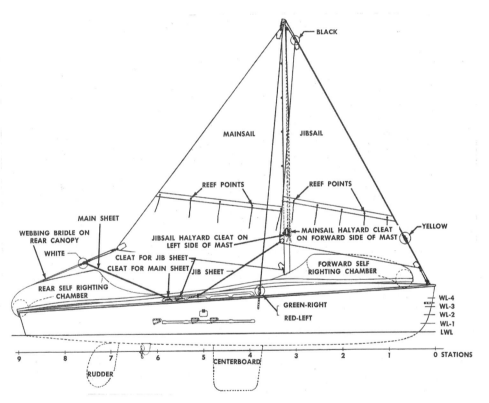

Diagram of the Airborne Lifeboat with sail hoisted and centreboard
and rudder deployed. (USAAF via A. McLeod)

A Typical ASR Course Programme

No. 279 Sqn was called upon, from time to time, to run ASR courses for visiting aircrew to give them an insight into procedures and equipment. The course programme below is typical of the type of course being run in 1942.

(1) Report to Adjutant's Office to: -

(a) sign Movements Book,
  (b) collect programme of course,
  (c) collect leaflet re – 'ditching'.

(2) See one of two Flight Commanders to arrange programme for flying either on search or cross country.

(3) Collect parachute and Mae West from Squadron Stores.

Every endeavour will be made to give officers a flight on air sea rescue work or at any rate a cross country trip. Accordingly the times for talks and demonstrations will not be definitely fixed beforehand but will be arranged as and when officers are not flying.

It is strongly recommended that notes be made of interesting points.

Respirators will be carried at all times both inside and outside of the camp.

Signed
Wing Commander, Commanding
No. 279 Squadron, RAF

Programme

Introduction to Squadron Commander		No. 1 Hangar
Medical aspect of life in a dinghy	Station Sick Quarters	Station or Squadron Medical Officer
Contents of Lindholme Apparatus	No. 1 Hangar	F/SGT SKETT (Equip. Asst.)
Fixing and release of Lindholme Apparatus	No. 1 Hangar	SGT GRAHAM (Armoury)
How searches are carried out (with special Reference to Navigation)	No. 1 Hangar	NAVIGATION OFFICER
Operations Room procedure and channels through which information regarding aircraft in distress is passed	Operations Room	INTELLIGENCE OFFICER
Procedure before ditching (with special reference to Wireless including visit to MF/DF Station)	No. 1 Hangar	WIRELESS OFFICER
'K' Type dinghies and Mae West	Parachute Section	NCO i/c PARACHUTE SECTION
Pigeons	Pigeon Section	NCO i/c SECTION
History of No. 279 Squadron (with photographs)	No. 1 Hangar	SQUADRON ADJUTANT

APPENDIX IX

No. 279 Squadron Aircrew
as at 31 May 1942

Captain	Observer	WOp/AG	A/G
A Flight			
W/Cdr Lynham	F/Sgt Harrington	F/Sgt Singleton	F/Lt Barrett
S/Ldr Pye	Sgt Cave	Sgt Lees	P/O Puxley
F/Lt Fitchew	P/O Scott	Sgt Field DFM	F/Sgt White
P/O Whittaker	Sgt Edgley	Sgt Furness	Sgt Quinn
P/O Heywood	Sgt Slugoski	F/Sgt Orr	F/Sgt Clark
P/O Zumar	P/O Hicks	Sgt Adams	Sgt Wallis
Sgt Scott SK	Sgt Cheslyn	Sgt Webdell	Sgt White
Sgt Marchand	Sgt Durward	Sgt Preece	Sgt Evans
P/O McKimm	Sgt Frost	Sgt Mackenzie	Sgt Kitteringham
Sgt Faux	Sgt Campbell AW	Sgt Darwin	Sgt Campbell
B Flight			
S/Ldr Binks	F/Sgt Betts	P/O Cowling	P/O Everett DFM
F/Lt Tyrell	F/Sgt Cramp	P/O Hall	F/Sgt Carty
P/O Henderson	Sgt Birkett	Sgt Burness	
P/O Lacy	P/O Younson	Sgt Adams	P/O Calvert
F/Sgt Spencer	F/Sgt Radford	Sgt Brown	Sgt Niven
Sgt Somerville	P/O Boxall	Sgt Gannon	Sgt Saunders
Sgt Werrin	P/O Allan	Sgt Buller	Sgt Parsons
Sgt Watts	Sgt Mogridge	Sgt Shaw	Sgt Johnson
Sgt Jackman	Sgt McGregor	Sgt Bastow	Sgt Bishop
Sgt Guthrie	Sgt Bedale	F/Sgt Goodman	Sgt Hibberd

Supernumerary
Sgt Briggs – sick   Sgt Sprung – sick

No. 279 Squadron Aircrew
as at 31 July 1942

Pilot	Navigator	WOp/AG	A/G	A/G
A Flight				
W/Cdr Lynham	F/Sgt Harrington	F/Sgt Singleton	Sgt Burgess	P/O Greeggan
S/Ldr Pye	Sgt Cave	Sgt Lees	P/O Puxley	P/O Knight
F/Lt Fitchew	P/O Scott	F/Sgt Field DFM	F/Sgt Burns	F/Sgt Aslett
P/O McKimm	Sgt Frost	Sgt Mackenzie	Sgt Kitteringham	
F/Sgt Scott	Sgt Sheclyn	P/O Webdell	Sgt John	
Sgt Marchand	Sgt Durward	Sgt Preece	Sgt Evans	
P/O Heywood	F/Sgt Slugoski	F/Sgt Orr	F/Sgt Clarke	
F/Sgt Forge	P/O Stephenson	Sgt Stapleton	Sgt Groome	
F/Sgt Faux	Sgt Bedale	Sgt Darwin	Sgt Campbell	
P/O Zumar	P/O Hicks	Sgt Adams FA	Sgt Wallis	
P/O Whittaker	Sgt Edgley	Sgt Quinn	Sgt Furness	
Sgt Woolford	WO Lansdall	Sgt Beard	Sgt Barnes	

Pilot	Navigator	WOp/AG	A/G	A/G
B Flight				
F/Lt Tyrell	F/Sgt Cramp	F/Sgt Carty	P/O Hall	
Sgt Mogridge	Sgt Smith	Sgt Rusby	Sgt Kidd	
Sgt Watts	F/Sgt Martin	Sgt Shaw	Sgt Johnson	
F/Sgt Werrin	Sgt Cook	Sgt Buller	Sgt Powell	
P/O Lacy	P/O Younson	Sgt Adams W	P/O Calvert	
P/O Henderson	Sgt Birkett	Sgt Burness	Sgt Gribble	
Sgt Farrer HT	Sgt Granger JD	P/O Holloman JJ	P/O Waters LW	
F/Sgt Spencer	F/Sgt Radford	Sgt Brown	Sgt Niven	
F/Sgt Jackman	Sgt Macgregor	Sgt Bastow	Sgt Bishop	
P/O Somerville	P/O Boxall	Sgt Saunders	Sgt Gannon	
Sgt Mackie	Sgt Main	Sgt Voyzey	Sgt Pearson	
Supernumerary				
Sgt Willis	Sgt Heanly	Sgt Codmer	Sgt Sprung	Sgt Parsons
Sgt Sweeting	Sgt White	F/Sgt Hollingworth		

APPENDIX XI

No. 279 Squadron Aircrew as at 30 September 1942

Pilot	Navigator	WOp/AG	A/G	A/G
A Flight				
W/Cdr Lynham	F/Sgt Harrington	F/Sgt Singleton	F/Lt Creeggan	P/O Knight
S/Ldr Pye	Sgt Cave	Sgt Lees	P/O Puxley	F/Sgt Burns
F/Lt Fitchew	Sgt Cheslyn	F/Sgt Field	P/O Webdell	F/Sgt Hollingworth
P/O McKimm	Sgt Frost	Sgt Buller	Sgt John	
F/Sgt Marchand	P/O Stephenson	Sgt Preece		
Sgt Groom*	Sgt Evans	Sgt Gendron		
P/O Heywood	F/Sgt Slugoski	F/Sgt Orr	F/Sgt Clark	Sgt Stapleton*
P/O Zumar	Sgt Edgley	Sgt Adams FA	Sgt Wallis	Sgt McFadden
F/Sgt Faux	Sgt Bedale	Sgt Darwin		
	Sgt Campbell	F/Sgt Aslett		
Sgt Woolford	WO Lansdall			
Sgt Kitteringham*	Sgt Beard*	Sgt Barnes*	Sgt Bailey	

Pilot	Navigator	WOp/AG	A/G	A/G
B Flight				
S/Ldr Tyrrell	F/Sgt Cramp	P/O Hall	Sgt Burgess	Sgt Whitty
F/Lt Stevens	F/Sgt Colmer	Sgt Furness	F/Sgt Archer	P/O White*
P/O Lacy	P/O Younson	Sgt Adams	P/O Calvert	Sgt Silverside
F/Sgt Spencer	WO Cook	F/St Niven	F/Sgt Brown	Sgt Barry
F/Sgt Watts	F/Sgt Willis	F/Sgt Shaw	Sgt Johnson	
F/Sgt Mogridge	F/Sgt Smith	Sgt Rusby	Sgt Kidd	
P/O Somerville	P/O Boxall	Sgt Saunders	Sgt Gannon*	Sgt Groome
P/O Henderson	Sgt Birkett	Sgt Burness	Sgt Lumley	
Sgt Mackie	Sgt MacGregor	Sgt Bastow	Sgt Bishop	Sgt Pertus
*Crew members awaiting posting				
Spare				
F/Sgt Main	F/Sgt Hughes	Sgt Wildman	Sgt Thompson	
Awaiting Posting				
F/Sgt Werrin	P/O Allan	Sgt Powell	Sgt Gribble	
F/Sgt Jackman	P/O Hicks	Sgt Mackenzie	Sgt Quinn	
F/Sgt Scott	Sgt Voysey	Sgt Pearson		

APPENDIX XII

No. 279 Squadron Aircrew
as at 1 January 1943

Pilot	Navigator	WOp/AG	A/G	A/G
A Flight				
W/Cdr Lynham	F/Lt Gibson	P/O Webdell	F/Lt Creeggan	F/Sgt Clark
S/Ldr Pye	P/O Cave	F/Sgt Lees	F/O Knight	F/Sgt Hopkins
F/Lt Fitchew	F/O Scott	F/Sgt Field	F/Sgt Burns	F/Sgt Hollingworth
F/O McKimm	F/Sgt Frost	F/Sgt Buller	Sgt John	Sgt Groome
P/O Heywood	WO Slugoski	F/Sgt Saunders	F/Sgt Orr	
P/O Zumar	F/Sgt MacGregor	F/Sgt Adams F	F/Sgt Wallis	Sgt Gendron
F/Sgt Marchand	F/O Stephenson	Sgt Preece	F/Sgt Evans	Sgt Jackson
P/O Crawford	Sgt Postle	P/O Peters	P/O Godfrey	Sgt Betteridge
Sgt Whitney	P/O Tidswell	Sgt Paterson	Sgt Fletcher	Sgt Cullen
P/O Wilson	F/O Hender	P/O Knight RC	Sgt Seaman	
F/O Tait	P/O Bishop	Sgt Speers	Sgt Whalen	
Sgt Neil	P/O Whapham	Sgt Pennington	Sgt Gourlay	
Sgt Passlow	P/O Whitten	Sgt Clifford	Sgt Purcell	

Pilot	Navigator	WOp/AG	A/G	A/G
B Flight				
S/Ldr Mossford	Sgt Wiseman	Sgt Hudson	Sgt Macklin	
F/Lt Stevens	F/O Boxall	F/Sgt Archer	F/Sgt Furness	
F/O Henderson	F/Sgt Birkett	Sgt Burness	Sgt Pertus	Sgt Lumley
P/O Lacy	F/O Younson	F/Sgt Adams W	P/O Calvert	Sgt Silverside
P/O Spencer	WO Cook	F/Sgt Niven	F/Sgt Brown	Sgt Pegg
F/Sgt Watts	F/Sgt Willis	F/Sgt Shaw	F/Sgt Johnson	Sgt Smith
F/Sgt Mogridge	F/Sgt Smith	Sgt Rusby	Sgt Kidd	Sgt Whitty
Sgt Oakes	F/Sgt Colmer	Sgt MacFadden	Sgt Every	F/Sgt Aslett
Sgt Arnold WM	Sgt Sclater JD	Sgt Bannister RF	Sgt Paradise RW	
F/O Gibbs	F/Sgt Long	Sgt Povey	Sgt Bacon	Sgt Barry
WO Oldfield	F/Sgt Sprung	Sgt Connelly		
F/O Clark	P/O O'Gorman	P/O Cobcroft	F/O Hayes	
Sgt Smith W	Sgt Wrigley	Sgt Ralston	Sgt Robinette	

No. 279 Squadron Aircrew
as at 3 November 1943

Pilot	Navigator	WOp/AG	A/G	A/G
A Flight				
W/Cdr Corry DFC	F/Lt Gibson	F/O Webdell	F/Lt Creeggan	P/O Burns OV
S/Ldr Fitchew DFC	F/Lt Scott	F/O Field DFM	WO Burne WR	F/O Farrell
F/O Sherwood	F/O Tidswell	F/Sgt Saunders	Sgt Groome	WO Hull
WO Passlow	F/O Whitten	F/Sgt Clifford	F/Sgt Miles	F/Sgt Peagam
F/O Wilson DFC	F/O Hender	F/O Knight RC	F/Sgt Cullen	Sgt Allaway
F/Sgt Oakes	P/O Baker	WO Ellyatt	F/Sgt Paterson	F/Sgt Edwards
P/O Bedford	P/O MacFarlane	Sgt Cooke	F/Sgt Danson	
F/Sgt Palmer	F/Sgt Brawn	Sgt Bullough	F/Sgt Windsor	
WO Gale	F/Sgt Wiseman	Sgt Hudson	Sgt Macklin	
F/O Butt	F/Sgt Wrigley	Sgt Breeze DFM	Sgt Galloway	
F/Lt Crawford	P/O Postle	F/O Godfrey	P/O Jackson	F/O Lerway
F/Lt McKimm DFC	WO Frost	F/Sgt John	F/Sgt Burness	

Pilot	Navigator	WOp/AG	A/G	A/G
M/Sgt Courson	F/O Carpenter	Sgt Franks	Sgt Chapman	
P/O Nicholson	F/Sgt Waddell	Sgt Cullen SWJ	Sgt Schroeder	F/O Peters
Spare				
Sgt Dunkley	Sgt Gardner	Sgt Roff	F/O Devine	
B Flight				
S/Ldr Downer	F/O Major	F/Sgt Rood	F/Sgt Cochrane	F/Sgt Burrow
F/Lt Stevens	F/Lt Boxall	WO Archer	F/Sgt Furness	F/Sgt Grant
F/O Reade	F/O Stapleton	F/Sgt Boulton	F/Sgt Beatty	F/O Denniss
F/O Pedersen	F/O Stephenson	P/O Brown	F/Sgt Pegg	WO Humphrey
	F/Sgt Douthwaite			
F/O Watts	WO Willis	P/O Shaw	P/O Johnson	
WO Mogridge	F/Sgt MacGregor	F/Sgt Middlemiss	P/O Kidd	F/Sgt Jones
F/O Myatt	F/O Case	WO Aslett	F/Sgt Barry	
F/O Clark	F/O O'Gorman	WO MacFadden	P/O Every	
F/O Clift	WO Birkett	F/Sgt Lumley	F/Sgt Silverside	
	F/Sgt Mouland			
F/Sgt Curtis	F/Sgt Whittaker	Sgt Trapmore	Sgt Pearson	
Lt Coale	F/O Wilson J	F/Sgt Middleton	F/Sgt Chisholm	F/Sgt Smith
F/O Gray	F/Sgt Radcliffe	F/O Keeler	F/Sgt Reid	

Spare				
Sgt Knight	Sgt Hillyer	Sgt Henwood	Sgt Kerr	F/Sgt Parsons
F/O Drinkwater				

APPENDIX XIV

RAF Thornaby in 2005

Station Armoury.
(Angela Jobson)

Airmen's barrack
block. (Angela
Jobson)

Little remains of No. 279 Squadron's base at RAF Thornaby. The airfield itself is covered by housing developments. The technical site and accommodation sites, though, have seen extensive conversion of the buildings to other uses as offices and small industrial units. Angela Jobson and Norman Smith kindly provided numerous photographs of the remaining buildings on the old airfield site.

The MT section sheds. (Angela Jobson)

The NAAFI building. (Angela Jobson)

Another view of the NAAFI building. (Angela Jobson)

No. 1 hangar. (Angela Jobson)

Another view of the MT yard, now a motorcycle workshop. (Angela Jobson)

No. 2 hangar, heavily converted for industrial use. (Angela Jobson)

The parachute store. (Angela Jobson)

The RAF graves at Thornaby. (Angela Jobson)

RAF Thornaby
Station
Headquarters.
(Angela Jobson)

The memorial
erected in 1997 to
honour all those
who served at
RAF Thornaby
from 1930 to
1958. (Norman
Smith)

Appendix XV

Farewell to the Warwick

With the war coming to a close many Warwicks were scrapped immediately with only a few remaining in service with No. 6 (Coastal) OTU based at RAF Kinloss providing ASR training to Coastal Command crews. Even these only remained in service for a short while before they to succumbed to the axe and blowtorch of the scrapman. The views below are of the final fate of many of the ASR Warwicks operated by the RAF, some of them by 279 Sqn.

Vickers Warwick coded C8-K7 in the sunset at No. 6 (C) OTU, RAF Kinloss 1946. (J. Hughes)

A Warwick in store at No. 45 MU, RAF Kinloss in 1946. (J. Hughes)

Twenty-five Warwicks can be seen in this view at No. 45 MU in 1946.
Many of them are finished in the extra dark sea-grey/dark
slate-grey/sky colour scheme adopted by the ASR squadrons.
(J. Hughes)

Another view of the same line-up of stored Warwicks. (J. Hughes)

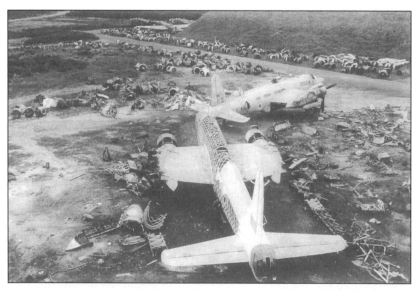

The end of the line for these two Warwicks at No. 45 MU. Note the
large number of engines lined up along the base of the L Type hangar
at RAF Kinloss. (J. Hughes)

Numerous Warwicks await their fate at No. 45 MU in 1946. (J. Hughes)

Acknowledgements

It would have been impossible to complete this history of No. 279 Squadron without the assistance of a large number of people: fellow historians, aircrew, ground crews and relatives of squadron members.

I am extremely grateful to all those who provided assistance with photographs, logbooks, letters and support. I would particularly like to thank Malcolm Barrass for producing the fine colour profiles of 279 Sqn aircraft for the book. My thanks also go to those listed below.

Air Historical Branch (RAF) Airfield Research Group
Gordy Alton Mike Banta
Helen Barnard Margaret Barnard
Malcolm Barrass Blair Bartholomew
Nick Berryman Gerry Berthiaume
Andy Bird Lee Bishop
Al Blue Ken Border
Tom Brittan Keith Bryers
James Burden Don Clark
Chris Charland Gary Cohen
John Cooper Chuck Craven
Robert Davies James Derk
Linzee Druce Cledwyn Evans
Michael Faley Ernest Farrow
Eddie Fell Ian Foster
Eunice Gambles Lyn Gambles
Simon Gifford Franek Grabowski
Hugh A. Halliday Frank Haslam
Jim Hughes Carl James
Angela Jobson Lee Kelly
Carolyn Kidd James Kidd

James Kidd Jr
Francis Marshall
Don Mabey
Ross McNeill
Sue Mortimer
Hank North
Steve Perri
Robert H. Powell
Peter Richardson
Michael S. Simpson
Norman Smith
Dave Stapleton
David Stinson
Raymond Towler
Vic Walzel
Henk Welting
Dougie Whittaker
Andy Wilson
James B. Young

Ken MacLean
Errol Martyn
R.S. McGill
Stein Meum
John Nicholls
Don Olds
James S. Peters
Fred Preller
Ted Russell
Len Smith
Nigel Spencer
Jenny Stephens
David Teasdel
Robert Truman
David Warren
W.G.A. White
Floyd Williston
David Wylie

Bibliography and References

Air 27/1609 279 Sqn Operational Record Book
Air 27/1610 279 Sqn Operational Record Book
279 Sqn Diary 16 November 41 – 30 November 43.
279 Sqn Diary 1 December 43 – 10 November 45.
279 Sqn Sortie Book 22 January 42 – 31 July 43.
279 Sqn Sortie Book 1 August 43 – 30 May 44.
279 Sqn Sortie Book 1 June 44 – 31 December 44.
279 Sqn Sortie Book 1 January 45 – 10 November 45.
Logbook of F/Lt B.P. Hollebone
Narrative Report of Operations 358th BG (H), dated 13 November 1943.
Extracts from HQ RNZAF form 765C-dated 30 November 1944 ref. W.O.
    Burrow & Grant.
The London Gazette (various issues).
The Times Digital Archive.

91st Bomb Group (H) by Bill Turcotte (www.91stbombgroup.com)
Airborne Lifeboats Reborn (www.torresen.com)
Avro Lancaster The Definitive Record by Harry Holmes (Airlife 1997)
Banff Strike Wing (www.scotshistoryonline.co.uk)
The Bomber Command War Diaries by Martin Middlebrook & Chris
    Everitt (Midland Publishing 1996).
Disused WWII Airfields in NE Scotland
    (www.geocities.com/Pentagon/Barracks)
Down in the Drink by Merle Olmsted (www.cebudanderson.com)
History of Air-Sea Rescue 1940–1952 (www.nobadlie.com/asr)
Mighty Eighth War Diary by Roger A. Freeman (Janes 1981)
Rescue from the Skies: *The story of the Airborne Lifeboat*. Stephen Daniels
    (1993).
Vickers Armstrong Warwick Variants by Norman Barfield (Profile
    Publications 1972)
Wireless for the Warrior by Louis Meulstee (www.home.hccnet.nl/meul-
    stee/gibsongirl)

USEFUL WEBSITES

RAF Commands at www.rafcommands.com

Mighty Eighth Public Message Board at www.com-web.com

Air of Authority at www.rafweb.org

www.americanwardead.com

Vickers Warwick information at www.uboat.net

RAF MOD website at www.raf.mod.uk/history

USAAF information at www.armyairforces.com

38 group information at www.raf38group.org

www.bomber-command.info

447th Bomb Group at www.447bg.com

WWII Ex-RAF Message Board at www.worldwar2exraf.co.uk

Halifax information at www.57rescue.org

44th Bomb Group at www.greenharbor.com

91st Bomb Group at www.91stbombgroup.com

626 Sqn at www.626sqn.org

457th Bomb Group at www.457thbombgroup.org

100th Bomb Group Foundation at www.100thbg.com

Index